Beyond Explicit

Beyond Explicit

Pornography and the
Displacement of Sex

HELEN HESTER

Published by State University of New York Press, Albany

© 2014 State University of New York

All rights reserved

Printed in the United States of America

No part of this book may be used or reproduced in any manner whatsoever without written permission. No part of this book may be stored in a retrieval system or transmitted in any form or by any means including electronic, electrostatic, magnetic tape, mechanical, photocopying, recording, or otherwise without the prior permission in writing of the publisher.

For information, contact State University of New York Press, Albany, NY
www.sunypress.edu

Production by Eileen Nizer
Marketing by Kate McDonnell

Library of Congress Cataloging-in-Publication Data

Hester, Helen, 1983–
 Beyond explicit : pornography and the displacement of sex / Helen Hester.
    pages cm
 Includes bibliographical references and index.
 Summary: "Develops a novel characterization of the pornographic as a cultural concept"—Provided by publisher.
 ISBn 978-1-4384-4961-6 (hc : alk. paper) 978-1-4384-4960-9 (pb : alk. paper)
 1. Pornography. 2. Pornography in popular culture. 3. Sex in popular culture. 4. Sex. I. Title.

 HQ471.H47 2014
 363.4'7—dc23   2013006613

10 9 8 7 6 5 4 3 2 1

Contents

Acknowledgments — vii

Introduction: Critical Voices in Porn Studies — 1

PART I: FEMINISM, PORNOGRAPHY, TRANSGRESSION — 17

1 The Sex Wars: Transgressive Politics and the Politics of Transgression — 21

2 Rethinking Transgression — 35

3 Sex and Disgust in Popular Culture — 49

PART II: INTENSITY AND PRURIENCE: PORNOGRAPHY AFTER SEX — 63

4 "Not All of it Will Get Your Dick Hard": Pornography and Displacement — 67

5 Prurience and Postmodernism — 87

6 Violence, Sympathy, Titillation: The Body in a State of Intensity — 103

PART III: PORNOGRAPHY AND THE REAL — 125

7 Pornography and the Appetite for Authenticity — 129

8 Autobiography and/as the Real — 141

9	Sex, Trauma, and the Authenticity Effect	157
	Conclusion: Pornographication and the Explosion of the Pornographic	181
	Notes	191
	Works Cited	207
	Index	231

Acknowledgments

I have been fortunate enough to have received exceptional support during the course of the preparation of this manuscript, and I would like to take this opportunity to thank all of those who have helped to make *Beyond Explicit: Pornography and the Displacement of Sex* happen. I am particularly indebted to Benjamin Noys, for his guidance and encouragement over the past years. He has been a significant influence on this text and, indeed, on my thinking more generally. I also thank the English Department at the University of Chichester for providing financial support throughout the early stages of the project, and Middlesex University for affording me so many wonderful opportunities to challenge myself as a teacher and a researcher. Thanks are due to Lisa Downing, whose work continues to be an inspiration, and Robert Duggan, who provided helpful comments at numerous stages in the development of *Beyond Explicit*.

An earlier version of Chapter 2 was originally published as an article in the Routledge *Journal of Lesbian Studies* (17:3), and I am extremely grateful to the journal's peer reviewers, who offered suggestions as to how I might develop the piece. I am similarly indebted to the two anonymous reviewers who considered this manuscript, and to Beth Bouloukos, Eileen Nizer, Kate McDonnell, and the rest of the team at SUNY Press, who have been unfailingly helpful and supportive throughout the publication process. I also thank all of those who have responded to my work or otherwise assisted and encouraged me during the writing of this book, including Alex Williams, Lucy Scholes, Michael O'Rourke, Alex Dymock, Adam Locks, Michael Amherst, Mark Mason, Caroline Walters, Sarah Harman, Abigail Pride, Mark Dishman, and Nick Srnicek. My thanks go to my family for their love, reassurance, and goodwill, and I dedicate this text to Diarmuid Hester, my first and best reader.

Introduction

Critical Voices in Porn Studies

This book represents an attempt to contribute to the branch of cultural theory known as *Porn Studies*. This emerging academic discipline takes as its object pornographic representations of various kinds, and aims to extend the understanding of a genre that has historically received too little in the way of sustained and dispassionate scholarly analysis. As a critical approach, Porn Studies is still relatively young; many of the edited collections that have been influential in shaping the discipline were first published in the opening decade of the new millennium, including Linda Williams' *Porn Studies* (2004), Pamela Church Gibson's *More Dirty Looks: Gender, Pornography, and Power* (2004), and Peter Lehman's *Pornography: Film and Culture* (2006). Nevertheless, Porn Studies has quickly gained a sense of its own identity and developed its own disciplinary conventions, and I address some of these conventions here.

The valuable work of Porn Studies in generating new strategies for talking about adult entertainment within an academic context has very much informed my own perspective on pornography. Like many Porn Studies scholars, for example, I am keen to go beyond repetitive and simplistic discussions about whether pornography should be viewed as either a positive or a negative phenomenon in terms of its cultural influence—discussions that are widely understood to be the legacy of the partisan feminist politics of the 1970s and 1980s. I agree with Williams when she states that these feminist debates have "impeded discussion of almost everything but the question of whether pornography deserves to exist at all. Since it does exist, however, we should be asking what it does for viewers; and since it is a genre with basic similarities to other genres, we need to come to terms with it" (*Hard Core* 4–5). *Beyond Explicit*, therefore, turns away from questions of whether we should be for or against adult entertainment in favor of a more nuanced analysis of the contemporary pornographic landscape.

This kind of approach unites much of the work currently being undertaken within a Porn Studies context, with historians and theoreticians staging "a partial escape from the dead-end of the feminist censorship debate" (Preciado 26). As Feona Attwood notes in her survey of new directions in twenty-first century research, contemporary theorists of porn have increasingly sought to move away from "a debate about whether pornographic texts have fixed and simple meanings, embody and encourage clearly oppressive power relations, produce direct and quantifiable effects and can be challenged only through the regulatory mechanism of the state" ("Reading Porn" 92), in favor of a "re-examination of pornography, sexuality and the politics of representation" ("Reading Porn" 92). This departure from the polemical feminism of old involves both a commitment to studying specific pornographic texts (rather than trying to generalize about pornography as a whole) and a new sensitivity to the diversity of adult entertainment as a genre. Porn is no longer discussed as if it is a single thing to be either condemned or defended, but is instead viewed as being as mutable and multifaceted as any other regime of representation.[1]

One of the first scholars to attempt a more nuanced and historicizing analysis of adult entertainment was Linda Williams. Her book *Hard Core: Power, Pleasure, and the "Frenzy of the Visible,"* first published in 1989, is arguably the founding text of Porn Studies, and represents a groundbreaking attempt to think critically about pornography as a moving-image genre. In *Hard Core*, Williams goes beyond generalizations and value judgments in an attempt to develop a more subtle critical vocabulary. She foregrounds the centrality of the "principle of *maximum visibility*" (*Hard Core* 48), for example, stressing that this principle "has operated in different ways at different stages of the genre's history" (*Hard Core* 48). It is testament to the quality and critical sophistication of Williams' work, I think, that it remains so influential and widely cited today; indeed, ideas regarding the frenzy of the visible will surface repeatedly throughout the present study, providing a valuable insight into the mechanisms of contemporary pornographic texts.

Problems Within the Discipline

Despite my engagement with and my esteem for certain of its central texts and theorists, however, there remain several key points on which

I am at variance with Porn Studies. For example, despite its admirable attempts to transcend the reductive arguments of previous approaches to pornography, I feel that much of Porn Studies is still mired in debates about whether adult entertainment is a good or a bad thing for the wider culture. Indeed, many of the discipline's most prominent figures are evidently still committed to the ideas of pro-sex or anti-censorship feminism—a movement highly invested in demonstrating the cultural value and political importance of pornography. Susanna Paasonen, Kaarina Nikunen, and Laura Saarenmaa are among those who have remarked on this heritage, arguing that although Porn Studies scholars have distanced themselves from "the binary logic of the porn debates to date," they have also "built on anti-antipornography perspectives" (17). Paasonen reiterates this point in her recent book *Carnal Resonance: Affect and Online Pornography*—one of the few examples of contemporary Porn Studies that seems genuinely wary of the "defensiveness and binary logic" that dogs the discipline (27). The influence of entrenched partisan feminist positions makes itself felt, she argues, in the manner in which pornography scholars continue "speaking past each other rather than trying to engage in productive dialogue" (27).

Although this relationship with pro-sex feminism does not appear problematic in itself, it has arguably resulted in a failure to obtain the standards of critical rigor by which the discipline seeks to define itself. As Jane Juffer notes, much of the recent work undertaken in relation to pornography has focused on countering "the victim status posited by anti-porn feminists and conservatives" ("There's No Place Like Home" 50), and a great deal of ink, therefore, has been spilled simply in attempting to convince people that "pornography is not the monolithic expression of phallic misogyny that it has been stigmatized as being" (Williams, "Second Thoughts on *Hard Core*" 58). This has arguably led to a certain partiality within Porn Studies. As Lehman puts it,

> In an effort to correct the fear and hysteria surrounding porn, some scholars have gone too far in the direction of simply embracing it as clearly not being the evil object so many writers and people in our culture imagine it to be, as if that means we should not be concerned about race, class, and gender depictions that we are so rightly concerned about in other genres. ("Introduction" 20)

This corrective emphasis on the positives of porn has resulted in a somewhat limited approach to adult entertainment—an approach that persistently over values the genre in an attempt to present it as subversive or liberating.

Williams, for example, largely disregards Foucault's claim that the extension of the discourses surrounding sexuality might represent "the encroachment of a type of power on bodies and their pleasures" (*Will to Knowledge* 48), and focuses instead on the idea that such discourses might provide a valuable tool for *resisting* power. Her reading of Foucault in *Hard Core* therefore ends up suggesting that the "less sex is spoken the more monolithic that speech is likely to be and the more that speech will tend to repress sexual minorities" (*Hard Core* 283). This approach rather sets the tone for Porn Studies as a whole, to the extent that there is now an apparent expectation that analyses coming from within the discipline will be largely affirmative when it comes to discussing the proliferation of pornography, and that they will keep unsympathetic comment to a minimum. As Lehman notes of his own experience of reading Williams' *Porn Studies* anthology, it is striking "how little criticism or even concern her former students show for any consequences of how anything is represented in porn" ("Introduction" 20).[2]

This tendency toward valorization within Porn Studies partly manifests itself via an emphasis on queer theoretical standpoints and potentially dissident pornographies. As Paasonen notes, "Proporn, anti-anti-porn, and prosex authors who approach the genre from a more positive angle have chosen independent, queer and artistic projects that challenge gender norms, porn clichés, and the commodity logic of the porn industry" (*Carnal Resonance* 42). By eschewing mainstream texts in favor of more transgressive fare, she argues, scholars are better able to position adult entertainment as the property of "the queer against the norm" (*Carnal Resonance* 247). There is indeed a growing body of research that discusses marginal pornographies, or that sets out to queer mainstream heterosexual porn. Scholars such as Thomas Waugh and Emily Shelton, for example, have addressed the issue of queer viewing contexts, including the idea that "straight sex in porn is anything but just straight," due to the fact that it "obsesses on the ability of heterosexual imagery to encode potentially homoerotic elements of homosocial spectatorship" (Shelton 139). Theorists such as Richard Dyer, Nguyen Tan Hoang, and Lee Edelman have written on the radical potential of adult entertainment texts aimed at a gay male audience, whereas Tanya Krzywinska ("Dissidence and Authenticity"), Heather Butler, and Julie Levin Russo are among those who have analyzed the pornographic subgenre of dyke porn. Katrien Jacobs, meanwhile, focuses on the political potential of non-normative adult entertainment, arguing that the producers of subcultural or independent pornographies "have inherited the gender roles and racial stereotyping inherent in commercial porn, yet have been skillful in trying to develop their everyday performing bodies into subversions of the plots" (76).³

I agree with Jacobs that, as porn has proliferated and diversified in the virtual age, a great deal of interesting, innovative, and politically engaged material has begun to emerge. I do not, however, focus on such material here. Instead, my analysis of adult entertainment will consider those examples that do not obviously invite the viewer to interpret them as subversively parodying heterosexist gender norms or as deconstructing phallocentric mythologies regarding sex. Indeed, I offer close analyses of several texts that eschew any overtly progressive agenda in favor of staging scenarios of male heterosexual power and aggression, without myself making any deliberate effort to queer these texts. It is not that these pornographic works are unavailable for queer readings; much of their hyperbolic display of masculine aggression seems ripe for the sort of analysis enacted by Shelton and others. However, I am keen to offset the redemptive, or at least overtly celebratory, tone evident within much of Porn Studies—a tone to which elements of the queer approach to pornography have contributed. As Paasonen suggests, much of this kind of work draws on the pro-sex feminist stance in producing analyses that are invested in the belief that pornography can have a positive effect on gender and sexual politics. This does little to broaden the critical landscape. I am of the opinion that not all pornographic material is radical, disruptive, subversive, progressive, or likely to have a positive effect on sexual minorities, and I believe that Porn Studies should do more to reflect and respond to this fact.

It would seem that the discipline's links with pro-sex feminist political agitation have resulted in a less than even-handed approach to pornography. Of course, it is important to note that much of this investment in the pro-sex position may stem from anxieties regarding the continued vulnerability of adult entertainment to censorship and repression. Indeed, recent evidence would suggest that such anxieties are well justified. There have been several high-profile obscenity prosecutions that have resulted in the incarceration of pornographers; a 46-month jail term was handed down to the controversial adult star Max Hardcore in October 2008 (Department of Justice, "Adult Entertainment Producer Sentenced"), for example, and the husband and wife behind the porn production company Extreme Associates both recently faced obscenity charges (Department of

Justice, "News Release"). The case ended with negotiations and a guilty plea in March 2009 (Deitch), and in July of that year, more than half a decade after their business premises were originally raided, the couple were sentenced to a year and a day in prison for violating federal obscenity laws (Ward). More recently, the "extreme" porn director Ira Isaacs—who "produced, sold and sometimes acted in films depicting scatology and bestiality" (Kim and Ahmad)—was convicted of five federal obscenity charges; he was sentenced to "four years in federal prison, three years of supervised release, and a $10,000 fine" in January 2013 (Griffo).

In the United Kingdom, meanwhile, there have been significant recent developments when it comes to censorship legislation. On January 26, 2009, the Criminal Justice and Immigration Act 2008 came into force in England, Wales, and Northern Ireland. Sections 63 to 67 of this Act address the "Possession of extreme pornographic images" (Part 5 Section 63), and represent the creation of a new offense punishable by up to three years in prison. In order to be considered an extreme pornographic image, a representation must be pornographic—that is, be "of such a nature that it must reasonably be assumed to have been produced solely or principally for the purpose of sexual arousal" (Part 5, Section 63, subsection 3)—and must also meet the Act's criteria for "an extreme image" (Part 5, Section 63, subsection 2). Extremity is defined in terms of a particular assortment of adjectives and acts, so that in order to fall foul of the offense, the material must be "grossly offensive, disgusting or otherwise of an obscene character" (Part 5, Section 63, subsection 6), while also portraying "an act which threatens a person's life," "which results, or is likely to result, in serious injury to a person's anus, breasts or genitals," or that involves sexual contact with a human corpse or an animal (Part 5, Section 63, subsection 7).

This legislation represents a new interest in policing the consumption of images in the United Kingdom—an interest that is no doubt deeply concerning to anti-censorship feminists. In terms of censorship and state regulation, the emphasis has historically been on policing the production and distribution, rather than the consumption, of pornographic texts. Walter Kendrick, writing in 1987, notes that "the possession of obscene materials has never been a crime in Britain, only their public display," and links this fact to the "traditional British—and American—respect for private property" (118). However, Sections 63 to 67 of the Criminal Justice and Immigration Act 2008 (along with developments in the area of child pornography legislation) indicate a new concern within legal discourse with the possession of those sexually explicit texts that are viewed as being particularly reprehensible.⁴ Of course, it is frequently the least normative representations of sexuality that are viewed as being the most "disgusting" or "grossly offensive," and it is no coincidence that much of the opposition toward the legislation has come from minority advocacy groups such as SM Gays and the Spanner Trust, which aim to protect the rights of those involved in the Bondage, Discipline, Dominance/submission, and Sadomasochism (BDSM) community (see Cohen).

There has, in fact, been a great deal of speculation about whether what is actually being targeted in the censorship of explicit images, both in the Act and more widely, are the specific pleasures of minority groups such as that represented by the BDSM subculture—that censorship, in other words, has "become a matter of scapegoating the more 'deviant' of the sexual representations that come on/scene" (Williams, *Hard Core* 287). Remarking on the Act's specification that, in order to be considered an extreme pornographic image, a text need not depict *genuine* acts of violence, but need only portray such acts in "an explicit and realistic way" (Part 5, Section 63, subsection 7), Julian Petley argues that the legislation "will criminalize the possession of [. . .] vast swathes of perfectly consensual BDSM material" ("Britain"). In the case of this extreme images legislation, at least, it appears that scholars are right to worry about the excessive effect of censorship on sexual minorities.

Porn Studies is very astute when it comes to recognizing the importance of adult entertainment for marginalized and non-normative groups—not only BDSM communities, but all ex-centric forms of sexual identity. Williams, for example, suggests that the increased visibility of sexuality, "in pornography no less than in all the arts, has become an important means of representing a wide range of sexual identities once labeled deviant—gay, lesbian, bisexual, sadomasochist, not to mention the female sexuality" ("Second Thoughts on *Hard Core*" 47).⁵ As we have seen, then, Porn Studies views discourse about sex as being broadly beneficial, and it may well be for this reason that hostile critical comment—which could potentially be interpreted as a justification for censorship—is largely avoided within the discipline. Theorists may feel that to criticize pornography within the current legal context risks creating an atmosphere that is conducive to censorship, and that this censorship will inevitably effect already stigmatized groups and communities. I acknowledge that the imagery of sexual minorities may be vulnerable to the mechanisms of censorship. BDSM pornographies, for example, seem particularly at risk, combining as they do the representation of violence with erotically charged scenarios. Concerns regarding the persecution of a specific community and its pornographies are entirely understandable, and political agitation is both welcome and necessary. However, although I would in no way suggest that anti-censorship activism is anything less than vital in drawing our attention to the continued vulnerability of the representations of sexual minorities, I would suggest that it can and should be kept separate from Porn Studies as an academic discipline.

Porn Studies needs to make a decision about what it is, or rather, what it wants to be. If its ambitions extend only as far as operating as a contemporary branch of the pro-sex feminism of the 1970s and 1980s, then its indulgent treatment of porn does not present a problem. If this is the case, of course, Porn Studies scholars rather give up their right to complain about the way in which the old feminist binaries have "impeded discussion" and dictated the debate (Williams, *Hard Core* 4–5). If, however, the discipline is serious about its stated aims of attaining a properly scholarly standard of critical rigor, and is invested in becoming an interesting, thorough, and genuinely valuable branch of cultural studies, then it needs to develop an identity distinct from that of pro-sex feminism, and must encourage the emergence of a more balanced and searching approach to adult entertainment. The discipline cannot evolve if it lets anxieties regarding censorship utterly determine the manner in which it responds to adult entertainment. This is, I would suggest, a recipe for propaganda rather than scholarly analysis.

An appropriately interrogative attitude to pornography is at risk of being quashed within the largely celebratory intellectual climate in operation within Porn Studies. As Attwood puts it, recent works on pornography "flatten out all opposition to pornography as a move towards censorship, against transgression" ("Reading Porn" 98), and in so doing, are in danger "not only of reproducing the rather worn-out questioning of pornography's potential for liberation and repression, but also of negating some important political issues raised in earlier accounts" ("Reading Porn" 98). Such defensiveness does not allow for a properly nuanced analysis of adult entertainment as a genre, and risks having a chilling effect when it comes to the emergence of thoughtful academic research on the subject. I suggest that, despite advances in censorship legislation, adult entertainment remains robust enough to withstand a proper critical commentary; indeed, considering the extent of the genre's cultural visibility, it surely deserves to be taken seriously, rather than to be cosseted by an overprotective critical apparatus.

Considering Porn Studies' attentiveness to the diversity of adult entertainment, one should be able to critique certain pornographic texts without being seen as damaging the reputation of others, or as slating the genre as a whole. It is worth remembering that, although some pornographies may be at continued risk for persecution and censorship, adult entertainment in general remains a multifaceted and widely available regime of representations. As Attwood remarks, "it is hard to feel that porn is the excluded other when it is so prevalent and so present in public" ("'Other' or 'One of Us'?"). The status of pornography (and of sex more generally) as dissident or liberating is by no means self-evident—I examine this topic in some detail in Part I—and it does not seem quite right to simply let the genre off the hook in the name of an anti-censorship activist stance that should, to my mind, function as a separate (if related) discourse.

New Directions in Porn Studies

Fortunately, a small number of critical voices do appear to be pushing through into the arena of Porn Studies. Such voices are recognizable in a number of accounts that theorize the role of race within visual pornographic texts. In her discussion of representations of black femininity in pornographic videos from the 1980s, for example, Mireille Miller-Young argues that such films "perpetuate the subordination of black bodies as spectacles for appropriation and consumption, even as they illuminate the profound anxiousness of cross-racial desire" (38). José B. Capino's largely celebratory look at the performance of race in "Asian pornography" is not afraid of claiming that the subgenre engages in the "symbolic management of 'foreign' bodies as well as the translation and marshaling of 'alien' desires" (213), whereas Daniel Bernardi provides a refreshingly unflinching account of "Pornography's Web of Racist Attractions" ("Interracial Joysticks" 220).[6]

It is perhaps more rare to find Porn Studies critiques like this emerging around issues of gender—a flash point issue, of course, for anti-pornography feminism—but the odd questioning voice is now being raised. Stephen Maddison, for example, writes about the "overwhelmingly sexist nature of the porn industry" (42), and argues that "we have to interrogate hardcore in a way that isn't foreclosed by what are increasingly becoming postfeminist preoccupations with entitlements to pleasure as a function of consumer empowerment" (50). Matteo Pasquinelli suggests that "Despite the rise of *alt-porn* and the activism of queer communities, pornography remains mainly the business of a male audience and a female (usually exploited) workforce" ("Libidinal Parasites" 221), while Tim Stüttgen remarks that porn is dominated by "white straight men, selling their boring and heteronormative desires through the ideas of liberalism and democracy" ("Before Orgasm" 10). There also is evidence of a generally more critical tone emerging within recent collections, as cautionary pieces are given space alongside more celebratory fare; Feona Attwood's *Porn.com* (2010) is a good example of this.

Texts *are* surfacing, then, that represent a more balanced, and a less defensively positive, position on the contemporary pornographic landscape.[7] This is, to my mind, a welcome move, as it encourages the development of an intellectual climate in which scholars are able and expected to write critically rather than polemically about sexually explicit cultural artifacts, even when those artifacts are potentially vulnerable to censorship or government regulation. I hope to draw and expand on elements of this emerging approach within the present work, by discussing adult entertainment texts that are not overtly dissident or readily available for recouping as politically progressive. This includes material ranging from the "mainstream heteroporn" proffered by Larry Flynt's *Hustler* (Paasonen, Nikunen, and Saarenmaa 18), to violent works of "extreme post-gonzo hardcore" (Maddison 39). I do not set out to celebrate "the transgressive text or the act of transgressing mainstream texts" (Juffer, "There's No Place Like Home" 50), but to discuss, without a pre-established agenda, the character of the contemporary pornographic.

In addition to this more rigorous critical focus, it is worth noting that I also diverge from the Porn Studies canon when it comes to the form or the media of the texts with which I engage. Although Porn Studies in general displays a conspicuous blind spot when it comes to the written word,[8] I draw on a number of different literary examples, some more overtly pornographic than others. Remarking on this blind spot, Jennifer Wicke suggests that perhaps pornographic books and magazines are "less visible as targets of critique or analysis because the prevailing figure for pornographic consumption lies so squarely in the arresting of the visual, in the enthralled spectatorship of the eye" (67). This idea also informs the work of Steven Marcus, an influential forerunner of Porn Studies and one of the few academics to consider examples of written pornographic texts (albeit examples from the Victorian era). Marcus suggests that pornography itself wants to avoid or escape the realm of the linguistic: "Language is to pornography a bothersome necessity; its function is to set going a series of nonverbal images, of fantasies—and if it could dispense with words it would. Which is why, one supposes, that the motion-picture film is what the genre was all along waiting for" (211). If images are indeed viewed as being the most suitable vehicle for pornographic representations, then the lacuna within Porn Studies is perhaps understandable.

We might also attribute this blind spot to the fact that Porn Studies often functions as a reactive discipline, seeking to intervene within public debate and counter censorious accounts of the damage affected by pornography on the lives of real people. This may have an influence in terms of the media that it elects to engage with. Visual pornographies seem to be much more vulnerable to aggressive critique than works of so-called literary erotica. As Kendrick notes, "None of the recent major battles over pornography has involved the naked word, and it seems unlikely that any future *Ulysses* or *Lady Chatterley's Lover* will be able to arouse the fury those books caused when they were new" (243).[9] Indeed, Sections 63 to 67 of the Criminal Justice and Immigration Act 2008 are solely concerned with representations of ostensibly "real" sexual acts and corporeal forms. It is clearly stated that, in order to be covered by the legislation, an image must portray a person engaging in extreme sexual acts in such a manner that "a reasonable person looking at the image would think that any such person [. . .] was real" (Criminal Justice and Immigration Act, Part 5, Section 63, subsection 7). The "practical effect of that requirement is that only photographs and films, and images which are indistinguishable from photographs and films, will be caught by the offence" (Ministry of Justice 3).

Cultural anxieties about photorealistic visual pornographies seem to be particularly pervasive, then, and attempts at censorship often target this area. Linguistic porn receives comparatively little negative attention, perhaps due to the fact that the graphic sexual scenarios it depicts do not depend upon the presence of real bodies—bodies that, in the popular imagination, could be vulnerable, or unwilling, or subject to damage. As Susanna Paasonen notes, "In contrast to audiovisual pornography that is, at least to a degree, anchored in an indexical relationship to that which has been acted out in front of the camera, [written] erotica—often authored by women—has been understood more as a realm of fantasy, play, and experimentation" ("Good Amateurs" 139). If the written word is positioned as being less of a problem within Western culture, then it is surely also less in need of strategic defense by Western scholars. Porn Studies academics may choose to focus primarily on visual pornographies because these are the representations most immediately in need of rehabilitative pro-sex intervention.

It is important, however, not to overlook the continued presence and significance of the written word in relation to porn. As Paasonen argues, a "tendency to understand porn in terms of the visual [. . .] fails to account for the diversity of contemporary practices" ("Good Amateurs" 139). Not only is there a continued commercial trade in pornographic fiction—from the output of small, specialist imprints like Silver Moon and X Libris to high-profile best sellers like E. L. James's *Fifty Shades of Grey*—but "erotic writing has proliferated online since the mid-1990s" (Paasonen, "Good Amateurs" 139). The Internet has facilitated new forms of engagement with linguistic pornography, and has enabled a culture of digital exchange to emerge among consumers and amateur producers. The possibility of seemingly unfettered distribution has arguably led to something of a resurgence of legal interest in the pornographic written word—a resurgence that Porn Studies is in danger of overlooking if it continues to focus its energies so intently on the analysis of visual culture. In Pittsburgh in 2008, for example, the woman behind the website *Red Rose Stories*—an online repository of written fiction "about abuse and torture of children" (Kernes)—pled guilty to six charges of obscenity trafficking. In the United Kingdom, meanwhile, text-based pornography also has found itself in the legal spotlight; Darryn Walker faced prosecution under the Obscene Publications Act 1959 for writing an explicit blog post about the rape, murder, and dismemberment of the British pop group Girls Aloud. Walker was cleared in June 2009 (see Swash), but cases like this indicate that concern about pornography goes beyond the use and potential abuse of real bodies, and extends to an anxiety about textual fantasies—specifically, "extreme" sexual fantasies that circulate relatively freely in the digital age.

In light of such cases and practices, it is clear that Porn Studies scholars should seek to extend the nature of the media with which they engage. Indeed, a limited number of critics *have* commented upon porn's "fundamentally intermedial nature" (Paasonen, "Epilogue" 165) in a manner that foregrounds the on-going significance of the linguistic. John Ellis, for example, sees pornography as a phenomenon in which "a particular area of signification is separated out across a wide range of media" (26), and suggests that it manifests itself "across a diversity of practices, each with its own means of marketing and dissemination, nevertheless unified by processes of self-designation into an institution of signification" (35). Paasonen, meanwhile, notes the following:

> Print magazines have been marketed with free bonus VHS tapes and DVDs since the 1980s; video and print publishing companies have branched out to online markets; online distribution has led to DVD production; the same companies are

involved in the production of websites, mobile entertainment and digital television channels; the same images are recycled in print and electronic formats while old porn films make their comeback as collector DVD editions. Pornographic texts and products transgress the boundaries of individual media, and content is recycled from one platform to another. ("Epilogue" 165)

There is no explicit mention of exclusively linguistic texts here, but the same logic easily can be applied.[10] Although there are various discourses surrounding photorealism that may effect the reception of specific pornographic artifacts, I can see no reason why the written word should be excluded from discussions of adult entertainment or the pornographic. Indeed, I not only use works of fiction to help further my analysis throughout this book, but, in Chapter 8, I take written works as the focus of my discussion of the pornographic. The texts that I examine in this chapter are not mass-market pornographic paperbacks, however, but works of memoir reframed within the context of contemporary understandings of the pornographic.

This leads me to a perhaps more significant point of divergence between my work and that conventionally produced within the confines of Porn Studies. The texts that I discuss at times differ from the discipline's typical objects of analysis not only in terms of their media, but also in terms of factors such as content, conditions of production, and intended audience. Porn Studies is predominantly interested in the genre of adult entertainment—a historically neglected area of popular culture well deserving of detailed scholarly attention. *Beyond Explicit*, however, engages with a broader conceptualization of porn—one that I argue reflects an idiosyncratic current of contemporary Western thinking on the topic. In addition to works of adult entertainment, my analysis encompasses literary and pop cultural representations of disgust, images of the violated body, and autobiographical accounts of trauma. These diverse texts are discussed here not because of any inherent link to adult entertainment—such links are often spurious at best—but because of their links to wider perceptions of the pornographic; as I seek to demonstrate throughout this book, pornography and adult entertainment must not be seen as synonymous.

Certain slippages have become apparent when it comes to the concept of the pornographic. In recent years, popular usage of the word "porn" has been extended, most noticeably in its deployment as a kind of descriptive suffix. "Porn" has become attached to a surprisingly diverse set of texts and affects, few of which actually put the sexual body front and center. The phrase "grief porn," for example, has been coined to refer to what the journalist Barbara Ellen calls the "mawkish" and "exaggerated" public reaction to death and illness. A category of reality TV programming depicting the urban working classes, meanwhile, is "increasingly being referred to as the 'poverty porn' genre" (Mooney and Hancock),[11] and the term *torture porn* has emerged to designate a certain type of horror film revolving around the spectacle of corporeal violation. As will be seen here, the phrases "misery porn" and "warporn" also are entering circulation. The fact that these discourses have acquired the porn suffix suggests that they are all popularly understood as being at least partially related to pornography, and yet (rather intriguingly) none of them necessarily include graphic representations of hard-core sex. It would appear that the word "pornography" has become somewhat detached from its etymological roots—as the *Oxford English Dictionary* remarks, the term originates from the Greek for "that writes about prostitutes"—and has become attached to materials that are somewhat outside of its traditional remit.

Whereas the term *pornography* seems to speak emphatically of sexuality, it has come to be associated with concerns that are not overtly sexual; and although "adult entertainment" appears to be a disingenuous and horribly euphemistic description, the materials and practices to which it refers can more reliably be seen to concern themselves with sex as a genital act. I use the term *adult entertainment* frequently throughout this text—not because it is a phrase in which I am particularly invested, but because it enables me to make a distinction between pornography as a representational genre and pornography as a capacious cultural concept. The word "adult" also has the benefit of being the name by which the pornographic film industry typically identifies itself. This is particularly helpful for my purposes, in that it de-emphasizes a celebratory and aggrandizing interpretation of porn as dissident, transgressive, and politically radical, and accentuates a more material set of concerns surrounding pornography as a business and a capitalist enterprise. Although adult entertainment is itself a multifaceted term, encapsulating many different types of sex-related commercial ventures, I use it in this book primarily to refer to one of its key manifestations as a visual and linguistic representational genre. Other 'adult' practices—such as stripping and lap dancing, for example—are not covered here.

In part, *Beyond Explicit* represents an attempt to think through the displacement of sex that is occurring within contemporary understandings of the pornographic. In order to achieve this, I not only engage with the kind of pseudo-pornographic texts just discussed, but also use a set of mobile and wide-ranging concepts in order to theorize the apparent explosion of the pornographic as a cultural concept. Part I explores the influence of feminism and transgression on perceptions of the pornographic. Chapter 1 argues that these three concepts—feminism, pornography, and transgression—are persistently conflated within popular and academic discourse, and interrogates the disruptive and undertheorized role played by transgression within the feminist sex wars of the 1970s and 1980s. Chapter 2 stages an examination of Charlotte Roche's controversial novel *Wetlands* (first published in Germany in 2008), and stresses the centrality of transgression to any attempt to position the novel as porn. It also argues that sex may be being gradually displaced as the privileged locus of transgression within contemporary Western society—that we may, as Elspeth Probyn puts it, be witnessing the "last gasp of the reign of sex" (215). It is in Chapter 3 that we begin to seriously examine the surprisingly diverse nature of both the material and the affective responses that our culture labels pornographic, and to consider what role transgression might play in the extension of the applicability of this concept.

Part II seeks to problematize the extension of the pornographic in relation to two key concepts—intensity and prurience. Chapter 4 explores pornography's surprisingly diverse history and considers a number of pornographic artifacts that can be seen to borrow from other body genres. Such texts appear to displace sex to some extent; I position this displacement in relation to the operations of intensity and, in Chapter 5, develop, explore, and historicize this post-Freudian notion. Drawing on the depictions of cyber-voyeurism in Margaret Atwood's dystopian novel *Oryx and Crake* (2003), I suggest that a generalized interest in the body in a state of intensity can be seen to intersect with certain anxieties about "prurience" in postmodern image cultures. Chapter 6 proceeds to address the conceptualization of the pornographic as a realm of representation that not only sporadically eschews or displaces sex, but that *need not be sexually explicit at all*. The counterintuitive, if not oxymoronic, notion of a nonsexual pornographic is an issue that lies at the very center of this book, and is sketched out with reference to a diverse range of political or documentary images and texts. I critically consider how and why this material comes to be connected with the pornographic, and relate this back to the emergence of intensity and prurience as key definitional criteria within a contemporary reconceptualization of porn.

In Part III, I further develop my analysis of the displacement of sex within contemporary understandings of the pornographic by considering the concept of "the authentic." Beginning with an examination of postmodern anxieties about authenticity, Chapter 7 outlines some of the many ways in which adult entertainment can be invested in ideas of the real, and analyzes how particular examples of adult entertainment generate an authenticity effect. Chapter 8 focuses on the popular literary phenomenon known as "misery porn," the subgenre of autobiographical works that are based on the author's real-life experiences of physical or emotional suffering. I interrogate exactly what it is about such works that makes them available for consideration as pornography, and consider what effect the ideas of genre and authenticity have on their reception. In the final chapter, I discuss the oeuvre and authorial persona of the literary hoax JT LeRoy. LeRoy's work exists at the intersection of various significant fault lines within contemporary thinking on misery memoir, and can be seen to trouble the distinction between misery porn and pornography proper. I conclude the section by thinking about how we might reframe the pornographic in relation to a dual emphasis on reality and the Real as *jouissance*.

Throughout this book, I draw on, question, and extend the approach of Porn Studies in an attempt to add to the growing number of academics who believe that this developing discipline needs to be more emphatic in its criticism of porn. I agree with Bernardi's suggestion that we must aspire to "a cinephile's golden mean, where critical analysis lies between two academic vices: excessive polemics on the one hand and deficient ideological analysis on the other" ("Interracial Joysticks" 223); we must, as Bernardi expresses it elsewhere, be "in favor of media literacy and ideological critique but against censorship and polemical positions on pornography" ("Racism and Pornography" 117). Critical voices are vital if Porn Studies is to evolve beyond a yea-saying exercise. To continue being taken seriously as a form of cultural theory, it must go beyond its investment in the political potential of sex and sexually explicit materials in order to become a more complex, nuanced, and rigorous discipline—one that can provide relevant insights into an ever-changing area of twenty-first century culture. It is to this kind of discipline that I, in addressing the pornographic as a wide-ranging and sometimes troubling cultural construct, aspire to contribute. If pornography isn't necessarily corrupting, violent, or oppressive, neither is it always progressive, healing, or liberating, and I would suggest that Porn Studies scholars owe it to their discipline to be less tentative about acknowledging that fact.

PART I

Feminism, Pornography, Transgression

This section contends that there is a clear clustering of issues detectable in contemporary responses to pornography, with certain key ideas suggesting and feeding off of one another in a manner that makes them difficult to disentangle. Specifically, there is an evident assumption that there is an organically occurring link between the concepts of the transgressive, the pornographic, and the feminist. We find something resembling this linkage in Porn Studies, with theorists frequently making a case for the significance of the genre of pornography by depicting it as oppositional to the values and standards of mainstream patriarchal culture. Laura Kipnis, for example, suggests that "Pornography provides a realm of transgression that is, in effect, a counter-aesthetics to dominant norms for bodies, sexualities, and desire itself" ("How to Look at Pornography" 121), and Constance Penley argues that "porn and its white trash kin seem our best allies in a cultural wars insurgency that makes camp in that territory beyond the pale" (328). The author and sex therapist Marty Klein, meanwhile, suggests that the "revolutionary implications of empowering people sexually challenge the cultural status quo" (254), and even goes so far as to state:

> Pornography's truths are subversive because they claim that people can empower themselves and create their own erotic norms. Political structures just hate when ideas or cultural products empower people. This is the recurring lesson of Copernicus, Guttenberg, Margaret Sanger, Lenny Bruce, and Timothy Leary. (254)

It is easy to appreciate the motivations behind this kind of celebratory account of pornography, even if we do reject the suggestion that its "truths" have the same kind of revolutionary import as the thinking of Copernicus. The limitations of analyses that set out to exalt pornography for its transgressive potential are obvious, however. By suggesting that porn's transgressions liberate "exactly those contents that are exiled from sanctioned speech, from mainstream culture and political discourse" (Kipnis, "How to Look at Pornography" 120), they encourage a largely uncritical understanding of transgression as a straightforwardly useful tool for feminism and liberal left-wing politics. This risks producing a partial and somewhat one-sided conceptualization of transgression as that which only ever violates the oppressive norms and rigid demands of heteronormative society. Transgression, of course, does not operate with this kind of politically correct fastidiousness. As Paasonen notes, contemporary pornography can be viewed as a genre in which "irreverence to social codes regulating appropriate behavior is rather programmatic and [. . .] the attraction of porn stems from its ability to disturb such codes. In other words, the incorrect becomes somewhat dogmatic" ("Repetition and Hyperbole" 69). Indeed, as is seen throughout this book, many pornographic texts appear to rely precisely on the *flouting* of those taboos surrounding the ethical, respectful, and appropriate treatment of others—such as taboos against sexual violence, underage sex, and the perpetuation of sexist and racist stereotypes—for much of their transgressive force.[1]

In addition to this failure to engage with the many possible objects and directions of transgression as it operates within pornographic discourse, many of the more simplistically "porn-positive" accounts tend to ignore the complex manner in which transgression and taboo necessarily interpenetrate—the fact that transgression "presupposes the existing order, the apparent maintenance of norms under which energy accumulates thereby making transgression necessary" (Klossowski 19). The importance of this co-dependence is made plain by such influential studies as Georges Bataille's *Eroticism*, in which the author remarks, "*The transgression does not deny the taboo but transcends it and completes it*" (63). In other words, the act of transgression actually reinforces the taboo that it violates because it depends on this taboo for its own subversive energy—indeed, for its very existence *as* transgression. As Bataille states:

> If we observe the taboo, if we submit to it, we are no longer conscious of it. But in the act of violating it we feel the anguish of the mind without which the taboo could not exist: that is the experience of sin. That experience leads to the completed

transgression, the successful transgression which, in maintaining the prohibition, maintains it in order to benefit by it. (*Eroticism* 38)

He makes a similar case in relation to periods of carnival or festival, stating that such periods represent "the cessation of work, the unrestrained consumption of its products and the deliberate violation of the most hallowed laws, but the excess consecrates and completes an order of things based on rules; it goes against that order only temporarily" ("The Festival" 249).

In using the notions of transgression and carnivalesque subversion merely in order to make a case for the dissident potential of pornography, Porn Studies often oversimplifies the relationship between the taboo and its own violation, thereby disregarding much of what is most compelling and complex about transgression as a concept. Linda Williams is a Porn Studies scholar with a more sophisticated understanding of transgression than most—her excellent work on race in "Skin Flicks on the Racial Border," for example, draws on Bataille to emphasize the centrality of taboos for the concept of eroticism—but even in her case, an investment in an anti-censorship position can manifest itself as a marked tendency to actively seek out the disruptive potential of pornographic discourse, while dismissing or overlooking some of its more troubling aspects.[2]

The discourses of pornography, feminism, and transgression are, as I shall endeavor to demonstrate throughout Part I, being persistently brought into conversation. Indeed, it seems that the usage of any one of these terms is haunted by the specter of the other two. We cannot hope to understand this clustering of concepts, I suggest, without looking back to some of the key debates surrounding sexuality and pornography that took place within the feminist movement in the late 1970s and the 1980s. These debates, known as the "sex wars," have had a lasting impact on our understanding of sexually explicit representations, and any comprehensive study of pornography cannot hope to avoid feeling their effects and acknowledging their influence on the study of the genre. In what follows, I offer an extended discussion of the feminist sex wars, particularly in relation to notions of transgression and pornography, before going on to look at what these debates often inadvertently obscure. In helping to tie sexuality to the violation of taboos, I argue, the sex wars skewed the way in which our culture understands transgression. These debates therefore contributed to a certain slippage in terms of the idea of the pornographic that, as I demonstrate, has led to the term loosing much of its specificity and meaningfulness.

1

The Sex Wars

Transgressive Politics and the Politics of Transgression

Anti-Pornography and Pro-Sex Perspectives

Carole S. Vance describes the feminist sex wars as "the impassioned, contentious, and, to many, disturbing debates, discussions, conferences and arguments about sexuality that continued unabated until at least 1986" ("More Danger, More Pleasure" xxii), and she remarks that these debates "often explicitly focused on the anti-pornography movement's fetishized Big Three—pornography, sado-masochism, and butch-femme roles" (xxiii). Mandy Merck, meanwhile, traces the origins of this "period of fabled conflict over the politics of sexual practice" (247) to three specific events: "the 1980 National Organization of Women's resolution condemning sadomasochism, pornography, public sex and pederasty; the 1981 'Sex Issue' of [the feminist journal] *Heresies*; and the 1982 Barnard conference 'Towards a Politics of Sexuality'" (247). Although the areas of dispute that came to the fore during the sex wars were in fact fairly numerous, I concentrate primarily on the intense debates that occurred around the issue of pornography. What were the key positions taken on porn? How did these positions use and exploit ideas of transgression and taboo, and what light can they shed on these complex concepts?

The anti-pornography feminism of the sex wars era was, as its name suggests, critical of the role that it believed pornography played in the subjugation of women, and strongly opposed to its continued existence and availability within contemporary society. Porn was perceived as possessing the power to have a profound and negative effect on the lives of real women, and in 1975, Susan Brownmiller felt moved to set herself against the proponents of the so-called sexual revolution by declaring that "Pornography, like rape, is a male invention, designed to dehumanize women, to reduce the female to an object of sexual access, not to free sensuality from moralistic or parental inhibition" (38). Many of the most high-profile advocates of the anti-pornography position similarly linked pornography with violence against women. Andrea Dworkin, for example, suggested in 1980 that the "basic action of pornography is rape: rape of the vagina, rape of the rectum, and now, after the phenomenal success of *Deep Throat*, rape of the throat" ("Women Lawyers and Pornography" 238), and she speculated that "the popularity of throat rape in current pornography" might lead to an increase in real deaths from suffocation (238). Although the debates surrounding the effects of pornography on violent behavior are still contentious, ongoing, and inconclusive, Dworkin here invokes the alarming specter of sexual deaths directly initiated by pornographic texts in order to provoke anxiety and to garner support for the anti-porn cause.

However, Dworkin suggests not only that pornography is a potential *trigger* for male sexual violence, but also that pornography is in and of itself a *form* of that violence. In *Pornography: Men Possessing Women*, Dworkin defines pornography in terms of the "dominance and violence" that she believes it necessarily involves (10), and she argues that sexually explicit visual materials "document a rape, a rape first enacted when the women were set up and used; a rape repeated each time the viewer consumes the photographs" (137). When it comes to pornography, then, not only is its production, like the behavior of its viewers, a near-inevitable site of male violence, but also the very process of looking at and gaining pleasure from a pornographic image is perceived as in itself constituting a form of assault.

If this position seems like an unsophisticated and somewhat extreme analysis of the hermeneutic process and of the relationship between reader and text, even more remarkable is the anti-pornography movement's simplistic equation of pornography with acts of historical violence. In her analysis of a photo spread originally published in the German edition of *Playboy* magazine, which depicts a racially ambiguous woman with "her ankles manacled, laser beams appearing to penetrate her vagina" (*Pornography* 153), Dworkin explicitly relates soft-core pornographic images to real-life atrocities. She suggests that the photographs, "like all pieces of pornography, do not exist in a historical vacuum. On the contrary, they exploit history—especially historical hatreds and historical suffering. The witches were burned. The Jews were burned. The laser burns. Jew and woman, *Playboy*'s model is captive, bound, in danger of burning" (*Pornography* 143). The images are here unequivocally equated with genocide, and this rhetorical tactic is not exclusive to Dworkin. Catharine A. MacKinnon, another high-profile anti-porn feminist and Dworkin's frequent collaborator, similarly evokes the specter of historical violence and mass death when she suggests that activism against pornography is a form of "resistance to a sexual fascism of everyday life" (23), and that any sexual pleasure generated by the consumption of pornography is akin to "masturbating to the violation of [. . .] human rights" (18).

Anti-pornography activism came to a head with attempts to push through new civil rights ordinances, authored by Dworkin and MacKinnon, in cities such as Minneapolis, Indianapolis, and Cambridge, Massachusetts. These controversial local ordinances sought to allow "victims" of pornography to bring a civil action directly in court, and defined pornography as "a form of discrimination on the basis of sex," and as "the sexually explicit subordination of women" ("Minneapolis Ordinance, 1983" 428). They tried to make it possible for people to take "the maker(s), seller(s), exhibitor(s), or distributor(s)" of pornography to court for "Discrimination by trafficking in pornography," "Coercion into pornographic performances," and "Assault or physical attack due to pornography" (429–30). They also were designed to allow "Any woman, man, child, or transsexual who has pornography forced on him/her" to take legal action against "the perpetrator and/or institution" responsible (430). These ordinances were either vetoed by municipal officials in the cities in which they were passed or eventually ruled unconstitutional, but even so, they drew significant attention to MacKinnon and Dworkin's brand of feminism and provoked substantial debate about the issue of pornography within the wider culture.

Located on the other side of the sex wars of the 1980s was the anti-censorship or pro-sex feminist position referred to in my introduction. Perhaps because of the extremely high profile of the anti-pornography feminist movement, much of the pro-sex feminism of this era feels reactive or defensive, with activists and critics directing much of their energy toward agitating specifically against the anti-pornography civil rights ordinances. Nan D. Hunter and Sylvia Law, for example, both members of the Feminist Anti-Censorship Taskforce (FACT), produced "The FACT Brief" in 1985. This document was expressly designed to

> mobilize, in a highly visible way, a broad spectrum of feminist opposition to the enactment of laws expanding state suppression of sexually explicit material; and to place before the Court

of Appeals for the Seventh Circuit a cogent legal argument for the constitutional invalidity of an Indianapolis municipal ordinance that would have permitted private civil suits to ban such material, purportedly to protect women. (207)

Similarly, in the early 1990s, Feminists Against Censorship, a group of British pro-sex activists, produced a slim volume entitled *Pornography and Feminism: The Case Against Censorship*. This pamphlet largely focused on encouraging people to oppose a bill, sponsored by the Labour MP Dawn Primarolo, which was designed to restrict the availability of certain types of sexually explicit material.

In addition to this kind of targeted activism, pro-sex feminists engaged in responding to and refuting the claims of anti-pornography feminism more generally. Carole S. Vance, for example, argued that "Women are vulnerable to being shamed about sex, and the anti-pornography ideology makes new forms of shaming possible" ("Pleasure and Danger" 6). Ellen Willis, meanwhile, suggested, "If feminists define pornography, per se, as the enemy, the result will be to make a lot of women ashamed of their sexual feelings and afraid to be honest about them. And the last thing women need is more sexual shame, guilt, and hypocrisy—this time served up by feminism" (83).

A primary strategy of pro-sex feminist resistance to the anti-porn movement can be found in the presentation of sexually explicit texts as agreeable and politically useful cultural objects, with critics such as Lisa Duggan, Nan D. Hunter, and Carole S. Vance arguing that "Just as the personal can be political, so can the specifically and graphically sexual" (59). One of the key ways in which this foregrounding of porn's political potential was achieved was via a certain gesturing toward pornography's radical or transgressive qualities—via an investment in, as Jane Juffer puts it, "inflating the importance of pornography as a transgressive text" (*At Home With Pornography* 34).[1] This is suggested by the frequent invocations of rebellion in the writings of the period. The influential pro-sex activist and "sex radical" Pat (now Patrick) Califia, for example, stated the following in 1986:

> Even given the constraints under which it is currently produced, pornography is valuable. It sends out messages of comfort and rebellion. It says: Lust is not evil. The body is not hateful. Physical pleasure is a joyful thing and should not be hidden or denied. It is not true that women have no sexu-

al hunger. There are other people who think about and do the things you dream about. Freedom is possible. There is a choice. ("The Obscene, Disgusting, and Vile Meese Commission Report" 52)

In a similar vein, Willis argues that pornography "expresses a radical impulse" (85) and that "a woman who enjoys pornography (even if that means enjoying a rape fantasy) is in a sense a rebel, insisting on an aspect of her sexuality that has been defined as a male preserve" (85). More recent pornography scholars have picked up this kind of celebratory account of porn, along with all its windy rhetoric. However, as I demonstrate here, this position is largely based on a misconception of, or an uncritical attitude toward, the concept of transgression. Indeed, I suggest that the complex operations and conceptualizations of transgression at work within the feminist sex wars render problematic the seemingly clear-cut division between the pro-sex and anti-pornography positions. These two standpoints, as will become apparent, are not engaged in separate, diametrically opposed political projects, but are in fact both engaged in the same endeavor—that is, in a concerted effort to redeem human sexuality.

The Operations of Transgression Within Pro-Sex Feminism

Although the pro-sex and anti-pornography positions outlined here may appear to be inherently antithetical, they do in fact have more common ground than one might assume. For example, Leo Bersani suggests that Dworkin and MacKinnon's "most radical claim is [. . .] that so-called normal sexuality is already pornographic," and he argues that the "ultimate logic" of their critique "would be *the criminalization of sex itself until it has been reinvented*" ("Is the rectum a grave?" 214). He is therefore able to position the anti-pornography strand of the feminist movement within a "more general enterprise, one which I will call the *redemptive reinvention of sex*" (214). I argue that this redemptive urge also can be detected within the work of certain pro-sex feminists.

In her essay "Desire for the Future: Radical Hope in Passion and Pleasure," Amber Hollibaugh suggests the following:

> Feminism must be an angry, uncompromising movement that is just as insistent about our right to fuck, our right to the beauty of our individual female desires, as it is concerned with

> the images and structures that distort it. This goal is not an end in itself but a means which will ultimately determine the future and direction of our desires. As feminists, we should seek to create a society limited only by those desires themselves. (409)

Hollibaugh's celebration of the sexual here is forward-looking and future-orientated. The acceptance of desire, passion, and pleasure within the feminist movement is perceived not as "an end in itself," but as the necessary origin of a radically reimagined society and economy of bodily pleasures. We also can see this emphasis on social change within Califia's work, as he claims that

> being a sex radical means being defiant as well as deviant. It means being aware that there is something unsatisfying and dishonest about the way sex is talked about (or hidden) in daily life. It also means questioning the way our society assigns privilege based on adherence to its moral codes, and in fact makes every sexual choice a matter of morality. ("Introduction" xii)

Being a sexual dissident, it seems, is not only about violating widely held norms in one's sexual life, but also is about actively and deliberately questioning contemporary society and its values.

Such contributions to the sex wars can be seen as belonging to the "immense body of contemporary discourse that argues for a radically revised imagination of the body's capacity for pleasure" (Bersani, "Is the rectum a grave?" 215). As Bersani argues, this discursive project is in fact predicated on "a certain refusal of sex as we know it, and a frequently hidden agreement about sex as being, in its essence, less disturbing, less socially abrasive, less violent, more respectful of 'personhood' than it has been in a male-dominated, phallocentric culture" (215).[2] Both the antipornography and pro-sex positions, then, which seem so divided over the issue of sexually explicit material, are in fact engaged in the same kind of redemptive project. Each in its own way rejects sex in its current form as inadequate and insufficiently egalitarian, and anticipates a new sexual world order that is less oppressive to women and vulnerable minorities.

An analysis of these positions in relation to the notion of transgression suggests further unexpected points of crossover. Pro-sex feminism, for example, can be seen as expressing an attitude that, far from embracing the pornographic, is in fact resistant to its troubling force. Benjamin Noys, in his discussion of the critical response to the often sexually explicit writings of Georges Bataille, suggests, "In an age that so admires excess Bataille has become more and more accepted, even lauded as the prophet of transgression" (*Georges Bataille* 1). The problem with this approach, Noys argues, is that it is actually "a profound *failure* to read Bataille" (1), and an "assimilation and appropriation" of his work (1). By adopting a simplistically laudatory attitude to Bataille's fiction, then, critics risk "confining" it "by admiration" (5).[3] It is easy to see how these insights could be extended and applied more generally to pro-sex feminism. In uncritically celebrating Bataille's writing, critics are in danger of ignoring or apologizing for its genuinely disturbing qualities, and of effectively resisting its power to disconcert. In other words, when we interpret Bataille's fiction in such a way that it becomes something thoroughly acceptable to our own personal value systems, we risk restraining, neutralizing, and rehabilitating him. Similarly, in enthusiastically praising the political usefulness of porn's transgressions—in becoming apologists for porn—pro-sex activists risk confining the troubling force of the pornographic text by rendering it safe. Indeed, as we shall see, it is not only the unsettling potential of sexually explicit representations that is limited and contained by this pro-sex strategy, but the very concept of transgression itself.

The *Oxford English Dictionary* entry for "transgression" defines the word both as "The action of transgressing or passing beyond the bounds of legality or right; a violation of law, duty, or command; disobedience, trespass, sin" and as "The action of passing over or beyond." The difference between these two definitions points to the fact that transgression is not necessarily loaded with the ideological weight of disobedience or rebellion, and can in fact take the form of a relatively neutral act of boundary crossing. As Peter Stallybrass and Allon White state, "there is no a priori revolutionary vector to carnival and transgression" (16), and it would therefore "be wrong to associate the exhilarating sense of freedom which transgression affords with any necessary or automatic political progressiveness" (201). To position an idea which has, as Noys puts it, "no secure conceptual identity" (*Georges Bataille* 87) as a handy political tool for undoing the effects of patriarchal repression is to underestimate the complexity of that idea and to attempt to impose impossible limits on it. Indeed, we would do well to retain a healthy skepticism when it comes to assessing the radical political potential of Bataille's model of transgression, not only because, as Lisa Downing and Robert Gillett remark, it "is at least as much about affirming the status quo as about challenging it" (93), but because the taboos being transgressed need not necessarily be bourgeois, patriarchal, or otherwise oppressive.

In pro-sex feminism, both pornographic representations and the supposedly transgressive force with which they are imbued are reimagined as instruments of social reform and as devices loaded with a politically useful transformative potential. One example of this kind of attitude can be found in Angela Carter's work on the Marquis de Sade (a name, incidentally, that will haunt the margins of this text). Carter writes that "Pornographers are the enemies of women only because our contemporary ideology of pornography does not encompass the possibility of change, as if we were the slaves of history and not its makers" (3), and she floats the idea of what she calls the "moral pornographer" (19).[4] This figure would use "pornography as a critique of current relations between the sexes" (19), thereby acting as a friend to the progressive gender political cause. The role of sexual arousal in this type of reconceptualization is, I suggest, frequently ignored, side-lined, and obfuscated in favor of emphasizing porn's potential as a vehicle of social reform.

Although apparently embracing pornography, pro-sex activists and critics are in fact protecting themselves against a regime of representations that, in its current form, is far from a utopian vision of an egalitarian sexual culture to-come. By focusing on the supposedly world-altering transgressive force of pornography, and by attempting to incorporate it into a politically progressive feminist system, the pro-sex approach limits, restrains, and largely ignores the realities of that which it purports to celebrate. I am not necessarily trying to suggest that there is anything wrong with this somewhat disingenuous approach. Instead, I argue that this supposed defense of pornography is in fact a shrewd and subtle form of resistance to it.

In "A Woman Writer and Pornography," an account of her experience researching and producing a book-length study on porn, Andrea Dworkin states:

> As a worldly writer—mired in time and meaning, infatuated and obsessed with the muck of real life—I decided that I wanted women to see what I saw. This may be the most ruthless choice I have ever made. But in the privacy of writing, it was the only choice that gave me the pleasure of writing, that greedy, arrogant pleasure: it was the only choice that enabled me to triumph over my subject by showing it, remaking it,

turning it into something that we define and use rather than letting it remain something that defines and uses us. (36)

This remark seems to me to offer as much of an insight into the pro-sex feminist position as it does into Dworkin's mindset and writing practices. In suggesting that attempts to remake and reimagine pornography can allow a writer to "triumph" over the genre, Dworkin unwittingly points toward the underlying, and perhaps unconscious, agenda of the pro-sex feminist stance.

If, as Dworkin suggests, the processes of examination and reinvention make it possible to prevail over the disturbing power of pornography, then the forward-looking, celebratory tendencies of pro-sex feminism, and its attempts to read pornography against the grain and reimagine it as an effective weapon for use against patriarchy, indicate not so much an acceptance of this realm of representations as an attempt to conquer or subdue it. These tendencies can thus be viewed as part of an attempt to obliterate porn as we know it from the cultural landscape—to eradicate it by strategically transforming it. Pro-sex feminism, which is often perceived as working in support of the realm of the pornographic, is therefore revealed as being resistant to contemporary pornography. Indeed, the version of the redemptive project which is enacted by pro-sex feminism has a clear advantage over that which is enacted by the anti-pornography movement, for in appearing to embrace and refusing to condemn pornography, the pro-sex position pragmatically circumvents many of the difficulties which come with attempting to resist an "industry that thrives on its designation as illicit" (Coward 315).

The Operations of Transgression within Anti-Pornography Feminism

Just as, in the case of pro-sex feminism, apparent acceptance can work as a circuitous form of rejection, so condemnation can function as a perverse form of validation or acknowledgment. To return to our exploration of the sex wars, for example, anti-pornography feminism can be shown to be alive to, and indeed productive of, that which it purports to wholeheartedly denounce. Dworkin includes a discussion of *Story of the Eye*, probably Bataille's best-known work, in her study of pornography. She summarizes the entire plot of the erotically charged novel in less than eight pages, and reduces the infamous bullfighting scene to a handful of flat sentences written in the past and present tenses:

> They went to numerous bullfights. They fucked in numerous environments, generally surrounded by stink and flies and urine. Simone demands the raw balls of a bull. Sir Edmond provides them. She wants to sit on them but cannot because of all the other people present. Sir Edmond, Simone, and the narrator become horribly excited. Simone bit into one of the raw balls. The bullfighter was killed. As the people screamed in horror, Simone had an orgasm. The bullfighter's eye was dangling from his head. (Dworkin, *Pornography* 173)

Noys remarks that this reading is "violently reductive, breaking down Bataille's writing into the staging of perverse scenarios," and argues that the "very violence of this reading and the horrified affect that Dworkin feels before Bataille is, in a strange way, a sort of respect for Bataille's writing" (*Georges Bataille* 88). That is to say, both despite and because of its condemnatory nature, this anti-pornography response to Bataille's fiction is in fact more receptive to its troubling and transgressive force than the laudatory readings that openly seek to defend it. Dworkin refuses to rehabilitate the text, claiming that its "language stylizes the violence and denies its fundamental meaning to women, who do in fact end up dead because men believe what Bataille believes and makes pretty: that death is the dirty secret of sex" (*Pornography* 176). She explicitly rejects—and in so doing, inadvertently foregrounds—the novel's disruptive affective power, its cultural significance, and its ability to produce effects in the extra-textual social world.

Of course, Bataille and Dworkin are in fact in agreement about what constitutes "the dirty secret of sex"; Dworkin, too, feels that eroticism in its current form connects all too easily with violence and death, and that pornography clearly demonstrates the fact "that male pleasure is inextricably tied to victimizing, hurting, exploiting; that sexual fun and sexual passion in the privacy of the male imagination are inseparable from the brutality of male history" (*Pornography* 69). As Noys points out, however, her "desire to categorize and condemn, to draw up firm boundaries and taboos, at once makes her feel the violence of transgression more and fail to appreciate the porous boundary between her own work and Bataille's" (*Georges Bataille* 88).

Similarly, anti-pornography feminism's creation and shoring up of certain taboos surrounding pornography can be seen as a perversely hospitable attitude toward the very realm of representations that it explicitly wishes to denounce. As I mentioned in my introduction to this section, it has been frequently and convincingly argued that transgression is inextricably linked to the forbidden, because it depends on that which it violates and "suspends a taboo without suppressing it" (Bataille, *Eroticism* 36). This notion of the interconnectedness of taboo and transgression has a long and auspicious history that stretches back many centuries before Bataille. Saint Paul, for example, explored similar ideas in his writings. As the New Testament scholar E.P. Sanders remarks, Paul maintains that "the purpose of the law is to provoke sin or to condemn all of humanity" (99), because this condemnation works to facilitate God's eventual salvation of mankind through Christ. In other words, the Apostle felt that "God himself had intended that the world be enslaved to Sin, so that he could save it" (Sanders 49), and therefore believed that the law had been handed down to mankind less because God wished it to be exactly and dutifully followed, than because He knew it would be broken and violated. God's law, then, was in fact designed to produce its own transgressions, and, as Alain Badiou puts it, its taboos can therefore be seen as "that through which the desire of the object can realize itself 'involuntarily,' unconsciously—which is to say, as life of sin" (*Saint Paul* 80).

Pauline thought demonstrates that the taboo has long been understood as generating the transgression that challenges or suspends it, and as provoking a desire for the very thing that it expressly forbids. We might therefore be prompted to question the efficacy of the anti-pornography movement's establishment of various "new feminist taboos" surrounding sexuality (Webster 387). In an article first published in 1982, Paula Webster examines the women's movement's recent history, and suggests that anti-pornography feminism's "list of taboos marked off more and more unacceptable terrain. 'Perverse' pleasures, like voyeurism, bondage, s/m, fetishism, pornography, promiscuity, and intergenerational, group, interracial, public or phone sex were presented as incomprehensible" (386). Bearing in mind "Paul's insight into how the prohibitive law creates sin" (Žižek, *The Puppet and the Dwarf* 15), this condemnatory attitude would appear to be a somewhat self-defeating political strategy. If the "law is required in order to unleash the automatic life of desire, the automatism of repetition. For only the law *fixes* the object of desire, binding desire to it regardless of the subject's 'will'" (Badiou, *Saint Paul* 79), then the anti-pornography movement, in setting up firm taboos around certain sexual practices, could be seen as inadvertently provoking the activities that it attempts to resist. The political activism of Dworkin and her colleagues risks simply creating more norms to violate, as well as rejuvenating something of the compelling aura of illicitness surrounding sexuality.

Indeed, we can find evidence of the unintended consequences of anti-pornography activism in some of the sexually explicit material produced during the period of the sex wars. Several of the texts that Dworkin analyses in *Pornography: Men Possessing Women* can be seen as exploiting feminism and the figure of the feminist in order to produce an erotic charge. In her interpretation of the pornographic novel *Whip Chick*, for example, Dworkin notes that the "dangerous female, now called an amazon or liberated woman, is ever present, ready to take over if the male lets up in his cruelty at all" (34), and she suggests that the book "targets feminists as the subgroup of women most threatening to male power, most in need of abusive, humiliating sexual treatment" (36). She also mentions a magazine feature "called "The Art of Dominating Women." It consists of four black-and-white photographs and a 'case history' with an introduction by a 'Dr.'" (160). She reports that this text, too, makes explicit mention of feminism; "The doctor explains that with the growth of the women's movement more men than usual seem to be sexually submissive but, never fear, the male will never give up or lose his role of leadership" (161).

Dworkin herself—as perhaps the most iconic representative of anti-pornography feminism—was also mentioned or depicted in pornographic works of the period. Indeed, in 1984 a "suit was brought against *Hustler* magazine for publishing features displaying Andrea Dworkin in a derogatory manner" (Nussbaum 142). These included references to Dworkin in cartoons depicting lesbian sexual acts and in captions for photographs featuring lesbianism and the fat female body. Martha C. Nussbaum opines that the "morally salient issue in the case [. . .] is one of harm, humiliation, and subordination. Dworkin is being treated as a plaything of male fantasies of humiliation and domination; in retaliation for her feminist criticism of men, *Hustler* is taking pleasure in portraying her as both disgusting and contemptible" (143). This may well be the case, but it seems to me that the pleasure of representing or encountering Andrea Dworkin within the pages of a pornographic magazine may also be a matter of self-consciously evoking the specter of feminist censure.

Hustler was, after all, a frequent target of Dworkin's ire—the publication provides the first of the examples that she subjects to close analysis in *Pornography: Men Possessing Women*—and we can therefore suggest that, in portraying Dworkin, the magazine is deliberately foregrounding its status as transgressive, renegade, and oppositional. This is not to suggest, of course, that there is anything politically progressive about the pornographic appropriation of Dworkin's persona; *Hustler*'s use of her name is an unsettling and deliberate attack on an individual by a corporation. As this section endeavors to illustrate, however, there is no *essentially* revolutionary aspect to any violation of taboos, and to say that *Hustler*'s actions are transgressive is simply to note that it self-consciously acts in an unseemly and inappropriate manner—by turning an anti-pornography campaigner into porn. It would seem that Dworkinite feminism, as a source of new standards of respectful and appropriate sexual behavior, inadvertently produces new prohibitions and therefore new possibilities for pornographers. Bataille suggests, "the essence of eroticism is to be found in the inextricable confusion of sexual pleasure and taboo. In human terms the taboo never makes an appearance without suggesting sexual pleasure, nor does the pleasure without evoking the taboo" (*Eroticism* 108). If we accept this argument, then to invent new sexual taboos is at the same time to generate at least the possibility of their pleasurable violation.[5]

This complex relationship of taboo and transgression means that the boundary between pornography and the political activism that seeks to resist it can sometimes seem remarkably fragile. Catherine MacKinnon has noted, for example, that the testimony of one of the women who spoke against pornography in the Minneapolis civil rights hearings "was published by *Penthouse Forum* without her knowledge or permission, selling her assault for sexual use" (12). Indeed, MacKinnon's work itself often has been seen as venturing perilously close to that which it most despises. Parveen Adams and Mark Cousins remark of *Only Words*— MacKinnon's study of pornography and hate speech—that "several reviews and comments have been struck by the appearance of passages in the book which are 'pornographic' "(63). This seems true also of Dworkin's readings of sexually explicit texts, which, in reducing pornography to its supposed essence in the humiliation and abuse of women, risk transforming works of conventional pornography into brutally erotic pieces of flash fiction. Harriet Gilbert has made a similar point about the proximity of Dworkin's writing to pornography. Discussing the polemical and autobiographical novel *Mercy*, which includes numerous depictions of rape and degradation, Gilbert notes that Dworkin at times adopts the "formal and imaginative language" of pornography (227). The prologue and epilogue "attempt to make it clear that *Mercy* should be read not for sexual excitement but as part of a feminist debate" (219), but as Gilbert remarks, "these context-providers (which would in any case make little sense to anyone unfamiliar with internecine sisterhood) occupy six of the novel's 344 pages" (219). She is thus prompted to question whether or not the text is in fact "prevented from being pornographic by its author's polemical bookends" (219).

An analysis of the feminist pornography debates demonstrates the ability of transgression to disrupt order and ideological position in numerous complex and unexpected ways. When one attempts to use transgression as a political tool, as pro-sex feminism sometimes does, one attempts to impose impossibly rigid limits upon what is in fact an endlessly mobile "a-concept" (Noys, *Georges Bataille* 87). It cannot, I suggest, be so easily pinned down and put to use. Following Bataille and Paul, transgression must be understood as the inevitable by-product of any attempt to impose order—as that which exceeds or disrupts a given system. It makes its presence felt in contradictions and disconnections—in the disavowed disavowal of sex that underpins an apparently celebratory account of sexuality, or in the resistance to pornography that is the hidden foundation of an ostensibly pro-porn position; in the respect for the disturbing power of the pornographic that lies beneath a horrified rejection, or in the invitation to transgress that comes with the enforcement of rigid taboos.

In the next chapter, I discuss the critical reception of a recent novel—Charlotte Roche's controversial and sexually explicit *Wetlands*—in order to consider how the contemporary association of pornography with transgression draws on the legacy of the feminist sex wars. I argue that it relies on a certain erroneous conceptualization of pornography as a straightforwardly dissident realm positioned in opposition to mainstream culture, and suggest that, in its own way, it represents another attempt to limit transgression. I also sketch out some of the ways in which contemporary discourses of pornography and transgression gesture toward an expanded understanding of the pornographic, and begin to consider the role of affect and the displacement of sex within current understandings of this concept.

2

Rethinking Transgression

The Critical Reception of Charlotte Roche's *Wetlands*

Wetlands, the debut novel by Charlotte Roche, is narrated in free direct discourse by 18-year-old Helen Memel, and takes place during the protagonist's stay in the proctology wing of the Maria Hilf Hospital. Having cut herself while "lady-shaving" (Roche, *Wetlands* 3), Helen is suffering from an infected anal lesion, and finds that her "swollen hemorrhoids are also pushing with all their strength against the razor wound, ripping the lesion open even farther" (4). With the narrator confined to her hospital bed, and the novel's diegesis therefore restricted to a world of medicalized bodies, corporeality emerges from the start as an explicit and central theme.

However, the text does not address the body solely as a source of suffering. Helen's actions during her stay in the "ass unit" (Roche, *Wetlands* 4)—including an abortive attempt to, as she puts it, "quietly give myself a handjob hidden under the bed" (158)—reveal a character with a marked interest in the aroused and sexually active female form. This fascination is further emphasized by the passages of retrospection and external analepsis that punctuate the narrative, offering the reader an insight into the protagonist's day-to-day relationship with her relatively healthy body. We learn, for example, that Helen uses her "smegma the way others use their vials of perfume. I dip my finger into my pussy and dab a little slime behind my earlobes" (14). We also are regaled with accounts of a number of her sexual exploits, including her first same-sex "hooker-fuck" (115).

It is, I argue, Roche's treatment of the sexualized, rather than the medicalized, human body that has captured the journalistic imagination both in the United Kingdom and on the continent. *Wetlands* reportedly caused "a delicious outrage" when it was first published in Roche's adopted homeland of Germany in early 2008 (Caesar, interview with Roche), with one national newspaper denouncing it as a "masturbation pamphlet" (Burke).[1] The features on *Wetlands* that have appeared in the mainstream British press also have tended to fixate on the novel's sexual content, particularly in terms of its relation to pornography. Joan Smith in *The Times*, for example, argues that the novel has managed to "reignite a longstanding debate about pornography," and Jason Burke of *The Observer* suggests that "For fans it is an erotic literary classic and an exploration of contemporary concepts of cleanliness and sex and femininity; for critics it is crude and cleverly marketed pornography." An article in *The Telegraph*, meanwhile, dwells on the fact that the book "was rejected by one German publisher on the grounds that it was too pornographic" and gleefully reports that "Roche's literary readings are restricted to the over-18s, and in Germany there were several reports of over-excited fans fainting upon hearing certain excerpts" ("Wetlands erotic novel goes on sale in Britain").

This overheated media coverage also has focused on the novel's alleged transgressive power, with the very "pornographic" character of the novel prompting critics to view it as charged with a certain subversive energy. Roche has been labeled "an unlikely shock artist" (Caesar, interview with Roche), and *Wetlands* has been described as "phlegmatic" and "taboo tearing" (Burke). Tony Paterson of *The Independent* argues that the text "is both an assault on the sexual and behavioral taboos that inhibit young men and women and an at times excruciatingly explicit account by the female narrator of how she goes about systematically breaking them." The author herself at times seems keen to encourage this kind of association between sex and transgression when it comes to her work. In an interview with the journalist Ed Caesar, for example, she remarks, "It happens that people faint in my readings. They get so worked up in it [*sic*]—it's either the sexual stuff or the stuff about menstruation. They are such taboos in people's heads that, when I go there and keep going there, they can't take it. I'm proud that I make people faint with words." Also, in response to a question by Philip Oltermann of *Granta*, Roche claims that she rather enjoys the image of "Me flying over Germany, throwing sex bombs into people's minds." These comments arguably suggest a woman who sees herself, or who wants to be seen as, being particularly open to the transgressive power of sex, and who deliberately positions herself as reveling in the violation of those patriarchal social norms that seek to control the feminine body.

The general tendency to interpret this literary text's sexual explicitness and its proximity to the pornographic as a measure of its potential transgressive force is, of course, based on some rather simplistic assumptions about the role and centrality of transgression in pornography—assumptions of which I am myself highly critical.[2] Yet however dubious such presuppositions may be, Roche's work is evidently positioned as shocking or unsettling, and (as Paterson's comments suggest) is frequently seen as political in its challenge to the conventions and norms of patriarchal society. The interlinking of feminism, transgression, and the graphic representation of sex is important here. The notion of a feminist agenda underlying Roche's depiction of the female body frequently crops up in reviews of her work, and this agenda often is related to ideas regarding both the novel's sexual explicitness and its depiction of the violation of bodily taboos. Reviewers have described Helen as a "wistful feminist creation, a walking, talking, bleeding, masturbating, hemorrhoid-bedecked apologist for anal sex and home-made tampons" (Ellmann), whereas the novel itself has been characterized by some as "a serious feminist book" (Aitkenhead, interview with Roche). *Wetlands* is positioned as an assault on the taboos that restrain or oppress people (particularly women), and the novel's explicit treatment of sexuality often is seen as important precisely because of these wider gender political implications.

It is easy to imagine why Roche's publishers might decide to emphasize both the book's overtly sexual content and its supposedly feminist agenda; after all, as Danuta Kean notes, "In publishing, where there's muck there's brass. Robust declarations that match literary aspirations with taboo-breaking feminism are a tried-and-tested publicity ploy." Such maneuverings also work to position the text within a very lucrative niche of the publishing market. Bryony Gordon, for example, sees *Wetlands* as one of a wave of fictional and nonfictional texts "in which women lay bare their most intimate experiences for the reading public in shockingly labored prose," and links it to recent lucrative bestsellers by authors such as Belle de Jour, Melissa P., and Abby Lee. It is less clear to me why journalists and critics would wish to emphasize this proximity. It seems to me that, although the journalistic response to *Wetlands* is aware of the fact that pornography is being cynically evoked by publishers in order to attract consumer interest, it cannot itself resist the lure of the incitement to speak about sex and porn as two of the primary sources of imagined transgression.

Representing the Abject Body

To some extent, *Wetlands* particularly invites interpretation as a literary work invested in the ideas of sex and transgression. As I have already indicated, the protagonist of *Wetlands* is not averse to providing explicit and titillating details of her sexual life, and it takes her less than two pages to reveal that, despite her hemorrhoids, she has "had very successful anal sex for many years" and can "come with just a cock up [her] ass" (Roche, *Wetlands* 2). There are detailed depictions of sexual acts of various kinds within the novel, and Helen examines and describes the sexual bodies that she encounters with precision and thoroughness. Indeed, in her discussion of her experiences with the women at the brothel, she even remarks that she doesn't get drunk before having sex with sex workers because "I worry that I won't remember afterward what the pussies look like. In which case it would all have been for nothing. That's why I'm doing this, after all. Studying pussy" (116).

There is plenty within the text to encourage a focus on its "pornographic" qualities, then. Indeed, the author herself also has done much to steer the critical response to her work in this direction. She has declared in interviews, for example, that she "definitely wrote a few scenes in the book to make people horny. For the reader it should make you sort of blush and get warm, like when you watch a scene like that on TV" (Roche to Aitkenhead), and she also has explicitly announced her support for and enjoyment of porn: "I am very much for pornography [. . .] I consume pornography with my husband, we like it very much" (Roche to Aitkenhead). However, I argue that the sexual elements of the novel are frequently overemphasized, and that this overemphasis often comes at the expense of the novel's more genuinely disconcerting elements. In focusing on the supposedly taboo-violating risqué content, the journalistic response in fact ignores those elements of the text that are most disturbing and most transgressive. I contend that the novel's strongest appeals to the body of the reader manifest themselves as nausea rather than arousal, with the moments depicting the ingestion of abject substances appearing expressly designed to sicken and revolt. The most prominent instance of this, perhaps, occurs in an incident involving medical waste.

Before undergoing anal surgery, Helen asks her anesthesiologist if it would "be possible for [her] to see what they cut away during the operation" because she would like "to hold it in [her] hand and examine it" (Roche, *Wetlands* 8). This damaged bodily material is dutifully delivered to her hospital room in a zip-locked plastic bag, just as Helen is settling down to eat a pizza. "Do I need rubber gloves to pull this thing out?" she wonders of the medical waste, before reasoning that "It's from my own body. So I can't catch anything, no matter how bloody it is. I touch what used to surround this clump of flesh—my gaping wound—all day long without gloves" (75). Helen expresses some disappointment that the contents of the bag is made up of "Lots of little pieces" (76)—"rectal goulash" (81) rather than "a magnificent anal fillet" (76)—but still professes to be "happy to have seen the pieces before they're cremated" (76). She then realizes that her "fingers are covered with blood and goop" (76), and decides that, rather than wiping her hands on the bedclothes or on her hospital gown, she will "lick [her] fingers off one at a time" (77). "I'm always proud of myself when I come up with an idea like that" (77), Helen's narrative informs us in a typically flat and even tone: "It's better than sitting helplessly in bed and hoping somebody happens by with wet wipes" (77).

Roche has stated that she believes she has "invented someone who is much cooler than I am, who is much more free and open-minded than I am, who could explore all the taboos" (Roche to Caesar), but her protagonist does not strike me as being a representation of a particularly "free spirit" at this point. Helen may display an apparently relaxed attitude toward bodily and food hygiene in this encounter with her discarded flesh, but it is clear that this approach is founded on a great deal of anxiety and psychic discomfort. Immediately before she asks the doctor whether she can see the bodily matter that will be removed from her anus in the operating room—"Dear anesthesiologist, would it be possible . . ." (Roche, *Wetlands* 8)—Helen prays that the surgery will not result in anal incontinence—"Please, dear nonexistent God . . ." (8). It seems to me that this desire to view the bodily by-products of her surgery, manifesting itself as it does during a real peak of anxiety, is part of a strategy to gain a sense of agency and to manage the corporeal form over which she is no longer fully in control. In encountering her own medical waste, Helen is hoping to regain an illusion of control over her disobedient physical form.

The character displays a similar attitude to her body when, soon after her operation, she asks a male nurse to "take a picture of [her] ass and the wound on it" because she wants "to see what it looks like" (Roche, *Wetlands* 40). Again, Helen's bold request of a virtual stranger may suggest a relaxed, confident standpoint regarding the human form, and a daring attitude to the confrontation of social norms or taboos. However, this request is similarly couched in terms of anxiety and a will to manage the errant body. She tells the nurse that she'll "go crazy" unless he helps her (40), because "There's no other way for me to tell what they did back there [. . .] Please. I can't tell from the feeling. I've got to see it" (40). The desire to see and to understand can again be viewed as part of a desire to regain control.

As the anthropologist Mary Douglas famously suggests, "dirt is essentially disorder. There is no such thing as absolute dirt: it exists in the eye of the beholder" (2). If dirt can be defined as "matter out of place" (Douglas 44), as a structural category rather than as an empirically verifiable set of unclean things, then that which we perceive to be threatening, polluting, or dangerous can be viewed simply as that which cannot be incorporated into the particular systems of classification that we use to order the world. Dirt, as Douglas puts it, "is never a unique, isolated event. Where there is dirt there is system. Dirt is the by-product of a systematic ordering and classification of matter, in so far as ordering involves rejecting inappropriate elements" (44). Helen's response to the collection of flesh in the zip-locked bag—the manner in which she calmly licks its bloody residue from her fingers—indicates that, for her, it does not have the power to pollute. It is not conceived of as matter out of place or as a troubling eruption within the classificatory system. She has come to terms with and conquered her unhealthy body in the form of medical waste.

Helen, it would seem, has the drive to examine threatening or dirty things until she is able to overcome them. She may appear to revel in the disgusting, but this is a symptom of her desire to prevail over and to neutralize her sense of the threat it might pose. Through a concerted effort of will, Helen refuses to view the bloody, pus-y by-products of her body as abject in Julia Kristeva's sense of the word; that is, as "something to be ejected, or separated" (127). For Kristeva, we avoid the abject because we "prefer to foresee or seduce; to plan ahead, promise a recovery, or estheticize" (209). In Helen's case, that which we might think of as abject— medical waste, an oozing wound—is deliberately sought out in the service of some of these very same preferences. The character uses the abject not to experience the limits of subjectivity or the precariousness of the body, but to help reassure and placate herself, and in order to plan ahead and visualize her own recovery.

Incidentally, we can detect a similar response to abjection in comments made by Helen's author. Roche has stated "I am not a person who would say, 'Oh, this is disgusting' and look away. I would look at the disgusting thing and describe it in a very detailed way. Maybe even to overcome the disgusting. You look it as long as you can and then it's not disgusting anymore" (Roche to Power). In this quotation, Roche suggests that her feelings regarding the disgusting exceed the operations of mere curiosity. Her openness to that which is unsettling or taboo is described as an attempt to "overcome" feelings of discomfort. This appears similar not only to Helen's behaviors in the novel, but also to the pro-sex redemptive strategies discussed in Chapter 1. Whilst pro-sex feminism sought to prevail over the troubling realm of contemporary pornography by ostensibly embracing and yet effectively limiting its transgressive potential, Roche celebrates the power of her writing to disconcert or to shock, and yet also articulates the idea that the endurance of the abject is a useful strategy for dealing with and surmounting disgust. In accepting and even welcoming a troubling presence, her comments suggest, one is better able to defend oneself against it and to strip it of its disruptive or self-shattering potential.

The effect that *Wetland's* treatment of the abject provokes in the reader, however, may be considerably less reflective or cerebral and a good deal more visceral. Roche's novel depicts the body *not* as a straightforwardly titillating object, but as a source of both repulsion and intense revulsion. Even in health, the female form is represented as being charged with the potential to disgust, and we encounter the abject even in Helen's reminiscences concerning her typical bodily habits outside the hospital. She refers to her vaginal discharge—"the nice light-yellow crust [. . .] which during the course of the day gets thicker as it continually gets re-moistened" (Roche, *Wetlands* 120)—as "a delicacy" (120); "Sometimes a bit of the crust will hang like a dreadlock from your pubic hair, spun around the hair like pollen on a bee's leg" (120), Helen says, and not only does she "like to pull this pollen off and eat it" (120), but she also ensures that "all of it makes its way into my mouth and gets slowly chewed between my front teeth so I can really taste it" (121). Roche's narrator also informs the reader that she once "drank someone else's puke. Mixed with my own. In big gulps" (*Wetlands* 59), and that

> When I pop pimples and get pus on my finger, I happily eat that. And when I squeeze a blackhead and the translucent little worm with the black head comes out, I wipe that up with a finger and then lick it off. When the sandman leaves puslike crumbs in the corners of my eyes, I eat them in the morning, too. And when I have scabs on a cut, I always pick off the top layer in order to eat it. (77)

It is moments like these that, to my mind, have the most pronounced ability to elicit visceral reactions; as I have suggested, it is nausea rather than arousal that constitutes the novel's most forceful appeal to the body of the reader. And yet, although one or two British reviewers do touch on the role of the disgusting in Wetlands,[3] it is almost always the sex that is pushed to the fore. This is clearly demonstrated by the headings and the subtitles used in articles, interviews, and reviews: "Publishers battle to sign up Europe's sex sensation" (Burke); "Novelist Charlotte Roche talks [. . .] about her sexually frank debut" (Aitkenhead, interview with Roche); "The British-born author is hot in Germany but her novel [. . .] has been criticized as literary porn" (Caesar, interview with Roche). The mainstream press coverage primarily focuses on Wetlands' explicit sexual content, and positions it as an elicitor of arousal, and therefore as the site of a subversive sexual politics and of a specifically sexualized type of affect. As a result, much of the affective power of Roche's descriptions of the revolting body has been ignored in favor of detailing the novel's supposedly transgressive treatment of sex. How are we to theorize this, then? What might this much-overlooked displacement of affect tell us about current popular thinking on disgust, sexuality, and transgression? And why has sex been overemphasized to such an extent in accounts of the text's transgressive potential?

The Contemporary Over-Valuation of Sex

It might be helpful at this point to take a closer look at contemporary understandings of transgression; that abjection and disgust are so infrequently invoked in reviews of the novel seems to me to be the consequence of a particular strand of Western intellectual history. As we have seen, the discussions of the novel's sexual content are frequently couched in terms of the violation of certain taboos, and the novel is presented as transgressive precisely because of its frank interest in sex and the sexualized body. The perceived interpenetration of sex and transgression is, of course, a familiar feature of our cultural landscape. Indeed, the ongoing tendency to conflate these two concepts could be seen as part of what Foucault identifies as "the centuries-long rise of a complex deployment for compelling sex to speak, for fastening our attention and concern upon sex, for getting us to believe in the sovereignty of its law" (*The Will to Knowledge* 158).

Sex is still widely assumed to be the privileged locus of transgression, and this is surely a result of what Foucault refers to as the "repressive hypothesis" (*The Will to Knowledge* 10); the notion that, with the development of capitalism and after "hundreds of years of open spaces and free expression" (5), our "natural" sexuality has been subdued and distorted. It is for this reason that "Something that smacks of revolt, of promised freedom, of the coming of age of a different law, slips easily into" the discourse on sexual oppression (Foucault, *The Will to Knowledge* 7), for if one conceptualizes sex as something which is "repressed, that is, condemned to prohibition, nonexistence, and silence, then the mere fact that one is speaking about it has the appearance of a deliberate transgression" (6). It is thanks to the lingering influence of the repressive hypothesis, then, that "we are conscious of defying established power" whenever we talk about sex (Foucault, *The Will to Knowledge* 6), and I would argue that contemporary Western culture has channeled its quest for the pleasures of transgression into this area more than any other.[4]

As we have seen, the journalistic response to Roche's debut novel certainly displays a tendency to (mis)read the sexual as the inherently transgressive, and to remain silent on the topic of disturbing representations of the abject body. There is an intense and insistent focus upon *Wetlands*' depiction of sexuality, with the journalist Sophie Harrison going so far as to suggest that the text's "basic premise is that Helen has had sex, feels great about that, and is generally at home and easy with human fluids in a way that the rest of us are not" (2009). This emphasis falls especially on sexual content as the primary site of the book's shocking or taboo-violating qualities, and this response is a symptom of a culture in which the concepts of sex and transgression have become so thoroughly conflated that all other forms of transgressive activity have been rendered largely invisible. In other words, the critical reaction to *Wetlands* is influenced by the repressive hypothesis and is tied to the now-conventional notion of sex and sexual speech as culture's privileged locus of transgression. It is for this reason that the role of disgust in the text remains largely ignored.

Indeed, this is perhaps reflected in some of Roche's own comments about reactions to her work. When asked by Nina Power whether she considers *Wetlands* to be pornographic, for example, Roche replies as follows: "I think 'pornographic' is the wrong word. We use 'pornographic' because we don't have enough words to describe what it is. I wanted to write something original, [to] be honest, and the way I write things is explicit because that's the way I see things." We see in this response, then, an awareness that the disgusting—those graphic depictions of the abject body—have been inappropriately labeled as pornographic. The transgressions associated with disgust, and the reader's affective responses to them, have been rendered almost invisible in journalistic discourse, because they have been conflated with ideas of the sexual via the use of the adjective pornographic.

The coverage of *Wetlands* could arguably be seen as yet another example of an unconscious attempt to regulate transgression by confining it to one of its most accepted, attractive, and marketable materializations. Although, as Noys notes, "Transgression can function in places we did not expect, and perhaps to be transgression can only function in places we did not expect" ("Transgressing Transgression" 317), this coverage, influenced by the repressive hypothesis, is tied to the now conventional notion of sex and sexual speech as our culture's privileged locus of politically radical transgression. This is despite the fact that, as Foucault so influentially put it, discourses on sex do not "multiply apart from or against power, but in the very space and as the means of its exercise" (*Will to Knowledge* 32), and

> one should not think that desire is repressed for the simple reason that the law is what constitutes both desire and the lack on which it is predicated. Where there is desire, the power relation is already present: an illusion, then, to denounce this relation for a repression exerted after the event; but vanity as well, to go questing after a desire that is beyond the reach of power. (81–82)

But not only does much of the critical response to Roche's novel in some way reinforce the association between writing about sex and a resistance to power, but it fails to take into account the decreasing ability of sex to retain even the illusionary force that Foucault once attributed to it.

Sex after Transgression

Since the first volume of *The History of Sexuality* was published in 1976, there is a sense that the conflation of sex with transgression has lost much of its luster, and gone some way towards exhausting itself. Slavoj Žižek's comments about "today's deadlock of sexuality or art" (*The Puppet and the Dwarf*) capture this perfectly:

> is there anything more dull, opportunistic, and sterile than to succumb to the superego injunction of incessantly inventing new artistic transgressions and provocations (the performance artist masturbating on stage, or masochistically cutting himself; the sculptor displaying decaying animal corpses or human excrement), or to the parallel injunction to engage in more and more "daring" forms of sexuality? (35)

This is further evidenced by hints of a move away from notions of sexual acts, practices, and identities as the source of a radical and politically transformative transgressive potential within the work of academic specialists. Virginia L. Blum, for example—a literary scholar with research interests in women's writing and gender studies—has remarked that "What sex/sexuality/intimacy academics often share is an urge to project progressive politics onto our intimate lives at the same time that intimate lives are imagined as potential springboards for successful democratic practice" (87), and she views the scholars in her field as being "committed to extracting a story of liberation from materials that may not be quite so emancipatory as we hope" (88–89). Tim Dean, meanwhile, also gestures toward the exhaustion of transgression as a concept, stating that "the vocabulary of transgression has permeated academic discourse to such an extent—influencing not just lesbian, gay and queer studies but the humanities and social sciences more broadly—that much of its original force has been blunted" (66).

There is also an increasing awareness of the manner in which the notion of sex as transgression is particularly vulnerable to being exploited by the operations of capitalism. Those groups that the pro-sex activist Gayle Rubin referred to (somewhat romantically) as "vulnerable sexual populations" (200), "erotic minorities" (211), and "populations of erotic dissidents" (225) are increasingly being viewed less as a thorn in the side of power than as a handy prop for the mechanisms of capital.[5] As Badiou remarks,

> each identification (the creation or cobbling together of identity) creates a figure that provides a material for its investment by the market. There is nothing more captive, so far as commercial investment is concerned, nothing more *amenable* to the invention of new figures of monetary homogeneity, than a community and its territory or territories. (*Saint Paul* 10, original emphasis)

As Badiou puts it, then, the "subjective and territorial identities" (*Saint Paul* 10) created when individuals use a shared sense of their sexual illicitness in order to coalesce as minority communities "never demand anything but the right to be exposed in the same way as others to the uniform prerogatives of the market" (11). To position these communities as transgressive often involves ignoring the senses in which they very much capitulate to the dominant ideology of late capitalism.

At the heart of this, I think, is Foucault's argument that the existence of power

> depends on a multiplicity of points of resistance: these play the role of adversary, target, support or handle in power relations. These points of resistance are present everywhere in the power network. Hence there is no single locus of great Refusal, no soul of revolt, source of all rebellions, or pure law of the revolutionary. Instead there is a plurality of resistances, each of them a special case. (*Will to Knowledge* 95–96)

Just as power and resistance to it can be seen as part of a pervasive network rather than as something centralized, so transgression can be viewed as operating at the local, situation-specific level. I have already suggested that transgression is a structural inevitability that can be experienced as political or apolitical depending on the system being exceeded, opened, or challenged. It is also the case that, being a local phenomenon, transgression does not operate with uniformity, and just because a certain act violates one of the taboos enforced by the agencies of mainstream culture does not automatically mean that it will violate another. Hence, erotic dissidents can also be exemplary consumers of commodities (including, of course, pornographic texts), and theorists and cultural critics are increasingly recognizing this.

Even as the association of sex with transgression is endlessly reiterated, it is showing signs of wearing down and losing its hold over the contemporary imagination. Sex is beginning, perhaps, to lose its status as a particularly privileged and iconic site of transgression. Certainly, if we take the capacity to elicit a visceral affective response as a sign of being psychically unsettled, and if we take this discomfort to be a symptom of the violation of our most deeply felt, culturally cherished, and ideologically loaded taboos, then, in the case of Roche's novel at least, the sexually graphic has given way to what Helen refers to as her "hygienic transgressions" (Roche, *Wetlands* 145). I would contend that—despite the narrow, sensationalizing reactions of the reviewers—many Western readers will be able to process the sexual imagery without registering it at the corporeal level as a transgressive affront, whereas the depictions of the abject human form are far more insistent and substantially more intrusive upon the reading body.

In my opinion, the most intriguing thing about *Wetlands* is not the explicitly sexual content, but the other ideas that get dragged into its orbit. This seems to me to be connected to a more general change that has taken place within the territory of the contemporary pornographic—a particularly volatile cultural space. When Roche argues that her novel is "more than just porn. For a start, it's not really sexy, it's also quite disgusting" (Oltermann), and when she says that she thinks ""pornographic" is the wrong word. We use "pornographic" because we don't have enough words to describe what it is" (Power), she is actually gesturing toward a certain slippage that has taken place within the realm of the pornographic itself. I would argue that Roche is prompted to bring the disgusting under the banner of the pornographic not simply because of a linguistic deficiency, but because the urge to encounter the disgusting—to be "grossed out"—is itself increasingly being conceptualized as in some way related to porn and the pornographic.[6] This notion of a certain set of slippages surrounding the idea of the pornographic is one to which I shall be returning throughout the course of this text. In Chapter 3, however, I specifically want to explore the role played by disgust in terms of an exploded notion of porn, and to critically consider how ideas regarding transgression might inform and contribute to an enlarged understanding of what pornography is and means.

3

Sex and Disgust in Popular Culture

The Pornography of the Gag Reflex

In the discussion of Charlotte Roche's *Wetlands*, we encountered scenes of everything from vomit drinking to pus licking, discharge chewing to scab eating. These representations of abjection were complex, affecting, and diverse, but our analysis was far from comprehensive. There is more to be said on the topic of contemporary engagement with revulsion, and more to explore when it comes to the link between disgust and the pornographic. No twenty-first century account of sexuality and the ingestion of abject bodily substances would be complete, for instance, without some reference to the Internet phenomenon that is "2 Girls 1 Cup." Since 2007,[1] this video—a trailer for a full-length porn film—has achieved substantial cultural visibility. References to it surface within pop cultural texts such as *Family Guy* ("Back to the Woods") and Lil Wayne's rap record *I Am Not a Human Being*. Indeed, *The Sex Education Show* (a high-profile, prime-time program screened by the British broadcaster Channel 4) recently described the video as "cult viewing, with millions of hits" ("Episode 1"). So, how are we to make sense of "2 Girls 1 Cup," and what exactly does this meme involve? Here is 15-year-old Ryan helpfully interpreting it for the benefit of *The Sex Education Show*: "I've seen some pretty grim stuff. I've seen two women and they were taking a dump, and they, er, were eating it. But then they, er, made out with each other and they were throwing up while they were making out." He neglects to mention the presence of the titular cup (receptacle of both feces and vomit), as well as the now-infamous surging piano soundtrack.

The video was initially intended as nothing more or less complicated than a work of adult entertainment, and it was expressly produced for a niche market of scatophiles. Its creator, the Brazilian pornographer Marco Antonio Fiorito, is a self-proclaimed "compulsive fetishist" who, in a statement intended for the US Federal Justice Department, claims that "money is not the main reason" behind his choice of career and subject matter ("2 Girls 1 Cup," *The Smoking Gun*). Despite any original intentions, however, "2 Girls 1 Cup" did not gain its notoriety by eliciting arousal from the wider public. In becoming viral, it transcended its primary pornographic usage to function as a rather different form of entertainment, and disgust, rather than arousal, became the chief draw for many viewers. This is evidenced by the numerous "reaction videos" posted on user-generated content websites such as *YouTube*. Such videos (in which the responses of those viewing "2 Girls 1 Cup," often for the first time, are recorded for posterity) have become hugely popular in and of themselves. Possibly the original contribution to this micro-genre—fartenewt's *YouTube* post "2 Girls 1 Cup Reaction #1," from September 2007—has generated well over 14 million hits at the time of writing. Some participants in this cultural phenomenon appear to willingly subject themselves to the viewing experience. *YouTube* user centerback14, for example, films his own reaction video with a webcam, and provides a verbal introduction before he begins to screen the infamous clip. This kind of viewer is presumably spurred on by a mixture of curiosity, a desire to be affected, and an investment in being part of a distinctive community of virtual spectators. Others participants, such as the viewers in fartenewt's "2 Girls 1 Cup Reaction #9" or Jacqueline7oX's Grandma Marlene, seem less aware of what they're letting themselves in for; Grandma Marlene's face registers alarm and anger during the course of her reaction, while raucous laughter rings out off-camera. The video ends with a message of apology: "Sorry Grandmom! I love youuuuu! :)"

Although "2 Girls 1 Cup" is obviously not operating as adult entertainment within these clips, one could argue that the reaction videos *do* fit into a certain radically expanded notion of the pornographic. That is to say, these reaction videos might themselves be seen to possess pornographic qualities, despite the obvious de-emphasizing of sexual arousal that occurs within them. Certainly, these texts demonstrate an abiding preoccupation with involuntary bodily responses. We witness flinches and facial contortions, and hear exclamations of shock and horror. The most spectacular corporeal reaction to feelings of disgust—the gag or the dry heave—seems to be particularly cherished in these videos; in fartenewt's "2 Girls 1 Cup Reaction #1," the camera operator leaves his or her position behind the computer monitor in order to pursue one loudly gagging viewer in his hurry to leave the room. In a follow-up post titled "2 Girls 1 Cup Reaction #5," the camera pulls away sharply from the primary viewer seated in front of the computer in order to capture the violent retches of a nearby onlooker who was previously positioned out of shot. In kevinsnyder's clip of the reactions of a group of young American servicemen, meanwhile, one particularly violent heave is flagged up for the viewer with the help of a text balloon reading "Woh [sic] guy! Swallow that shit!!!"

This fascination with largely uncontrollable bodily experiences such as the heave or the shudder has strong links with certain characterizations of the pornographic. Williams, for example, touches on the importance of the bodily spasm in her discussion of porn's predisposition toward making sex as visible as possible. As Williams notes, this focus on rendering sex visually accessible is problematic for porn, for "while it is possible, in a certain limited and reductive way, to 'represent' the physical pleasure of the male by showing erection and ejaculation, this maximum visibility proves elusive in the parallel confession of female sexual pleasure" (*Hard Core* 49). The woman's corporeal experience of sexual ecstasy—for Williams, a key object of fascination for the heterosexual male consumer-viewer—proves frustratingly difficult to demonstrate. As Gertrude Koch puts it, due to the "expressive poverty of its naturalistic style, pornographic film necessarily reaches its limit literally *ante portas*, before achieving its goal of seeing the secret place where woman's pleasure resides" (41).

This quest for the unobtainable image of female pleasure is, in Williams' analysis, hugely influential on adult entertainment as a contemporary genre. She argues that the "animating male fantasy of hard-core cinema might [. . .] be described as the (impossible) attempt to capture visually this frenzy of the visible in a female body whose orgasmic excitement can never be objectively measured" (*Hard Core* 50), and she suggests that the excessive emphasis on depicting the male climax is in some ways "a substitute for what cannot be seen" (*Hard Core* 95). In short, Williams suggests that adult entertainment represents "the obsessive attempt of a phallic visual economy to represent and 'fix' the exact moment of the sexual act's involuntary convulsion of pleasure" (*Hard Core* 113), and displaces its interest in the supposedly invisible female orgasm onto the fetishized representation of external ejaculation. In the "2 Girls 1 Cup" reaction videos, I contend, the pornographic frenzy of the visible is transferred from the paroxysms of the male body at the moment of ejaculation onto the paroxysms induced by nausea and disgust. In this sense, it is doubly displaced, shifted as it is from the obscure spasms of the female orgasm onto the more visible penile ejaculation, and then from this male cum shot onto the state of involuntary corporeal convulsion triggered by the experience of disgust. These reaction videos represent what one might call the pornography of the gag reflex.

Positioning Sexually Explicit Digital Memes

Despite these points of intersection, however, I stress again that the "2 Girls 1 Cup" phenomenon cannot be dubbed pornographic in any common-sensical or straightforward fashion. As Paasonen suggests in her very astute work on the topic, "There is no reason to imagine that the affective complexities of shock porn sites and viral videos would automatically be experienced as sexually arousing or that people would relate to porn's imageries in a literal manner" (*Carnal Resonance* 243). Although the meme may be considered a work of porn in terms of its original context of production and the intentions of its production team, it does not circulate as adult entertainment; the viewing conditions, not to mention the affective responses generated, are markedly different from those associated with porn as a moving-image genre. The reactions posted on *YouTube* obviously speak more of abjection than of sexuality,[2] calling to mind as they do some of Kristeva's famous remarks: "Loathing an item of food, a piece of filth, waste, or dung. The spasms and vomiting that protect me. The repugnance, the retching that thrusts me to the side and turns me away from defilement, sewage, and muck [. . .] The fascinated start that leads me toward and separates me from them" (2).

Steven Jones makes a similar point in one of the few academic articles attempting to address the topic of sex or sexualized content in viral videos: "Because of their similarity to some types of pornography, it may be inferred that these images are meant to sexually arouse the viewer. However, while the images themselves are not incompatible with this reading, the context of distribution is" (129). The way the consumer-viewer encounters and contextualizes images of course impacts upon the reception and the affective power of these images. So, although the initial "2 Girls 1 Cup" video may fit the Criminal Justice and Immigration Act 2008's criteria for the pornographic—that is, it may be considered "of such a nature that it must reasonably be assumed to have been produced solely or principally for the purpose of sexual arousal" (Part 5, Section 63, subsection 3)—its viral aftermath merely uses it as part of a series of gross-out pranks intended to violently and visibly disgust.

In this sense, "2 Girls 1 Cup" can be seen to belong to a genre of digital images, both still and moving, which primarily relies on email, bulletin boards, and social networking sites for distribution and circulation. These representations can be seen as depicting the point at which "pornographic images become exemplary of the more generally affective, disturbing or confusing" (Paasonen, "Repetition and Hyperbole" 72). Other examples would include 2004's "Eel Soup," which depicts "two Japanese women and numerous eels" (Paasonen, "Repetition and Hyperbole" 72), or the "shock site video-loop known as "Meatspin," which focuses on the rotating penis of a man engaging in anal intercourse" (Jones, "Horrorporn / Pornhorror" 127-28). As Steven Jones remarks, these so-called virals frequently feature material "culled from pornography (especially porn involving urolagnia, coprophilia, or graphic homosexual imagery) or from medical contexts (pictures of bodily abnormalities, severe injuries, and corpses)" (124). They can therefore be seen as part of a contemporary regime of representation that brings together a number of divergent forms of imagery and repurposes them in attempt to generate disgust, offence, or shock.

It is no coincidence that many of these kinds of images appear as "shock sites," often linked to Internet trolling. As the online encyclopedia of viral phenomena *Know Your Meme* remarks, people often are unknowingly directed to the websites via "bait and switch." That is, people are lured to them by online tricksters, who suggest "that they should open the link because of some incentive" (Ogreenworld), typically the promise of useful information or services. The sexually graphic or otherwise shocking nature of the imagery encountered then combines with the users' disorientation and confusion to deliver a powerful affective kick. Our attention is drawn once again to the context-dependent character of transgression here, discussed in detail in the previous chapter. It is not simply that the content of this material violates certain taboos around the depiction of the human form—although it could certainly be seen as providing a "counter-aesthetics to dominant norms for bodies" (Kipnis, "How to Look at Pornography" 121) via the active courting of horror and disgust. It is also, crucially, the manner in which the imagery is encountered—the way that it is aggressively sprung upon the viewer—which links it to transgression. Anal sex of the kind represented in "Meatspin," for example, can hardly be viewed as inherently transgressive, especially when placed in the context of a pervasive and diverse culture of online pornography; what makes it feel like a shocking taboo violation is the fact that it appears unbidden, while browsing for other materials. It is imposed on the viewer, opening, disrupting, and exceeding the boundaries of the anticipated viewing experience. The intrusive nature of the extreme imagery deliberately and gleefully runs against the expectations of the net user and temporarily violates the norms associated with the browsing experience.[3]

To position "2 Girls 1 Cup," and materials like it, as pornographic, is to ignore many of the significant details regarding the reception and the social function of this imagery. After all, as Laurence O'Toole insists in his book on adult entertainment, "the hard and soft-core truth is that arousal is porn's main event" (298). If arousal is marginalized or displaced from its position as the favored affective response, then we have to question to what extent the designation of "porno" still applies. To label these digital images as pornographic, then, would require us to consider the implications of this adjective beyond its popular usage; we would need to conceptualize porn in ways that would adjust, extend, and perhaps undermine many of the existing conventional and legal understandings of the term. This is an idea that I explore more comprehensively in the next section.

Bearing in mind this complication of the pornographic in relation to digital memes, I question *The Sex Education Show*'s treatment of "2 Girls 1 Cup." For me, the coverage registers as not only disingenuous but also as somewhat hypocritical. In the show, first broadcast in 2008, teenagers' use and enjoyment of adult entertainment is repeatedly, not to mention sensationally, problematized. Within the first minute of the first episode of the first series, the viewer is informed that Britain has "the worst ever rate of sexual diseases among young people; over twenty school girls get pregnant every day; and, most alarming of all, teenagers have unlimited access to extreme pornography." Here, a spurious claim about young people's unfettered encounters with certain representations is presented as eclipsing numerous (unwanted?) pregnancies and even the transmission of sexually transmitted diseases in terms of its importance for the health of the nation. The concrete consequences of teenage porn use are clearly meant to be self-evident, as no discussion or statistics are deemed necessary. It is within this hysterical context that "2 Girls 1 Cup" is mentioned.

The infamous clip is shown to a group of parents, including the aforementioned Ryan's mum and dad, and is billed as an example of the kind of extreme porn that today's young people are downloading and using. The adults are clearly concerned about the material that they have been confronted with; one worried mother says "If I caught them watching this, I would have to take their computers off of them. I'd just be so angry." Ryan's mother, meanwhile, is visibly anxious and upset, walking away from the screening at one point, before declaring that she is "totally freaked out." The gathered parents are presented as being thoroughly horrified by the idea that their offspring might be obtaining their sex education from this kind of non-normative material. However, as we have seen, "2 Girls 1 Cup" should not be understood as circulating as adult entertainment. Rather, considered in its meme-etic incarnation, it should be considered as a viral phenomenon loaded with alternative kinds of affect.

Indeed, *The Sex Education Show*'s coverage implicitly gestures toward the trailer's status as a meme by showing its viewers the faces of the parents as they watch. The show, in other words, stages its own reaction video. The set-up is almost identical, with the camera positioned behind the computer monitor in a manner reminiscent of the static webcams so frequently used by those uploading videos of viewers' reactions. The collective viewing context also recalls many of the most widely viewed responses, such as those posted by fartenewt, where multiple participants both watch the clip and watch one another watching it. And, of course, the reactions are also largely the same. There are the usual verbal and visual indicators of distaste—wrinkled noses, groans and exclamations—with a number of the unsuspecting parents instinctively looking away at times. There is one key element missing in this particular reaction video, however, and that is levity.

Perhaps the most frequent bodily paroxysm evident in the *YouTube* videos is the shudder of laughter; involuntary convulsions of gaiety can be detected in numerous online examples. Pornography's bodily contagion of arousal—the way in which its scenes of sex try to beget sensations of sex—is reproduced in these texts via the infectious laugh, which spreads among the on-screen participants and which pierces the screen to contaminate the viewer. Unlike the vast majority of the other recorded responses, however, there is no laughter on screen in *The Sex Education Show*. The show simply refuses to let the assembled parents in on the joke. For most of its audience, "2 Girls 1 Cup" is not experienced as adult entertainment in any meaningful way. As with Roche's *Wetlands*, then, we find that a text which deals primarily with hygienic transgressions is being misread as dealing primarily with sexual ones; we find that a text that predominantly elicits reactions of disgust is being erroneously assumed to predominantly elicit reactions of sexual arousal. "2 Girls 1 Cup" is a work of adult entertainment that is no longer typically interpreted in the manner intended by its creators. It is in some ways undoubtedly pornographic, and yet, for the vast majority of its mass audience, its raw proximity to the realm of abjection means that it lacks any kind of a masturbatory function. It is therefore somewhat anomalous in terms of conventional understandings of what porn is and does.[4] I finish this chapter by muddying the waters even further via a discussion of another anomalous example—a visual text that somehow manages to be simultaneously both non-sexual and pornographic.

Medical Porn: Pornography Without Sex?

The text I am referring to is another Channel 4 show, *Embarrassing Bodies*, which started as *Embarrassing Illnesses* back in 2007 and which is currently ongoing. The show usually airs in the 9 PM slot, in "among the soaps and sitcoms of primetime Channel 4" (Benedictus), and features a team of doctors offering the British public advice about a range of supposedly embarrassing ailments. Certain episodes even go out live, enabling viewers at home to share and discuss their health problems via a webcam. Like our previous example, the show centers on representations of the abject body. Unlike "2 Girls 1 Cup," however, it explicitly does not set out to arouse the viewer. The disgusting body is medicalized rather than eroticized, and this is stressed on the *Embarrassing Bodies* website: A message at the head of the page warns us that the site "contains images of an explicit medical nature and nudity in a medical context." The depictions of vulvas and penises, breasts and rectums, occur within what are obviously clinical examination situations, and the sexual organs do not make an appearance in each and every segment. Conditions featured during the most recent fourth series, for example, include skin tags, tonsillitis, leg ulcers, earwax, acne, and sweaty palms ("Embarrassing Bodies: Back to the Clinic").

Despite this self-consciously nonsexual treatment of the body, however, certain cultural critics have found cause to label the show "pornographic." An article in the *Guardian*, for example, quoted a doctor as describing the program as "medical porn" (Benedictus). Kevin Maher in the *Times*, meanwhile, commented on the "crypto-pornographic nature of the show. The way it trails and teases with the prospect of high-value money-shots—the big genital close-ups, dripping and oozing in biological glory." There seems to be something interesting going on here, which relates back to our previous analysis of disgust in *Wetlands*; there is a certain displacement occurring in terms of the use of the idea of pornography. In the journalistic response to *Embarrassing Bodies*, porn is being characterized neither as a representational genre, nor as a product of lascivious authorial intentions, nor as the elicitor of a certain kind of erotic response. Content that does not identify itself as adult entertainment, and that does not set out to solicit the viewer's arousal, is being talked about as if it is an example of the pornographic. How can this be?

We might argue that the concept of transgression is once again a crucial factor here. As shown in Chapter 2, there is a residual (and increasingly anachronistic) tendency to characterize transgression as primarily related to the sexual realm, and to run together the ideas of pornography and the violation of cultural taboos. Perhaps the frequent breaches of the conventional boundaries set up around self-exposure help to make the show available for this kind of reading. That is to say, it may be that *Embarrassing Bodies*, like Roche's novel, is interpreted as pornographic simply because it deals with certain facets of the abject body, the representation of which is typically prohibited within mainstream Western culture. Certainly, many of the noisy objecting voices raised in response to the show would seem to support this hypothesis. The *Guardian*'s Sam Woolaston, for example, has repeatedly pointed to the "horrid and unnecessary" disregard shown for the norms of decorum by the show's participants: " 'I'm just going to pop some gloves on and have a little look,' are just about the scariest words you'll ever hear. They should be spoken by the doctor, and heard by you and no one else. But no, these people want to share." Woolaston objects to the violation of norms of bodily propriety enacted within *Embarrassing Bodies*. The scenes of clinical examination are viewed as dirty, in precisely Mary Douglas' sense of being matter out of place: "I'm very pleased these people are taking their problems to the doctor. But that's where they belong, at the surgery, with no one else there" (Woolaston).

Although the participants' contravention of norms regarding who gets to see our bodies, in what locations, and in which states, may well contribute to the manner in which *Embarrassing Bodies* has been interpreted, I suggest that we need to look beyond the perennial dynamic of transgression if we wish to understand why the show has been seen as pornographic. After all, as we have seen, transgression is such a capacious concept that one can detect its operations almost anywhere; if we agree that it is a structural inevitably (or at least possibility) within any given set of circumstances, then we must confront the fact that its meaningfulness may be limited for any concrete act of analysis. It gives us no absolute reference point, and we may simply find ourselves becoming ever more entangled within the "spiral" of transgression and the limit (Foucault, "A Preface to Transgression" 35). Transgression's usefulness in terms of helping us to palpate the slippage of the concept of the pornographic should not be overestimated, and our discussion deserves to be augmented with reference to a range of separate (although undoubtedly frequently related) concepts and ideas. How else, then, can we begin to understand the idea of the nonsexual pornographic? What is it, aside from the violation of taboos, that prompts commentators to posit ideas such as "medical porn"? I finish this chapter by sketching out some of the alternative factors in operation when it comes to a distended idea of the pornographic, and by outlining some of the key ideas to be advanced in Parts II and III.

Conclusion: Lines of Enquiry

In addition to making hostile comments about the transgressions enacted within *Embarrassing Bodies*, critics also focus on factors such as its relationship with its audience, its imagined appeal, and its effect on the body of the spectator. Those who conflate the program with pornography often gesture toward its power to provoke intense (and largely unpleasant) affective responses, for example. Dina Murphy remarks that its graphic representations of surgical brutality "did turn my stomach," whereas Leo Benedictus draws our attention toward what Kristeva might describe as the powers of horror: "Among my memories of consultations past, it is the abscesses and prolapses that live the longest." The experience of being moved by the image is positioned at the very heart of the viewing experience here. Indeed, submitting to an episode of this so-called medical porn is presented as a similar kind of affective experience to that induced by submitting to the viral phenomenon of "2 Girls 1 Cup." It is perhaps as a result of this emphasis on powerful, visceral, and seemingly disagreeable affects that commentators appear so suspicious of the show's audience.

The overriding journalistic response to the program's popularity is that it reflects very poorly on contemporary television audiences. Articles question the motives of those who would chose to watch something so overtly distasteful, and proffer theories as to the real pleasures of this particular text. Ian Collins, for example, declares *Embarrassing Bodies* to be "TV porn, pure and simple," reasoning that "viewers tune in specifically for the money shot—the over-pendulous testicles, the festering anal boils, the girl whose breasts exist in two separate postcodes." For him, the show "is not medical education. It exists for the voyeur and the chronically immature—a

21st century Freak Show for the chattering classes." Here, it is the show's ability to court the prurient interests of the viewing public—its indirect appeal to the ghoulish aspects of human curiosity—that is seen to warrant the adjective "pornographic." Collins sees *Embarrassing Bodies* as using an ostensibly educational agenda to obscure an appeal to a less wholesome form of epistemophilic desire.[5] The show becomes entangled with the idea of porn, then, not as a result of its medicalized nudity or frank sexual discussions, but because of certain anxieties about how it might be received—that is, because of the morbid and lascivious forms commentators imagine viewer engagement will take.

A similar kind of critical attitude is evident in Eva Wiseman's comments about the show's tabloid format—which "relies on suspenseful ad breaks and the promise of genital close-ups"—as well as in Leo Benedictus' insistence that "gawping is why the show remains so popular. It revives the disgusted thrill that many of us remember from our biology textbooks—a thrill very similar to the one that sent 2.6 million viewers to Channel 4 for Britain's Fattest Man, or the one that causes cars to decelerate past traffic accidents." As with Collins, then, we see the freak show emerging as a paradigm for viewer engagement here. It is easy to see the logic of these claims, even if we are suspicious of their disparaging tone and lack of supporting evidence. Indeed, one could argue that *Embarrassing Bodies* itself makes reference to the ideas of voyeurism and prurient interest via the visual language of its studio set; a substantial, articulated medical privacy screen provides the background for a number of shots. This screen functions not only as an ironic reminder of the deeply private nature of the issues under discussion (and under public scrutiny), but as a visual token of the spectator's investment in witnessing corporeal abnormalities and bodily "horrors" that are typically kept hidden. This, I argue, is a key factor in the alignment of *Embarrassing Bodies* with contemporary conceptualizations of the pornographic.

Affect and prurient interest, along with transgression, all appear to feed into journalistic characterizations of so-called "medical porn." However, there is (at least) one other idea that I believe is at play here, and it is an idea that is crucial to both the reception of the program and to understandings of porn. Underpinning the entire discussion about *Embarrassing Bodies*, I argue, is an emphasis on the authentic—on the real ailments of real people. This reality is crucial. As Dr. Paula Franklin of the reproductive health care charity Marie Stopes puts it, the show "doesn't shy away from real issues that are a concern to people. It's frank, it's honest, and it presents the information in an accessible way. If you're someone with a real issue, it can be very reassuring that other people have the same or similar concerns to you" (Benedictus). Those aspects of corporeality that are not widely discussed and that are typically left unrepresented outside of the doctor's surgery are brought to the fore in *Embarrassing Bodies*. More than this supposedly edifying mission of being "honest" about "real issues," however, the focus on authenticity is visible in the documentary emphasis on actual, extra-textual bodies. The close-ups and descriptions of the ailments featured would lack both their affective charge and their appeal to a prurient interest if they were not grounded (and guaranteed) in the living, suffering, and grimace-inducing flesh of the participants. Indeed, these bodies perhaps come to seem authentic precisely through their evident suffering; this is an idea to which I return in the discussion of trauma and *jouissance* in Part III.

Authenticity is yet another reason why *Embarrassing Bodies* has found itself being labeled as pornographic. As with the genre of adult entertainment, the viewer is presented with real bodies really experiencing corporeal phenomena on screen. The difference is that it is not arousal, sexual pleasure, and orgasmic climax that undergird the discourse but uncomfortable sensations, physical suffering, and bodily malfunction. We might argue that, as with the case of "2 Girls 1 Cup," the show represents something of a displacement of the sexual. Just as the gag reflex comes to stand in for another bodily paroxysm in the "2 Girls 1 Cup" reaction videos, so an interest in the authentic bodily experience of sex is displaced onto a fascination with the authentic bodily experience of illness in *Embarrassing Bodies*. We have already seen both Collins and Maher describe the show's unflinching imagery of ailments as a kind of "money shot," indicating a somewhat unconventional understanding of this pornographic convention. That an image need no longer feature the act of external ejaculation in order to be labeled a money shot—that pus, mucous, or inflammation might just as easily come to stand in for semen in an expanded notion of porn—suggests an urgent need to start recalibrating ideas about contemporary understandings of the pornographic.

To summarize, the claims that *Embarrassing Bodies* is "crypto-pornographic" (Maher), or that it represents a kind of "hypochondriac porn" (Murphy), seem to me to be grounded in at least three factors in addition to its perceived transgressive qualities. These are the intensity of the affective experience it induces in the viewer; the prurient interest it can be seen to exploit; and the corporeal reality of the various abject bodies it represents and examines. These issues will prove central to the argument advanced throughout the rest of *Beyond Explicit*. Over the course of the next six chapters, I explore them in detail as I attempt to "flesh out" the concept of a pornographic that is synonymous neither with adult entertainment nor with the sexually explicit. In Part II, then, I broaden my discussion of both transgression and the contemporary pornographic in an attempt to develop a firm set of alternative definitional criteria for an exploded characterization of porn.

PART II

Intensity and Prurience

Pornography After Sex

As shown in Part I, the complex interpenetrations of feminism, transgression, and pornography have resulted in something of a diversification when it comes to contemporary understandings of the pornographic. In the case of Charlotte Roche's *Wetlands*, representations of abject bodily substances, along with the affects that such representations might produce, have, as the result of a particular set of cultural operations and terminological difficulties, been brought under the rubric of the pornographic. In this section, I consider the manner in which responses and representations that are not typically viewed as sexual or sexually explicit can be seen to intersect with the pornographic. I move away from reactions of nausea and disgust in favor of examining the sometimes discomforting conjunction of prurient interest and depictions of the violated human form within contemporary Western visual cultures.

Chapter 4 examines a number of examples of adult entertainment and considers their engagement with a sphere of interests that exceeds the conventionally sexual. In particular, I address the surprising centrality of other, nonsexual body genres to a marginal subset of pornographic works. Beginning with a brief look at the history of pornography, my analysis will deal with such infamous and well-established contemporary pornographic artifacts as Larry Flynt's *Hustler* magazine, as well as with material that has yet to achieve this degree of cultural visibility, including examples of the emerging cultural discourse known as "warporn." Central to my discussion is the idea of intensity, and its role within sexually charged representations. Using Leo Bersani's post-Freudian account of the significance of powerful affective processes for the formation of human sexualities, I ask whether theories of intensity might help us to account for the at times surprisingly diverse nature of adult entertainment's interest in the body.

The other key theorist of intensity is, of course, Jean-François Lyotard, whose analysis of the philosophy of desire in *Libidinal Economy* frequently positions libidinal intensities as zones of radical possibility. For Lyotard, the "operator of disintensification is exclusion: either this, or not-this. Not both. The disjunctive bar" (14), whereas "every intensity, scorching or remote, is always *this and not-this*" (15). Like Bersani, he extends the ideas of sexuality and intensity beyond the genitals; indeed, the genitals themselves are displaced in a reading that views the body as a vast surface in which there "are no holes, only invaginations of surfaces" (21). However, he has a rather looser understanding of the idea of intensity than does Bersani. I find that, in Lyotard's (admittedly rather beautiful) rhapsodies, the concept of intensity becomes increasingly slippery, expansive, and difficult to use effectively as a critical tool—a critique that this book will also level at the explosion of the pornographic itself.

Lyotard argues, for example, that "intensities may withdraw from the skins of bodies [. . .], and pass onto the skins of words, sounds, colors, culinary tastes, animal smells and perfumes" (256), thereby exploding the idea to a point of near meaninglessness. He stresses that the "demand for clarity must be strongly denounced" (258), for the demand that one define the intense is "the first imprint of power on the libidinal band" (258). This anarcho-libidinal conceptualization of the liberating power of affect is seductive, but also seems to bring politics into a wholly eroticized realm, and to reduce it to the libidinal in a manner that feels somewhat anachronistic at a time when the transgressive possibilities of sexuality are increasingly being called into question. Bersani also displays an investment in sexuality's potential—in the possibilities for rethinking and decentering the self that come with ego-shattering experiences of *jouissance*, for example—but this is matched by a certain spirit of skepticism in the face of broad claims about the political implications of sexual practices (see his comments on parody and queer S/M in "Is the rectum a grave?"). This skepticism, combined with his more precise and restrained style, is why I find Bersani so useful, and why I favor his work in my analysis of intensity throughout this section.

Chapter 5 builds on Bersani's work to further develop, interrogate, and historicize this concept of intensity. Drawing on the depictions of cyber-voyeurism present within Margaret Atwood's dystopian novel *Oryx and Crake* (2003), I suggest that a generalized interest in the body in a state of intensity can be seen to intersect with certain anxieties about contemporary image cultures. Atwood's novel, I contend, presents an unwholesome interest in, and a disaffected engagement with, representations of the affected body as an indication of a damaged culture, and in so doing, stages an engagement with apprehensive accounts of the postmodern. The novel's depictions of a morbid and lascivious interest in the body also prompt a reassessment and a repurposing of the idea of prurience here. This largely derided (and apparently somewhat outmoded) concept might, I argue, prove particularly helpful in attempts to discuss certain marginal currents in evidence within today's visual cultures, as well as in efforts to theorize the role of intensity within pornographic representational practices.

Developing this examination of intensity and prurience, Chapter 6 addresses the conceptualization of the pornographic as a realm of representation that not only sporadically eschews or displaces sex, but that in fact *need not be sexually explicit at all*. The counterintuitive, if not oxymoronic, notion of a nonsexual pornographic is an issue that lies at the very center of my analysis of the pornographic, and that is sketched out with reference to a diverse range of political or documentary images and texts, including several that might be said to intersect with the warporn phenomenon. The materials engaged with here range from eighteenth- and nineteenth-century British abolitionist propaganda, to sentimentalizing anti-pornography feminist polemics, to the images at the center of the recent Abu Ghraib torture scandal. How, I ask, have these images come to be connected with the pornographic? For what reasons and to what ends?

By highlighting adult entertainment's nonsexual concerns before proceeding to emphasize the growing association of certain types of nonsexually explicit representation with the realm of porn, this section demonstrates that the meaning of the contemporary pornographic is progressively mutating, even to the point where it can be said to exceed any straightforward notion of the sexually explicit. At the heart of this mutation, I argue, lies a cluster of diverse but related ideas, including transgression, intensity, and prurience.

4

"Not All of It Will Get Your Dick Hard"

Pornography and Displacement

Pornography's Historical Diversity

In his essay "'Choke on it Bitch!': Porn Studies, Extreme Gonzo and the Mainstreaming of Hardcore," Stephen Maddison identifies a tendency within certain pornographic texts to engage with the idea of corporeal spectacle in a manner that might be said to exceed the domain of the strictly sexual. This engagement, he suggests, manifests itself in the use of the representational conventions of other genres—genres that, although displaying a marked interest in the human form, do not typically prioritize the sexual body and its performances over other forms of corporeality. Taking the output of Extreme Associates in general, and Lizzy Borden's *Forced Entry* in particular, as illustrative of this tendency, Maddison argues that such works of pornography "combine gonzo hand-held camera work and low-tech style with conventions derived from slasher movies, the reality TV genres of *Jackass* stunts and gross-out and fly-on-the-wall documentaries" (38). So Borden's porno, for example—which was a key text in the recent *United States v. Extreme Associates* obscenity case—might be said to in some ways imitate the slasher film genre, representing as it does the activities of a serial killer and his accomplices as they assault, rape, and murder a number of women.[1]

Meanwhile, Extreme Associates' *Cocktails* series, the second installment of which also featured in their obscenity indictment, might be said to recall the gross-out style of programming that became so popular on youth and music television outlets during the first years of the new millennium. The series depicts porn actresses drinking abject bodily substances such as semen, saliva, and vomit, in a manner that recalls famous affecting moments from the *Jackass* franchise, such as cast member Ehren McGhehey eating urine-doused snow in 2002's *Jackass: The Movie* or Dave England consuming a regurgitated omelet during a scene from 2009's *Jackass: The Lost Tapes*. Interest in the body is, in the case of *Cocktails*, seemingly displaced from the realm of the arousing to the realm of the repulsive, as reflected by the elements of apparent generic slippage.

Indeed, the subterranean connections between the genres of adult entertainment and the stunts-and-pranks format of some reality television is made even more explicit by websites such as *Fear Factor Fuck* (which was renamed *Sicko Games* after the makers of the NBC reality show *Fear Factor* contacted the site regarding trademark infringement), and *Porn Jackass* which, as the homepage declares, offers "CUNNING XXX STUNTS BY STUNNING XXX CUNTS." As one critic from the adult entertainment reviews website *Rabbit's Reviews* states, the material here combines explicit depictions of sexual acts with scenes of less sexual bodily feats such as women inserting fireworks into bodily orifices or being shot by paintball guns. The reviewer's verdict on this peculiar fusion of content is, tellingly, that it is "fun to browse through, but not all of it will get your dick hard" ("Porn Jackass review").

We might be surprised to learn that the genre of adult entertainment is capable of eschewing the sexual in this manner. After all, as Laurence O'Toole remarks, "Modern porn is about fantasy and arousal. Anything else [. . .] is strictly secondary. And should it ever start to be more than that, it's most likely getting in the way, and then it's probably no longer porn we're talking about" (4). Adult entertainment, then, is largely conceptualized and defined as being precisely about sex; to use the gender-biased phraseology of *Rabbit's Reviews*, the genre should at least aspire to "get your dick hard." The idea that it might want to set aside this aspiration, even temporarily, in favor of engaging with different genres or with alternative conventions for representing the body might perhaps strike us as a rather novel development for the genre.

However, as O'Toole himself recognizes, porn has not always had such a "one-track mind" (13):

> Previously, throughout early modern European history, "pornography" was used chiefly to satirize, criticize, to tilt at the

Church, the state, the monarchy. This was political porn: product of the birth of print culture and the beginning of an urban market society where increasing numbers of people, partly distanced from laws of kinship, met to trade ideas, as well as commodities, and inevitably to question the values of traditional authorities who they now rivaled in the power game. Porn was controlled during this period not because it was obscene but because it was seditious, blasphemous or defamatory. (1)

This idea is also stressed within *The Invention of Pornography: Obscenity and the Origins of Modernity, 1500–1800*, a hugely influential collection of essays edited by the historian Lynn Hunt. The contributor Joan DeJean, for example, remarks that the "classic French pornographic tradition places pornographic literature at the intersection of sexual explicitness or obscenity and political dissidence" (121), before going on to add that, in early modern France, "writing obscenity on or across the female body was always also writing on the body politic" (122).

Other contributors to Hunt's volume use discussions of early modern England to help emphasize porn's historical diversity. Rachel Weil notes that, in the seventeenth century, "stories about royal or court sexuality were a legitimate part of political discourse, not cordoned off into a separate category" (142), whereas Randolph Trumbach dissociates much of early English erotic writing from the modern pornographic, which he traces back only as far as John Cleland's *Memoirs of a Woman of Pleasure*: "Cleland principally aimed at sexually arousing his reader, in a context that was neither satirical nor humorous. With that purpose and by those means, Cleland established in England the modern pornographic genre" (253). Pornography as a separate cultural category narrowly defined by a particular field of interests is understood here to be a relatively contemporary invention. As these critics suggest, sexually explicit material that engages with nonsexual content, affects, and intentions was at one point the norm, rather than the exception.

Perhaps the best-known example of the interpenetration of sexual and nonsexual themes within the history of pornography is the work of the Marquis de Sade. In their guise as porn, Sade's "exceptionally ferocious fictions" (Steintrager 353) exceed what a contemporary reader might assume to be their remit in terms of both affect and subject matter. They present genital sex acts, certainly, but they also are apparently linked to a revolutionary political project,[2] and their frequent segues into politico-philosophical discourse mean that they are perhaps just as likely to frustrate, to irritate, or to bore as they are to arouse. Indeed, Robert L. Mazzola, perhaps failing to take into account the genre's history of diversity, suggests that Sade's work should be viewed as exceeding the realm of the pornographic precisely because of its higher or more cerebral qualities, and should instead be considered "pornogonic." Sade's *Eugénie de Franval* and *Philosophy in the Boudoir*, Mazzola argues:

> are traditionally viewed as pornographic in that both elicit a degree of sexual excitation in the reader. However, where the pornographic text usually stops once its onanistic purpose has been served, the "pornogonic" text produces a pornographic reading that could stop at that point—the writerly text allows for the reader's choice here—or continue on toward other goals. These other goals in Sade are also deviant since they aim at derailing the socio-sexual contract. (117–18)

If, as Hunt suggests, a pornography consisting of "mass-produced text or images devoted to the explicit description of sexual organs or activities with the sole aim of producing sexual arousal in the reader or viewer" is a comparatively recent phenomenon ("Pornography and the French Revolution" 305), then the presence of this ostensibly more sociopolitical content in Sade should come as no surprise, and certainly should not prompt us to call into question its status as pornographic. Pornography has not always been viewed as being limited to erotic titillation or to the depiction of genital mechanics and, as we have seen, the genre actually has a remarkably rich history when it comes to engaging with the realm of the political.[3]

In addition to "using the shock of sex to criticize religious and political authorities" in the manner so characteristic of early modern pornography (Hunt, "Introduction" 10), however, Sade's work also subsumes sex within a range of other corporeal and transgressive activities. Indeed, Pierre Klossowski suggests that the dynamic of transgression represents the "node of the Sadean experience" (18), and the act of violating any and all taboos can arguably be positioned at the center of the Marquis' fictions. In *The 120 Days of Sodom*, for example, the Duc declares that "crime has of itself such a compelling attractiveness that, unattended by any accessory activity, it may be itself suffice to inflame every passion and to hurl one into the same delirium occasioned by lubricious acts" (426); for the Duc, then, violating the law holds the same kind of appeal (and bodily affects) as violating the body. Sex is explicitly positioned as just one form of a generalized tussling with the limit here. It functions as part of a larger project—an all-encompassing investigation of extremity—which, I suggest, cannot be understood solely in terms of a satirical impulse. That is to say, if the preoccupations of Sade's work cannot be reduced to sex, neither can they be reduced to sex with an admixture of politico-philosophical discourse.

We can see that Sade's work exceeds the conventionally sexual in a plethora of ways—sometimes quite unpleasant and disturbing ways—other than critique. It depicts human suffering and the abject body, and features a world in which disgust "is both sought after and overcome by the agents, and aggressively aroused in the reader" (Frappier-Mazur 216). We encounter a different kind of supplement to sex within the worlds of Sade's narratives, then—a supplement that does not revolve around political and social meanings, but around different ways of representing the (vulnerable, permeable) body and the reactions that such methods of representation can provoke. Just like the example of Roche's *Wetlands*, sexual arousal is frequently displaced in this fiction by other, less obviously enjoyable forms of affect, and its sexually explicit qualities are frequently eclipsed by other forms of corporeality. That the sex need not form the focal point of an interpretation of Sade will come as no surprise to those who have read his fiction. After all, as Walter Kendrick has stated, "No one has ever condemned Sade's books chiefly as a source of lascivious excitation; they are literally too extreme, in all directions, for that rather mild rebuke" (103–04). It may be that Sade remains infamous neither because of his politics nor because of his sexual explicitness, but because of his insistent engagement with the powers of horror.

Sexuality and/as Intensity

Yet although Sade's extremity has long been linked to perversity through the supposed pathology that bears his name, it could be argued that the Sadean interpenetration of sexual and other bodily experiences, such as violence and abjection, may in fact reflect ideas about the nature of normative sexuality itself. That is, sexuality is sometimes positioned as necessarily concerned with factors that might appear to be nonsexual. Freud attempts to outline the obscure and diffuse nature of this element of human experience in his *Three Essays on the Theory of Sexuality*. In

Section 7 of his discussion of infantile sexuality, for example, he tries to pinpoint some of the sources of sexual excitation in children. As well as stimulation of the skin, muscular activity, and the experience of "games of passive movement, such as swinging and being thrown up into the air" (121), Freud highlights the role of what he refers to as "affective processes" within the realm of childhood sexuality. "It is easy to establish," he claims, "whether by contemporary observation or by subsequent research, that all comparatively intense affective processes, including even terrifying ones, trench upon sexuality" (123). He then suggests that the "sexually exciting effect of many emotions which are in themselves unpleasurable, such as feelings of apprehension, fright or horror, persists in a great number of people throughout their adult life" (123).

Sexuality, then, is positioned as being influenced by and founded on sources that in themselves exceed that which we might think of as the strictly sexual. It is not a matter of sex per se, but of any and all possible states of powerful agitation. If for Freud "sexual excitation arises as a byproduct, as it were, of a large number of processes that occur in the organism, as soon as they reach a certain degree of intensity, and most especially of any relatively powerful emotion, even though it is of a distressing nature" (157), then we might suggest that there is no area of experience that is fully divested of the potential for operating in relation to the sexual—and that the sexual as a concept is in fact quite different from the sexual as an act of genital stimulation. As Bersani observes, Freud is moving toward a vision of sexuality in which sexual excitement is triggered by those moments "when the body's 'normal' range of sensation is exceeded, and when the organization of the self is momentarily disturbed by sensations or affective processes somehow 'beyond' those compatible with psychic organization" (*The Freudian Body* 38). The sexual, as Bersani so eloquently puts it, emerges "as the *jouissance* of exploded limits, as the ecstatic suffering into which the human organism momentarily plunges when it is 'pressed' beyond a certain threshold of endurance" ("Is the rectum a grave?" 217). Sex is displaced via dispersal here; it can be located at diverse sites, but only at the cost of losing its genitally erotic specificity.

For Bersani, this line of thinking leads to the suggestion that sexuality can be thought of as "that which is intolerable to the structured self" (*The Freudian Body* 38), and the concept can therefore be viewed as "a tautology for masochism" (39).[4] More significantly for our current purposes, however, the suggestion that any intense experience—whether that experience be of pain, pleasure, or of some other affecting state—is inherently open to becoming entangled with the subject's experience of sexuality provides some explanation as to why sexual and ostensibly nonsexual themes have so frequently been brought into conversation throughout the history of Western art and literature, not least in the writings of Sade. This confluence need not be seen as an inappropriate clashing of discrete cultural categories (sex and violence, sex and suffering, sex and disgust, etc.), but as a reflection of the elusive and perversely nonsexual character of human sexuality itself.

It may be rather easier, however, to accept the implications of Freud's insights in relation to examples of early modern pornography—with their more diverse political, social, and philosophical aims—than to do so in relation to today's pornographic landscape. Historical artifacts may incorporate both sexual and ostensibly nonsexual elements in a manner suggestive of the workings of intensity, but surely adult entertainment as a contemporary genre is far less ambiguous in its focus and intent. As we have seen, a "truly modern pornography" often is characterized by critics in terms of its *divergence* from the political porn of the period from 1500 to 1800 (Hunt, "Pornography and the French Revolution" 305), and is characterized precisely by a focus on sexual arousal as an end in and of itself. Likewise, although we might expect the high-cultural discourses of art or the avant-garde to bring sexual themes into conversation with other kinds of material,[5] adult entertainment is seen as being a far narrower kind of genre with a much more limited aim.

Porn's market identity is widely perceived as being founded on the production and distribution of material that displays naked, eroticized bodies and sexual acts and, as such, might today be expected to have no greater aim or wider intention than to provide a sexual service. Despite porn's history, any claim that contemporary pornographic materials might be seen to display an interest in nonsexual or nongenital concerns will likely register as somewhat counterintuitive, if not far-fetched. Yet, as our opening remarks about Extreme Associates and *Porn Jackass* demonstrate, that which presents itself as adult entertainment is not necessarily required to involve the representation of explicit sexual acts, or even to stage an attempt to facilitate a state of sexual arousal in the consumer-viewer. In these a-typical examples, it would seem above all to be the provocation of corporeal intensity—in all its multifarious forms—which is the focus. If this may be more immediately achieved by incorporating content that is not directly sexual into the world of adult entertainment, then so be it. It would seem that other forms of bodily spectacle easily could be imported to accompany and displace conventional representations of genital sexuality, and to thereby court more diverse forms of affect.

It is worth remarking, I think, that this idea of displacement—of a certain slippage of representational interests—has long been discussed in relation to one of adult entertainment's most high-profile subgenres; sadomasochistic pornography (a particular bugbear of many anti-porn feminists). Linda Williams, for example, refers to S/M's "displacement of a hard-to-see pleasure onto an easier-to-see, and apparently similarly involuntary, response to pain" (*Hard Core* 203). The very possibility of this displacement would seem to suggest that the affective kick that comes with witnessing the involuntary reactions and convulsions of the human body is not connected exclusively to the activities of genital sexuality, but may segue into other varieties of bodily reflex. Indeed, Williams notes that the very experience of orgasm has been linked to a markedly different kind of corporeal paroxysm, for the term "*petite mort* links the involuntary shudder of pleasure to the involuntary shudder of death—both are spasms of the ecstatic body 'beside itself'" (*Screening Sex* 65).

Williams even suggests, in reference to both horror films and extreme pornographic texts including elements of violent aggression, that what is "particularly disturbing about such visions [. . .] is the sense in which a new form of the 'frenzy of the visible'—here, an involuntary spasm of pain culminating in death—becomes imaginable as a perverse substitute for the *invisible* involuntary spasm of orgasm that is so hard to see in the body of the woman" (*Hard Core* 194). She adds that, when read in the generic context of pornography as opposed to that of horror, "a flinch, a convulsion, a welt, even the flow of blood itself, would seem to offer incontrovertible proof that a woman's body, so resistant to the involuntary show of pleasure, has been touched, 'moved' by some force" (194).[6] Despite these observations about the potential lures and affective powers of violence, Williams is ultimately positive about the political usefulness of violent pornography for feminist theorists, linking this realm of pornographic representations to what she views as a potentially subversive sadomasochistic subculture:

> The rise of sadomasochism in the full variety of its forms may very well indicate some partial yet important challenges to patriarchal power and pleasure in the genre of film pornography. S/M's emphasis on oscillating positions over strict sexual identities and its extension of sexual norms to include sadomasochistic play and fantasy suggest a rising regime of relative differentiations over absolute difference. Some of the apocalyptic force of much sadomasochistic pornography undoubtedly derives from these challenges to phallic laws that stand for strict dichotomization. (*Hard Core* 226)

This specific attitude toward S/M might be theorized as part of the wider tendency among scholars of pornography, as mentioned in my introduction, to emphasize and glorify the supposedly transgressive nature of pornographic texts. More relevant to our current discussion, however, are Williams' ideas regarding the displacement of desire. The flow of real blood from real injuries is hardly a predominant feature of the contemporary pornographic landscape, but as we saw in the case of Borden's *Forced Entry*, an interest in simulating and playing with the *mort* in *petite mort*—an interest in experimenting with the visceral charge attached to other body genres—can be detected within certain marginal and willfully transgressive pornographic texts.

This displacement of genital sexuality is not limited to the realm of violence and violation, however. It is worth noting that, as shown in the discussion of disgust in Chapter 3, a fascination with the moved body can manifest itself in a variety of ways besides the representation of pain. The frenzy of the visible, which Williams positions at the heart of her analysis of the pornographic, might therefore be viewed as being connected less with sexually explicit images than with generalized depictions of the out-of-control body, and might be associated less with physiologic arousal than with the experiencing of a broader spectrum of intense affective responses. That is to say, some varieties of adult entertainment at times both represent and seek to elicit nongenital forms of intensity. In the examples that follow, I further interrogate the unexpected blending of themes and tropes within a genre that would, at first glance, appear to have some of the most narrowly defined subject matter and authorial intentions in the whole of contemporary visual culture, and thereby demonstrate the centrality of intensity to the pornographic. I begin now with possibly the most significant (and infamous) contemporary forerunner of the trend for exploiting the potential of nonsexual imagery in an avowedly pornographic context—Larry Flynt's *Hustler*.

"Post-PC, Bad Taste Aesthetics": *Hustler* Magazine

Before Flynt's more recent attempts to assimilate himself into corporate America,[7] *Hustler* magazine had a long and noted tradition of publishing material which, aside from being sexually explicit, appeared expressly designed to provoke a diverse range of intense affective responses in its readers. As Laura Kipnis has noted,

> *Hustler*, from its inception, made it its mission to disturb and unsettle its readers, both psycho-sexually and socio-sexually, interrogating, as it were, the typical men's magazine codes and conventions of sexual representation: *Hustler's* early pictorials included pregnant women, middle-aged women (horrified news commentaries referred to "geriatric pictorials"), overweight women, hermaphrodites, amputees, and in a moment of true frisson for your typical heterosexual male, a photo spread of a pre-operative transsexual, doubly well-endowed. ("'Male' Desire and 'Female' Disgust" 135)

Despite Flynt's attempts to adapt to mainstream norms, and to incorporate them into his company's publicly expressed values, he can still be seen to flirt with controversy in his attempts to provoke. Indeed, that the ghosts of the old days of dissident posturing still linger around Flynt's publication is evidenced by the recent furor over *Hustler*'s attempts to acquire a set of crime scene photographs.

In March 2010, reports emerged of an open records request that had been filed with the Georgia Bureau of Investigation by the *Hustler* contributor Fred Rosen, who was seeking to obtain images of the decapitated body of the young murdered hitchhiker Meredith Emerson. Although the rationale behind *Hustler*'s wish to get hold of these images remains somewhat obscure,[8] this would appear to be another case of adult entertainment seeking to engage with material that would conventionally be judged as being outside of its remit. Political figures and members of the state Legislature were predictably quick to condemn Rosen's activities in the strongest possible terms. The CNN website, for example, quoted the House Speaker David Ralston as saying that it was "sickening, disgusting, vile and [. . .] very, very hurtful" (Grinberg). Whatever Rosen's and Flynt's actual intentions for the images, I think it is fair to say that the controversy surrounding the request was to some extent triggered by the magazine's position as a pornographic artifact, and by the concomitant expectation that it conform to established understandings of what the contemporary pornographic signifies and entails. Such documentary images may, like pornography, help the viewer to pry open the "fleshy secrets of normally hidden things" (Williams, *Hard Core* 191), but that does nothing to reduce the cognitive dissonance brought about by this situation.

I argue that although adult entertainment proves to be open to influences ranging from reality TV to crime scene photography, it is, for many people at this historical juncture, profoundly unsettling to think of discrete cultural realms being combined in such an apparently indiscriminate manner. For contemporary real-life tragedies to, in some way, be brought into conversation with sexually explicit material raises some rather discomforting questions about whether these seemingly disparate forms might in fact prompt similar varieties of tabooed pleasure, and what it might say about us if this is the case.[9] As William Ian Miller, in positioning pornography as but one source of *jouissance*, has remarked:

> Something makes us look at the bloody auto accident, thrill to movies of horror, gore, and violence; something makes porn big business and still draws people to circus sideshows. Is there no moral offensiveness that doesn't by some dark process elicit fascination, if in no other way than in the horror, wonderment, and befuddlement such depravity evokes? (112)

From the examples that we have touched on so far, it would appear to be true to say that not all forms of twentieth- and twenty-first century adult entertainment are solely preoccupied with the representation of naked bodies and energetic sexual performances. In fact, certain texts within the genre appear to take sex acts as just one instance (albeit the primary and privileged instance) of a more general set of possibilities for transgressing dominant and widely held norms. Indeed, the one factor that appears to unite all of the contemporary pornographic representations discussed thus far is an overt interest in staging the violation of a range of taboos. O'Toole is not unaware of this trend, despite his insistence that "porn is a sex thing" (342). He somewhat undermines his own argument when he suggests that pornographers at the beginning of the new millennium are "cranking out hard-core videos for twenty-somethings in the shadow of *Beavis and Butthead*, Quentin Tarantino and Jerry Springer, of *South Park*, Howard Stern, *There's Something About Mary*, *Doing Bad Things*, *Smack My Bitch Up*, etc." (359). These materials may use or incorporate sex, but sexually arousing the viewer is not their principal aim. As O'Toole puts it, "right now the broader culture [. . .] has a weakness for post-PC, bad taste aesthetics" (359). In certain instances, the joyfully puerile pleasures of such transgressions have arguably come to usurp the specifically sexual quality of porn's assumed content and affects.

The *Porn Jackass* website, for example, exploits the potential of reality television's carnivalesque interest in the excessive and grotesque body—in the transgression of the norms of bourgeois decorum and corporeality—by adding a stunts-and-pranks dimension to what Constance

Penley identifies as "the porn world's now decades-long use of trashy, militantly stupid, class-iconoclastic, below-the-belt humor" (324). Extreme Associates' pornographic output, meanwhile, can be seen to push against culturally potent taboos regarding violence (particularly sexual violence, particularly in pornography) directed toward women, and *Hustler* magazine still retains something of an anachronistic association with antiestablishment ideals and subversive intent. As Kipnis remarks, surely in reference to the magazine's near-mythical 1970s glory days, "*Hustler* basically just wants to offend—anyone, of any race, any ethnic group. Not content merely to offend the right, it makes doubly sure to offend liberal and left sensibilities too, not content merely to taunt whites, it hectors blacks" ("'Male' Desire and 'Female' Disgust" 150). Linda S. Kauffman agrees, arguing that the magazine routinely ridicules "society's most cherished illusions. Romance, youth, beauty, truth, democracy, justice, equality, success, and capitalism are all targets of Larry Flynt's satire" (244).

Kipnis contends that "on *every* front *Hustler* devotes itself to producing generalized transgression" ("'Male' Desire and 'Female' Disgust" 136), and although I question that assertion in relation to some of Flynt's more recent business decisions, I certainly detect an interest in the operations of transgression at work within the texts that I have been discussing here. Indeed, if we discount or deemphasize sexual explicitness and the provocation of arousal as common or defining factors, I suggest that a pervasive desire to transgress any and all norms—bar those immediately necessary for the continued existence and profitability of the genre itself—is the one thing that most obviously characterizes these (admittedly a-typical) examples of commercial adult entertainment. That is to say, in those cases where an interest in genital sex per se appears to be somewhat diluted, a fascination with transgression (and its affective charge) clearly remains.

Warporn:
"The Hybridization of War Documentation and Pornography"

One area of visual culture that has recently brought particular attention to pornography's engagement with tropes and themes that would not conventionally be positioned as sexual is the emerging phenomenon known as *warporn*.[10] What exactly is designated by this term is open to debate,[11] but I use a general definition of *warporn*—deployed by Katrien Jacobs in her 2007 study *Netporn: DIY Web Culture and Sexual Politics*—as "the hybridization of war documentation and pornography" within contemporary visual culture (118). As is seen later in the chapter, this hybridization has numerous vehicles and appears in diverse contexts, but within the specific confines of adult entertainment, I suggest that it manifests itself most frequently as an overtly sexualized adaptation of news reports and documentary images, or as an attempt to pornographically exploit current political events.

Warporn within the realm of adult entertainment might simply take the form of a repackaging of preexisting material, as evidenced by certain military-themed sex scenes circulating on free porn sites under salacious and opportunistic titles, such as "TOP SECRET What Solders [sic] Do With Iraqi Prisoners." The content of the version of this clip posted on the free adult movie website *Need Bang* is not, in fact, a direct exploitation of the recent human rights abuses in Abu Ghraib and elsewhere. Instead, it appears that a new title has been grafted onto an older moving-image scene, featuring a woman having sex with three men dressed as American G.I.s. The fact that the (seemingly white) actress is initially costumed in a conical Southeast Asian hat, and is at one point referred to as being "slant-eyed," would suggest that the content of this scene is seeking to exploit the cultural legacy of the war in Vietnam rather than to comment on prisoner abuse in the twenty-first century Middle East. Nevertheless, as part of the process of hybridization so central to the operations of warporn, recent prurient interest in factual accounts of "What Solders [sic] Do With Iraqi Prisoners" is deliberately and self-consciously exploited, and the scene is repackaged under a title that has a more profound set of contemporary resonances.

Warporn may also take the form of recently commissioned works of adult entertainment that seek to incorporate recent political and military developments into their pornographic world. Indeed, such texts may not only be inspired by current events, but also may end up playing a significant part in them. Simon Hardy discusses one such example, remarking the following:

> a photo-shoot on the *Iraq Babes* website shows porn actors dressed up as American troops and "raping" Iraqi women, thus allowing the average American citizen to vicariously share in the tradition of invading armies that rape the women of a defeated power. The images were withdrawn once they began to circulate as authentic in the Arab world. (16)

These photographs, inspired by contemporary events and produced as part of "a sub-genre of trash porn—still relatively unknown, coming from the dark side of the net" (Pasquinelli, "WARPORN WARPUNK!"), began circulating as documentary images in 2004, and ended up effecting the very political landscape that they originally intended merely to exploit. Indeed, it was not only in the Arab world that these hybridized representations were mistaken for legitimate images of war crimes. *The Boston Globe* newspaper "gave readers a jolt at the breakfast table by printing the sexually explicit photographs, clearly showing men in camouflage penetrating unidentified women" (Bone), after a local councilor took the images for authentic and used them as the basis for a press conference during which he called for the resignation of the then-US Defense Secretary Donald Rumsfeld.

Another example of adult entertainment texts being deliberately commissioned as warporn can be found in *Gag Factor 15*—the fifteenth installment of an ongoing heterosexual porn series centered on irrumatio (the act of rough deep throat fellatio). Distributed by JM Productions in 2004, the very year that the Abu Ghraib prisoner abuse scandal broke, the opening scene of *Gag Factor 15* not only makes explicit reference to the controversy, but also attempts to co-opt it for the purposes of sexual arousal, in a particularly clear demonstration of the way in which the events in Iraq can be exploited and utilized by adult entertainment. As with early modern pornography, then, we see political events being incorporated into the pornographic landscape. Unlike historical examples of pornography, however, there would seem to be little in the way of a satirical impulse in operation here.[12]

The scene opens on a group of five actors, all apparently white yet all wearing the same version of an Arab terrorist costume—long, loose-fitting black garments with black head and face coverings that leave only the eyes exposed. The man positioned down stage right "rants angrily at the camera in gibberish intended to sound Arabic" (Maldoro), while the man next to him translates this as: "Listen to us now, for you will be sorry, you Western devils. We will do to your women what you have done to our men. Look what you have done to my fellow brother." At this point, Polaroid pictures restaging some of the more iconic Abu Ghraib images are briefly shown to the camera. They depict the scene's female star, Ashley Blue, in the Lynndie England role, dressed in a khaki t-shirt and camouflage-print combats, giving the camera the thumbs up and resting her booted foot on the back of a male prisoner, who is naked but for his black hood and white socks. Over one of the photos is scrawled the message "We conquered you." In another image, Blue is shown holding the end of a leash attached to the prisoner's neck, in obvious imitation of one of the most infamous images to emerge from the prisoner camp.[13]

The dialogue continues: "The Western scum will pay. You have degraded our people, and now we will degrade yours. The streets will spill over with spit, semen will flow from your pores, and you will know the true wrath of the Arab world." The ringleader and the translator then step aside to reveal Blue, dressed in the same military attire, seated on the floor behind them. One of the terrorist figures brandishes a sword, as if threatening Blue with decapitation, before the hard-core action of multiple rough blowjobs begins.

It is not just the tortures of Abu Ghraib that inform this piece of commercial pornography, but also their aftermath—the high-profile hostage-beheadings that followed in the wake of the scandal. As Jacobs notes, the decapitation of the American civilian contractor Nicholas Berg by Islamic militants in May 2004 "received worldwide attention because it was filmed and the footage was subsequently released on the Internet" (117). The aesthetic of the video, stills from which often accompanied online news reports about the murder, has filtered into Western cultural consciousness, to the extent that many are now familiar with the image of Berg, seated before a line of masked militants, in the moments before his death. Indeed, Matteo Pasquinelli has described the dissemination of the video as a kind of "capillary diffusion" ("WARPORN WARPUNK!"), emphasizing the pervasiveness and speed with which the imagery spread across the global mediascape. I argue that the fact that *Gag Factor 15* includes the scenario of a group of anonymous, black-clad terrorists, faces obscured, addressing a camera as they surround the seated figure of an American would in itself be enough to recall the execution video, even without the explicit inclusion of the threatening gesture with the sword.

The opening segment of this installment of JM Productions' *Gag Factor* franchise hybridizes pornography as a genre by incorporating references to both amateur images of prisoner abuse and homemade works of terrorist propaganda that are disseminated via the Internet and made culturally visible through mainstream news coverage. The extent to which these authentic, documentary discourses can be thought of as sexual is unclear, and their appearance within a work of adult entertainment is perhaps a further discomforting example of pornography's diversified, and to some extent nonsexual, interests. What, we might be prompted to ask, makes the imagery of contemporary warfare so open for a pornographic revisioning? Why is it that war, as a visual discourse, can be so easily repurposed and converted into commercial porn?

Once again, I stress the importance of transgression for the genre here. JM Productions, like Extreme Associates, is a company that seems to have woven the idea of an ostentatious vulgarity into the very fabric of its market identity. This is reflected not only in the content and the concept behind the series, but also in paratextual features such as the series' logo and DVD box covers. The brand tends to deploy garish colors and gross-out imagery, such as photographs that include details like spit bubbles or globules of mucous. The box cover for *Gag Factor 31*, for example, shows a heavily made-up blonde with blood-shot eyes, situated over the body of her male co-star in something like the 69 position, looking into the camera. Her lips are around the head of his erect penis and a thick string of viscid mucous descends from her nose, running the length of the shaft of the penis and down onto the testicles. There is also a bead of cloudy white mucous (or is it ejaculate?) hanging from a strand of her hair. This is not dissimilar from the images used on other box covers in the series. The *Gag Factor* logo and branding, meanwhile, use a white, viscous-looking font that recalls the image of freshly ejaculated semen. In this way, a willfully crude and tasteless aesthetic is foregrounded; one that seems designed to provoke reactions of bourgeois disgust. After all, as Miller notes, "the gust in disgust was very early on, in both English and French, not a narrow reference to the sense of taste as in the sensation of food and drink, but an homage to the broader, newly emerging idea of "good taste"" (170). In setting out to transgress the standards of good taste, JM Productions appears to be courting a sense of disgust. Indeed, we might suggest that the series markets itself as much as an inciter of repulsion as an elicitor of lust, and that *Gag Factor's* appeal to disgust might therefore be viewed as yet another manifestation of adult entertainment's diverse, nonsexual concerns.

These aesthetic transgressions are complemented by, and to some extent reflect, other forms of taboo violation, many of which appear to exceed the realm of the conventionally sexual. Indeed, I am tempted to suggest that, even taking into account the explicit attention paid to corporeal mechanics and bodily paroxysms,[14] much of the affective charge of the first sex scene of *Gag Factor 15* is the result less of its explicit depiction of sex, and more of its preoccupation with the transgression of a range of social and cultural norms. These include certain politically correct standards of racial sensitivity, disregarded in the joyfully exaggerated imitation of Middle Eastern accents and speech patterns, and, of course, the familiar prohibition applied to the representation of suffering and sexual violence within a pornographic context; Robert Jensen reports, with no little distaste, that the producer of the *Gag Factor* movies takes "great pride that his [. . .] series was the first to feature exclusively aggressive "throat fucking"" (44).

The transgression most obviously enacted by the scene, however, is one common to much of adult entertainment's contribution to the realm of warporn; that is, the violation of those normative standards of decency that require that war, particularly its atrocities and its victims, be treated with an appropriate level of respect and reverence. *Gag Factor 15* seems intent on breaching this taboo, incorporating the still-raw events surrounding Abu Ghraib into its pornographic purview with politically incorrect glee. The fact that this scene—and indeed the action of purchasing, watching, and enjoying this scene—violates our society's deeply felt need for respectful seriousness when it comes to discussing the ongoing events of war is, it would appear, precisely the point. After all, as Bataille puts it, a "prohibited act invites transgression, without which the act would not have the wicked glow which is so seductive" (*Tears of Eros*, 67), and, of course, a particular thrill of violation attaches itself to the act of transgressing standards to which one still whole-heartedly subscribes—to those moments when "the taboo still holds good and yet we are yielding to the impulse it forbids" (Bataille, *Eroticism*, 38). To quote Tim Dean, for an act of transgression to be truly meaningful, not only must the prohibition itself be breakable, but also "breaking it must qualify as more than mere theatrics" (67).

As with Larry Flynt, Extreme Associates, *Porn Jackass*, and other examples, we find that *Gag Factor 15* and other manifestations of warporn are not only concerned with the sexually explicit, but also are invested in the generalized violation of taboos made possible by the operations of transgression as an objectless and endlessly mobile "a-concept" (Noys, *Georges Bataille* 87). How can we theorize the apparent significance of transgression for adult entertainment as a genre? Why incorporate this fascination with violating any and all taboos into a realm of representation that, according to popular understandings, is primarily interested in depicting the sexual? The obvious answer in the case of commercial pornographic examples is the quest for profit. Even within an industry whose unique market identity is predicated on offering a degree of explicitness rarely available in other generic contexts, transgression appears to hold a special kind of marketability. But this raises the question of why the adult entertainment industry might assume that generalized transgression will attract consumer-viewers. What exactly is the imagined appeal for spectators? What is it about the violation of taboos that generates the perceived demand behind the supply?

In her essay "Pornography and Fantasy: Psychoanalytic Perspectives," film scholar Elizabeth Cowie contends that sexual desire, seen as standing in opposition to a realm of order and control, is most truly itself when it is most "other" to social norms, when it transgresses the limits and exceeds the "proper." The result is a hotchpotch, formed only by its status as the forbidden; it is characterized not only by the now more conventionally acceptable transgression of barriers of race or class, but by the transgression of the barriers of disgust—in which the dirty and execrable in our bodily functions becomes a focus of sexual desire. (134)

An interest in generalized forms of transgression, Cowie asserts, is very much linked to the functioning of normative and nonpathological forms of desire, and her comments position sexuality as to some extent synonymous with transgression. This suggestion that desire is "a hotchpotch, formed only by its status as forbidden" might in itself appear to shed some light on the peculiarly diverse nature of some of adult entertainment's current representational preoccupations, but it may also act as a starting point for a deeper examination of the supposed conjunction of sexuality and transgression. After all, as we saw throughout Part I, the transgressive nature of sexuality is frequently overemphasized and overstated. The two may be widely perceived as deeply, if not fundamentally, entangled, but the operations of transgression as a concept can be seen to go well beyond the confines of the genital realm.

I suggest that the manner in which modern thinkers discuss the affective force of transgressive experience may offer some valuable insight here. Miller, for example, suggests that the experience of "transgressing the barrier itself produces the sense of excessiveness that provides pleasure as well as disgust and shame for it, all felt in some strange simultaneity, pleasure and aversion augmenting each other in a kind of ecstasy" (120), whereas Bataille, ever-enlightening on such issues, notes that "If we observe the taboo, if we submit to it, we are no longer conscious of it. But in the act of violating it we feel the anguish of mind without which the taboo could not exist: that is the experience of sin" (*Eroticism* 38). Such remarks stress the sheer affective power of transgression, suggesting that the experience of violating taboos can manifest itself as a profoundly felt shattering of the self, and that one of the chief characteristics and clearest symptoms of such an experience is the production of psychic disturbance.

Let us return here to comments made at the start of this chapter regarding the perversely non-sexual nature of sexuality itself. As we discovered, any and all forms of strongly felt experience can, according to Freud, become vehicles for sexuality, provided that they "reach a certain degree of intensity" (157). As such, "many emotions which are in themselves unpleasurable, such as feelings of apprehension, fright or horror" are apt to become exciting as a result of their enormous power to affect the subject (Freud 123). Transgression, being as it is a source of anguish and ecstasy, would seem to be a particularly rich site of psychic disturbance and affective force. It is, as theorists of transgression intimate, very much intertwined with those self-shattering experiences which pass "beyond certain quantitative limits" (Freud 124), and which are therefore capable of segueing into an expanded realm of the sexual. After all, if "sexual pleasure may be a component of all sensations which go beyond a certain threshold of intensity" (Bersani and Dutoit 32), then to suggest that transgression is capable of provoking intense affective responses is necessarily to imply that it to some extent speaks to our ideas about the nature of sexuality.

In simpler terms, transgression is intense and can therefore be linked to sexuality.[15] Of course, to talk about sexuality is not necessarily to talk about sexual acts, and the nature of transgression may not always be such that it triggers the obvious physiological responses of sexual arousal—as the *Rabbit's Reviews* website puts it, "not all of it will get your dick hard." Yet its fundamental involvement with intensity firmly aligns it with the ephemeral realm of self-shattering *jouissance* that, from a certain post-Freudian perspective, is known and understood as sexuality. This may go some way toward explaining the often discomforting presence of transgressive (and not necessarily genital) subject matter within certain marginal varieties of adult entertainment. To see the images at the heart of a recent torture scandal reimagined as part of a puerile and self-consciously adolescent porn franchise may provide some of the unsettling and volatile pleasure that one associates with the willed violation of those cultural taboos to which one still adheres.

Indeed, this idea of intensity may help to shed some light on the queasy appeal not only of pornographic texts that play on cultural trauma, but also of images of cultural trauma themselves—those elements of contemporary visual cultures that thrive on reactions of shock and horror. As Pasquinelli argues:

> Underneath the surface of the self-censorship belonging to the radical left (not only to the conformist majority), it should be admitted publicly that watching Abu Ghraib pictures of

pornographic tortures does not scandalize us, on the contrary, it rather excites us, in exactly the same way as the obsessive voyeurism that draws us to videos of 9/11 [. . .] We show our teeth as monkeys do, when their aggressive grin looks dreadfully like the human smile. ("WARPORN WARPUNK!")

Of course, the images are capable of both scandalizing *and* exciting a contemporary viewer. Indeed, it may be that the scandal is the very thing that most excites us, adding the luster of transgression to our prurient (but also conflicted) desire to watch. Beneath this hard to admit and truly self-shattering excitation lies intensity, as Slavoj Žižek's comments make particularly clear:

> When, days after September 11 2001, our gaze was transfixed by the images of the plane hitting one of the WTC towers, we were all forced to experience what the "compulsion to repeat" and *jouissance* beyond the pleasure principle are: we wanted to see it again and again; the same shots were repeated *ad nauseam*, and the uncanny satisfaction we got from it was *jouissance* at its purest. (*Welcome to the Desert of the Real!* 11–12)

I return to the issue of our interest and investment in these kinds of depictions of trauma in the coming chapters. For now, however, it is enough to note the crucial role that ideas of intensity play in relation to representation. It is intensity that arguably underpins the incorporation of certain nonsexual themes into conventionally pornographic texts and contexts, and intensity that makes the existence of a discourse such as warporn at least partially fathomable.

5

Prurience and Postmodernism

Affect and Contemporary Image Cultures

War, as demonstrated in Chapter 4, intersects with the contemporary pornographic in a number of affecting ways. However, despite operating under a new name, engaging with highly contemporary events, and frequently circulating in technologically advanced virtual forms, it is worth noting that warporn is not an exclusively twenty-first century phenomenon. Indeed, Carolyn Dean's work would appear to suggest that a certain conflation of discourses of war and pornography first manifests itself in the immediate aftermath of World War I:

> While it is true that eroticized violence was a predominant theme in underground pornography in England and North America during the nineteenth century, contemporaries generally viewed it as a manifestation of its authors' and readers' weakness of moral will; its violence was one among many examples of the human susceptibility to sin which was evident in all pornographic material. After the Great War, however, there is a new continuity between the thematics of war and pornography, in which sexualized violence becomes the primary example of human moral failure. (61)

It is not only in an abstract or general sense that pornography and war can be seen to be brought into conversation during that uniquely volatile historical moment. Several of the concrete examples that Dean provides resonate profoundly with contemporary definitions and manifestations of warporn. Discussing a 1925 work by Georges Anquetil entitled *Satan Conduit le bal*, for instance, she notes:

> Trench journalists had already described the spectacle of dismembered corpses in macabre detail, but Anquetil implicitly eroticizes such images by juxtaposing flagellation scenes in brothels with anecdotes of war atrocities. The war is turned into a transnational brothel, another eroticized mise-en-scène in which the body's private pleasure and pain become public affairs. (63–64)

The "hybridization of war documentation and pornography" which characterizes today's warporn (Jacobs 118), then, would seem to be at least partly indebted to an inglorious cultural legacy stretching back to the birth of modern warfare.

Despite the existence and influence of such an inheritance, however, warporn often is discussed as if it is an entirely new development within representational culture, with Jacobs, for example, stating that "a new phase in netporn history has been written" with the circulation of such texts (9). Such claims of originality are entirely understandable, for much about warporn seems to lend itself to discourses regarding the contemporary age. It is easy to view warporn as somehow symptomatic of postmodern, image-driven cultures, and to associate it with those concerns about affect and the ethics of consumerism that typically characterize critical commentaries on such cultures. Brian Massumi has noted the following:

> There seems to be a growing feeling within media, literary, and art theory that affect is central to an understanding of our information- and image-based late capitalist culture, in which so-called master narratives are perceived to have foundered. Fredric Jameson notwithstanding, belief has waned for many, but not affect. If anything, our condition is characterized by a surfeit of it.[1] (27)

That is to say, affect is increasingly being positioned at the heart of characterizations and conceptualizations of the contemporary world. This recognition of the emphasis on affect within our culture is not always celebratory. Indeed, it is frequently somewhat suspicious, and can translate into specific anxieties about the consumer-viewer's engagement with representations. Affect's apparent primacy over belief comes to suggest not only the potential for a moral vacuum, but also a fierce desire to be moved by images—a desire so strong that it can lead to blind consumption. Such concerns are, as Jennifer Wicke points out, particularly obvious in apprehensive discussions of contemporary adult entertainment, for "All the valences of affect used to discuss consumer states of mind come into play with redoubled fervor and seeming relevance when translated into the arena of pornography consumption—satiety, passivity, absorption" (68).

Pornography, Spectacle, and the Generalized Affective Response

Anxieties about the lure of images in the postmodern age are evident not only in scholarly and theoretical works, but in popular, artistic, and literary works as well. In Margaret Atwood's depiction of a futuristic dystopia in *Oryx and Crake*, for example, the illicit but easily accessible images of virtual space are presented in such a way as to invite condemnation of some elements of our existing visual culture. Although the text's status as fiction means that we must be wary of using it as the basis of too many conclusions about the extra-textual social world, it does provide a valuable springboard for theorizing cultural anxieties about media spectacles and the "fabric of sharp gut reactions and affective jolts" (Paasonen, *Carnal Resonance* 224). Early in the novel, first published in 2003, we are given an account of some of the ways in which the protagonist Jimmy and his best friend Glenn (known as Crake, after his online game-playing handle) spend their shared adolescent leisure time; "When they weren't playing games they'd surf the Net—drop in on old favorites, see what was new" (81). The sites that they access are all predictably unsavory, but the distasteful digital content that Atwood imagines is far from uniform. Indeed, the diverse nature of the representations that Jimmy and Crake access would appear to resonate with the previous chapter's discussion of the various themes and affects evident within adult material, as well as to suggest that this diversification is linked with specific anxieties about late capitalist image cultures.

It is perhaps not surprising that Atwood should choose to have those sites providing access to pornographic material feature prominently on the characters' list of "old favorites." The narrative reports that the boys "checked into Tart of the Day, which featured elaborate confectionary in the usual orifices, then went to Superswallowers; then to a Russian site that employed ex-acrobats, ballerinas, and contortionists," before visiting

"HottTotts, a global sex-trotting site" (*Oryx and Crake* 89). The excessive or novelty elements of these sites might, when viewed without the framing of a specific predilection or fetish, disturb any notion of pornography as a genre simply seeking to elicit arousal and augment the spectator's sexual climax, while the suggestion that pedophilia is viewed as simply another niche in the adult marketplace raises certain issues surrounding the affect-seeking consumer's unethical passivity before the image. However, the author ensures that these sites are all recognizable as being in some way related to what currently is known as adult entertainment. That is, their titles imply that they feature, in explicit detail, nudity and hard-core sex acts.

Equally central to these shared online expeditions, however, are other forms of voyeuristic spectatorship. The characters are just as likely to engage with coverage of assisted suicides on "nitee-nite.com" (*Oryx and Crake* 83), streaming footage of executions, or "animal snuff sites, Felicia's Frog Squash and the like" (82), as they are to watch anything resembling today's adult entertainment. Jimmy and Crake's formative viewing experiences, then, consist of using so-called communications technologies to bring together the conventionally pornographic with other forms of transgressive depiction of the human or animal body. They are able to transfer their attention from "the Noodie News" (81), where current events combine with soft-core pornography, to a "cat being torn apart by hand" (82) without displaying any sign of cognitive dissonance. Indeed, what is most troubling about Atwood's presentation of these viewings is not only that seemingly diverse spectacles are brought into conversation, but that the unique affective responses that one might typically expect to attach themselves to each category of image do not emerge.

There is, for many contemporary readers, a perceived gulf between the discourses that Jimmy and Crake's surfing brings together. Adult entertainment, common sense continues to insist, is a genre primarily focused on sexual arousal, whereas documentary images of suicide, violence, and execution should provoke a different kind of affective response, be that horror, disgust, or repulsion. Instead, these affects become blurred in the novel. The following paragraph describing the boys' mutual surfing sessions is particularly telling on this point:

> So they'd roll a few joints and smoke them while watching the executions and the porn—the body parts moving around on the screen in slow motion, an underwater ballet of flesh and blood under stress, hard and soft joining and separating,

groans and screams, close-ups of clenched eyes and clenched teeth, spurts of this or that. If you switched back and forth fast, it all came to look like the same event. Sometimes they'd have both things on at once, each on a different screen. (*Oryx and Crake* 86)

Not only do the images appear to merge here, but so too, it is implied, do the reactions that they provoke. That Jimmy and Crake can screen pornographic visual texts alongside documentary images depicting the loss of human life suggests that, in some ways, the two are seen as complementary. They appeal, Atwood suggests, to the same desire to see, each enhancing and augmenting the operations of the other rather than generating a sense of discord; the affects produced by a diverse range of imagery appear to merge into a single reaction. The most appropriate label for such a generalized response is the rather unfashionable term *prurience*.

As Linda Williams remarks, *prurience* "is a key term in any discussion of moving-image sex since the sixties. Often it is the "interest" to which no one wants to own up" (*Screening Sex* 122). The notion of prurient interest first appeared in a legal context in 1973, in the influential Supreme Court case *Miller v. California*, which spawned the so-called "*Miller* test" for determining whether material can be deemed to be obscene. Prurient interest emerged in this case as part of an attempt to shore up the legal definition of obscenity but, as Williams notes, the Court did not

> helpfully go on to actually define prurience in the ruling itself. Rather, in a footnote to the decision the Court had recourse to Webster's New International Dictionary describing it as: "persons, having itching, morbid, or lascivious longings of desire, curiosity, or propensity, . . ." Further on, perhaps noting the vagueness of "lascivious longings," and the naturalness of "curiosity," it attempts to specify: "shameful or morbid interest in nudity, sex, or excretion . . ." (*Screening Sex* 122)

All this censorious and morally loaded talk of shame, lasciviousness, and morbid interest may obscure the contemporary usefulness of this term for describing modern forms of engagement. Indeed, prurience may be particularly helpful for discussing the seemingly incoherent blending of affective responses, for, like transgression, it is not limited to a particular object but has the potential to span categories. The law, for its own purposes, attempts to pin the term to something resembling the worst in pornography, but the concept itself exceeds any such limits. Prurience may, therefore, provide a basis for the unification of diverse forms of spectacle under a particular set of drives and sensations—the disreputable inclination to see and know does not discriminate between categories of representation.

The Quest for Intensity versus the Deadening of Affect

As suggested by Atwood's Jimmy and Crake, and by many of the other examples that feature in this section, prurience may be positioned as one element of the insatiable contemporary appetite for affect. The diverse forms of "moving" imagery that the boys encounter in *Oryx and Crake* would certainly seem to be designed to produce as intense a generalized affective response as possible, and Jimmy leaves the viewing sessions "feeling as if he'd been to an orgy, one at which he'd had no control at all over what had happened. What had been done to him. He also felt very light, as if he were made of air; thin, dizzying air, at the top of some garbage-strewn Mount Everest" (86–87). As Stephen Dunning puts it, the novel presents Jimmy and Crake as inhabiting a "culture of disembodied voyeurs, who can only 'experience' the shock of their own reality through ever more extravagant means." In this way, we might argue, the text reflects what Žižek, following Badiou, has described as the "authentic twentieth-century passion for penetrating the Real Thing (ultimately the destructive Void) through the cobweb of semblances which constitutes our reality" (*Welcome to the Desert of the Real!* 12).[2] That is, Atwood's novel reminds us of our lingering fascination with experiencing an affecting realm that exists beyond comprehension and representation, and which therefore stands in opposition to everyday social reality.

Ironically, however, this desire to be emotionally affected is also shown to have something of a deadening effect in the novel, perhaps further stressing the conjunction of anxieties about affect with suspicions regarding postmodern image cultures more generally. Jimmy and Crake are drawn to certain transgressive representations because, the novel suggests, they *could* be real; because they at least gesture toward the possibility of some authentic profilmic event. The narrative, focalized through the character of Jimmy, therefore foregrounds those aspects of the representations that most seem to verify the legitimacy of the actions depicted. With "hedsoff.com, which played live coverage of executions in Asia" (*Oryx and Crake* 82), for example, it's the setting—"someplace that looked like China" (82)—as well as the convincing presence of "thousands of spectators" (82). For the execution site alibooboo.com, footage for which is shot in "dusty enclaves which purported to be in fundamentalist countries in the Middle East" (82), it is the authenticating properties of the quality of the video footage that are emphasized:

> The coverage was usually poor on that site: filming was said to be prohibited, so it was just some pauper with a hidden minivideocam, risking his life for filthy Western currency. You saw mostly the backs and the heads of the spectators, so it was like being trapped inside a huge clothes rack unless the guy with the camera got caught, and then there would be a flurry of hands and cloth before the picture went black. (82)

Yet despite this fascination with affect-augmenting authenticity—the "Real in its extreme violence as the price to be paid for peeling off the deceptive layers of reality" (Žižek, *Welcome to the Desert of the Real!* 6)—the boys are depicted as unwilling or unable to respond to the images as if they are connected to an extra-textual reality. Instead, they seem markedly detached from what is occurring on screen, perhaps as a result of the distancing that occurs via technological mediation. As Libby Saxton notes, "Modern technologies of visual representation expose us to others' pain from a spatial and (unless the images are live) temporal distance" (64), and this works to disrupt "the chain reaction linking contemplation, compassion and action" (65). The mediated nature of the suffering to which the boys are exposed (or rather, to which they elect to expose themselves) produces a distinct kind self-reflexive approach, and their responses are marked by a skepticism that is suggestive of a certain type of media literacy or readerly sophistication. Crake, in particular, focuses upon undermining the reality effect of these sites, pointing out the ways in which such imagery may be attempting to provoke an affective response via inauthentic means—that is, via acts of textual trickery. Of the foreign execution sites, for example, Atwood has Crake claim that "these bloodfests were probably taking place on a back lot somewhere in California, with a bunch of extras rounded up off the streets" (*Oryx and Crake* 82).

This recalls Badiou's suggestion that "the real, conceived in its contingent absoluteness, is never real enough not to be suspected of semblance. The passion for the real is also, of necessity, suspicion. Nothing can attest that the real is the real, nothing but the system of fictions wherein it plays the role of the real" (*The Century* 52). The characters in the novel are seen to treat the footage that they encounter on their prurient quest for affect as Baudrillardian simulacra; they self-consciously think of it as providing what *Simulations* calls "an aesthetics of the hyperreal, a thrill of vertiginous and phony exactitude, a thrill of alienation and of magnification, of distortion in scale, of excessive transparency, all at the same time" (50). Indeed, as Richard J. Lane points out, "total involvement or immersion combined with alienating detachment" characterizes much of our engagement with representations for Baudrillard (96), and this is especially evident in the conceptualization of genres like pornography.

During a conversation between the boys about home-grown American execution sites "with their sports-event commentary" (*Oryx and Crake* 82), Atwood appears even to obliquely reference Baudrillard, at the very moment that Crake questions the reality of reality itself. Jimmy, thinking about the veracity of the deaths on screen, begins as follows:

"A lot of them look like simulations."
"You never know," said Crake.
"You never know what?"
"What is *reality*?"
"Bogus!" (83)

Jimmy and Crake therefore end up disavowing the very authenticity that drew them to the material in the first place. They deny, disown, and distance themselves from the legitimacy of the representations on screen. It is this disavowal, just as much as Atwood's deployment of Baudrillardian terminology, that recalls contemporary criticisms of certain conceptualizations of postmodernism.

Peter Barry, for example, is troubled by the postmodern tendency to over question the reality that is presented to us in a mediated form: "if we accept the 'loss of the real' and the collapsing of reality and simulation into a kind of virtual reality," he writes, "then what of the Holocaust? Could this, too, be part of the reality 'lost' in the image networks? In other words, without a belief in some of the concepts which postmodernism undercuts—history, reality, and truth, for instance—we may well find ourselves in some pretty repulsive company" (89–90). In his discussion of autobiography and postmodernism, Paul Lauritzen similarly argues that to "jettison the distinction between the real and the unreal, to be willing to collapse the distinction between fact and fiction, is [. . .] to play into the hands of the Holocaust deniers" (33), whereas the political scientist Richard Gilman-Opalsky suggests that Baudrillard makes too much of the role of the fake within late capitalist culture:

> I think he errs on the wrong side of the equation. Sometimes we can discover the difference between reality and simulacra, and sometimes we can make claims about reality. And whenever we cannot tell the difference, whenever we just don't know if it's a real or a fake, I think we should err on the side of a moral obligation to humanity. I for one would rather be fooled into thinking a fake death was real than into thinking a real death was faked.

Such responses to Baudrillard's work can run to overstatement but, although I question the idea that accepting his insights puts one on a par with a holocaust denier, the fears that these critics express are by no means irrational. If one's anxiety about being duped by a horrific image outweighs one's anxiety about responding humanely and ethically to the depicted horror itself, then one may need to question the level of one's investment in infallibly sophisticated strategies of reading.

The relentless skepticism of Jimmy and, particularly, Crake in Atwood's novel is certainly not presented as an appealing trait, and the idea that a prurient interest in affect might perversely result in a *disaffected* mode of spectatorship and image consumption seems to preoccupy the text in its early stages. It is rather telling of the author's attitude, I think, that she especially highlights Crake's ability to remain unmoved by these representations. The narrative states that he "didn't seem to be affected by anything he saw, one way or the other, except when he thought it was funny" (*Oryx and Crake* 86), and draws attention to his particular enjoyment of the nitee-nite.com suicide page: "Crake grinned a lot whilst watching this site. For some reason he found it hilarious, whereas Jimmy did not" (84). This nonchalant observation of virtual, mediated death prefigures Crake's later experience of the actual death of his own mother after she "picked up a hot bioform" (176). In one sinister episode, he discusses watching her demise through an observation window at the hospital, the window providing yet another distancing screen through which to view the horrors of the world:

> "It was impressive," Crake told Jimmy. "Froth was coming out."
> "Froth?"
> "Ever put salt on a slug?" (177)

Jimmy, the more responsive of the two when it comes to digital imagery, is shown to view himself as correspondingly sensitive to real-world events. The focalized narrative states that he "didn't understand how Crake could be so nil about it—it was horrible, the thought of Crake watching his own mother dissolve like that. He himself wouldn't have been able to do it" (177).

It is later revealed that Crake may have orchestrated his mother's death in a test run for the virus that he eventually unleashes on humanity, and this single act of spectatorship, not to mention his wider adolescent viewing practices, are rather overshadowed by his eventual ideologically motivated act of mass murder. Prurience is replaced by something far less itching, less morbid, and less lascivious as an apparent motivation; it is finally a clear-headed ambition to create a post-human world that drives Crake. Nonetheless, an ability to remain detached and emotionally unmoved by the idea of raw corporeal suffering is shown to run through the character even from his formative years, and his youthful disaffection before virtual texts is shown to lead to, or at least to foreshadow, his eventual act of cold and uncompromising ideological ruthlessness.

The critic J. Brooks Bouson even goes so far as to suggest that to understand Crake's lack of emotional responsiveness we have to look to his real name—Glenn, after "a dead pianist, some boy genius with two n's" (Atwood 70):

> In having Crake's father name him after the boy-genius pianist, Glenn Gould, Atwood provides a significant clue to her character's behavior, for Gould, as Atwood has speculated, probably had Asperger's syndrome—a high-functioning type of autism sometimes called the "little professor" syndrome, characterized by narrowly focused, obsessional interests and prodigious feats of memory, but also poor social skills and a lack of empathy.

> Pointing to the Asperger's-like traits of her character, Atwood provides a contemporary twist on the well-worn stereotype of the mad—and impersonal-amoral—scientist, creating in the process a puzzling, and troubling, character, one whose game-like approach to life ultimately leads to his gruesome destruction of humanity. (145)

It is impossible to say definitively whether Crake's lack of emotional response to pornographic and violent imagery is intended to be presented as a contributing factor in terms of his later behavior or whether Atwood imagines it as the symptom of a medical condition. What is apparent, I argue, is that such disaffection is presented as a cause for significant unease and is shown to bode rather ill for human society.

It is worth noting at this point that not only do the boys *react* to the images on their computer screens as if they are wholly unreal, but the account of these images provided by the narrative itself suggests that their authenticity is to be questioned. In other words, although the combination of prurient interest and a blasé lack of affect may appear unethical, or even pathological, the representations themselves would appear to invite it. The American execution sites are a prime example here: "Shortcircuit.com, brainfrizz.com, and deathrowlive.com" certainly appear to be living up to their names by providing streaming footage of "electrocutions and lethal injections" (*Oryx and Crake* 83). But although the deaths themselves appear real, significant artifice is apparent in the way that the events are staged. "Once they'd made real-time coverage legal," the text states, "the guys being executed had started hamming it up for the cameras" (83). This is shown to include such behaviors as "making faces, giving the guards the finger, cracking jokes, and occasionally breaking free and being chased around the room, trailing restraint straps and shouting foul abuse" (83). Not only is the presence of the camera shown to end up provoking the behavior that it is ostensibly there merely to record, but the existence of the inauthentic within the situation is said to run even deeper. Crake, ever the skeptic, "said these incidents were bogus. He said the men were paid to do it, or their families were" (83).

In true postmodern fashion, the images are shown to precede the very reality that they depict, at least partially. What is most significant about this idea, however, is not simply that the scenes are exposed as simulations. Rather, I would argue that it is the culpability of the consumer-viewer that is foregrounded here. Just as the supposedly authentic spectacles on offer online in *Oryx and Crake* are shown to fail to convince, so the less spectacular, more convincingly "real" representations are presented as lacking the power to entertain. For example, Crake suggests that the condemned men on the execution sites are encouraged to perform in order that their deaths may prove suitably entertaining for the remote viewer: "The sponsors required them to put on a good show because otherwise people would turn off. The viewers wanted to see the executions, yes, but after a while these could get monotonous" (*Oryx and Crake* 83). In the world of the novel, it is presumably the prospect of genuine, un-faked death which appeals to those who seek out footage of executions; that is, it is the element of reality which, being typically so taboo when it comes to portrayals of death, has the power to titillate.[3] In the hyperreal dystopia of *Oryx and Crake*, however, reality fails to live up to the standards of simulation, and we are presented with a situation in which the "life" of state execution is forced to mimic the "art" of reality television or WWE wrestling.

We encounter something within Atwood's novel, then, which resembles what Žižek identifies as "the fundamental paradox of the 'passion for the Real': it culminates in its apparent opposite, in a *theatrical spectacle*—from the Stalinist show trails to spectacular terrorist acts" (*Welcome to the Desert of the Real!* 9). Just as Jimmy, if not Crake, experiences his postmodern preoccupation with intangible digital imagery as a form of the passion for the real, so, Žižek suggests, "the passion for the Real ends up in the pure semblance of the spectacular *effect of the Real*" (9–10). In their desire to be moved—to be intensely affected on a bodily level—the spectators within Atwood's world demand more than reality itself can provide, and reality itself must therefore be augmented in order that it may provide a greater sense of the real.

This would once again seem to resonate quite profoundly with Baudrillardian ideas of postmodern image cultures, but as with so much that appears at first glance to be radically novel, the privileging of the semblance over the less spectacular real is hardly new. This, for example, is how Susan Sontag illustrates her discussion of the passion for the semblance:

> New demands are made on reality in the era of cameras. The real thing may not be fearsome enough, and therefore needs to be enhanced; or reenacted more convincingly. Thus, the first newsreel ever made of a battle—a much-publicized incident in Cuba during the Spanish-American War of 1898 known as the

> Battle of San Juan Hill—in fact shows a charge staged shortly afterward by Colonel Theodore Roosevelt and his volunteer cavalry unit, the Rough Riders, for the Vitagraph cameramen, the actual charge up the hill, after it was filmed, having been judged insufficiently dramatic. (*Regarding the Pain of Others* 57)

The perceived desires of the viewer are often embedded in the representations that he or she ends up viewing, and have been since the earliest days of moving-image photography. If historical documents such as the Battle of San Juan Hill newsreel can prove to be so very mutable, then it is perhaps no great surprise that the trash entertainment of *Oryx and Crake*'s fictional world also should prove somewhat flexible in the face of the imagined demands of the spectator. The prurient interest of the viewer is felt in the execution chambers, the porn studios, and the hospitals from which the diverse mix of transgressive digital material is recorded or transmitted, and yet despite this all-too-obvious imprint, Atwood's characters reflect not at all on their own complicity in its production and dissemination.

That Atwood should engage with this topic is a reflection of her connectedness to contemporary cultural concerns. After all, as Sarah Leonard remarks:

> In an era in which the tape of Daniel Pearl's execution-style murder at the hands of Islamic militants is available on a frequently visited website on the Internet, questions of the violation of the body, privacy and public consumption of images become matters of great concern. One source of this concern surrounds the status of events *as images*. Pearl's execution was produced as an image, that is, the act was secondary to the publicity that attended the act. Thus those who view the videotape are complicit in the event—for the event itself was produced for the image. (200)

In watching the imagery, of course, we do not become responsible for Pearl's death, just as in refusing to watch the tape we do not prevent the events depicted from having taken place or prevent the tape itself from existing. However, what Leonard is saying here is that the imagery was produced in expectation that it *would* be viewed and disseminated, and so the imprint of the consumer-viewer is firmly upon the event. As a result,

Leonard would have us pause and interrogate our desire to see before we engage with such a text.

Of course, the itching and morbid desires characteristic of prurience broke no appeal to ethics, and the guilt attached to the viewing of such troubling imagery may only exacerbate the intensity of its pull. The lure of violating taboos once again raises its head. However, at least an awareness of the fact that the act of viewing is, in this case, also an act of transgression encourages a critical engagement with one's own culpability, however dysfunctional the form of this engagement might be. In *Oryx and Crake*, however, the body has "set out on its own adventures [. . .] having ditched its old travelling companions, the mind and the soul" (85), for it has grown "tired of the soul's constant nagging and whining and the anxiety-driven intellectual web-spinning of the mind, distracting it whenever it was getting its teeth into something juicy or its fingers into something good" (85). With corporeality given more autonomy within culture's conceptualization of the human organism, the subject is free to satiate his or her bodily needs in relation to pornography with relative impunity, and with precious little need for reflection.[4]

The downside of this is the diminishment of transgression and its possibilities for intense affective charge—as we have seen, affect is hard to come by in the world of *Oryx and Crake*, and even the diverse barrage of extreme material that the boys set out to encounter is shown to be capable of eliciting only a relatively hazy and subdued response, even in the more empathetic Jimmy. As Bataille notes, "If the taboo loses its force, if it is no longer believed in, transgression is impossible" (*Eroticism* 140), and in a world where one is more or less free to encounter any image one wants, from a work of child pornography to footage of dying animals, the forms of intensity made possible by pornographic transgression become inaccessible. Disavowing the authenticity of the imagery and separating themselves from its affective charge is therefore a somewhat self-defeating move on the boys' part. In cultivating the diminishment of intensity—the diminishment of the thrill of transgression—via knowingness, cynicism, and jaded media literacy, Jimmy and Crake act in a manner counter to their apparent aims in searching out and viewing these moving-image texts. The upside for the boys, however, is that they are not immediately prompted to confront the discomforting fact of their own involvement in the production of exploitative images. They can remain passively unquestioning in terms of their image consumption, and do not have to acknowledge their complicity.

In her essay, "*The Handmaid's Tale* and *Oryx and Crake*, 'In Context,'" Atwood says that she likes to "make a distinction between science fiction proper—for me, this label denotes books with things in them we can't yet do or begin to do, talking beings we can never meet, and places we can't go—and speculative fiction, which employs the means already more or less to hand, and takes place on Planet Earth" (513). "Speculative fiction" is the label that she chooses to apply to *Oryx and Crake*, which would suggest that this text depicts a potential future; that is, it presents a cultural landscape and a social situation that Atwood believes could be born from the seeds of the early twenty-first century West. The author is self-consciously exploring current cultural trends within this fictive universe, then; she recognizes within our existing world the beginnings of a troubling and unpleasant alignment of pornographic representations of sex acts with other, less sexually explicit documentary images of the body—a domain of imagery that generally depicts "flesh and blood under stress" (86). What attracts people to this generalized domain in the novel is a powerful prurient interest that, when uncoupled from the intensifying properties of taboo, is shown to result in disaffection, a radical deadening of the sympathetic impulse, and an uncritical passivity toward the images one consumes. This, in turn, is implicitly associated with a near-pathological indifference to human suffering.

As a work of speculative fiction, *Oryx and Crake* seems to suggest that virtually circulated imagery has the potential to act as a catalyst for the destruction of mankind. By this reading, the novel would appear to stage a particularly extreme version of the media effects model, and its idea that "exposure to violent imagery [. . .] automatically leads to violent deeds" (Kauffman 134–35)! However, despite the apparent excessiveness of this logic, some of the seemingly more fanciful aspects of Atwood's dystopian vision *can* be linked to current regimes of representation. As we have seen, today's adult entertainment can at times appear to court a pervasive prurient interest in representations of generalized forms of transgression, and to combine the representation of sexual arousal with the representation of other corporeal states. As such, we must acknowledge that the troubling blending of affects that characterizes spectatorship in the novel is not entirely alien to our own visual culture. As Coral Ann Howells notes, Atwood possesses a "dystopian impulse to shock readers into an awareness of dangerous trends in our present world" (164), and, whether or not we share Atwood's perception of its danger, there is no doubting that it is a contemporary cultural concern with which she is engaging here.

In the analysis that follows, I continue to examine the generalized prurience that is such an apparent source of concern for Atwood. In fact, I approach representational territory that appears to be closer even than this section's previous examples to the imagery investigated by Jimmy and Crake, especially in that it takes documentary images of the violated body as its primary object. In light of the contemporary interest in prurience, affect, and transgression, is our sense of the adjective "pornographic" beginning to mutate? Chapter 6 attempts to answer this question via an analysis of both recent and historical documentary images of suffering and war, and reflects on the manner in which certain cultural commentators have responded to and engaged with these images.

6

Violence, Sympathy, Titillation

The Body in a State of Intensity

Another Meaning of Warporn

Perhaps one of the most powerful and disturbing things about Margaret Atwood's imagining of a post-postmodern visual culture in *Oryx and Crake* is the manner in which suffering, violence, and sexuality are brought together in the form of various spectacles catering to a prurient and uncritical desire to see,[1] and yet even some of the more troubling aspects of the author's vision have been mirrored by events in the contemporary world. In terms of content, dissemination, and viewing conditions, for example, Atwood's depiction of an illicit world of extreme imagery recalls the recent scandal surrounding the website *Now That's Fucked Up* (*NTFU*). This now-defunct bulletin board site, previously run by Florida resident Chris Wilson, "started out as a place for people to trade amateur pornography of wives and girlfriends" (Glaser). However, when Wilson discovered that "potential military customers in Iraq and Afghanistan couldn't pay for membership, because credit card companies were blocking charges from 'high-risk' countries" (Zornick), he began offering "soldiers free access to porn in exchange for posting pictures from both the Afghanistan and Iraq wars" (Jacobs 122).

Thus, taking "the concept of user-created content to a grim new low" (Zornick), *NTFU* opened a thread entitled "Pictures from Iraq and Afghanistan—Gory," where photos depicting "body parts, exploded heads and guts falling out of people" could be uploaded and viewed (Glaser). Jacobs notes that as of September 2005 "there were 244 graphic battlefield images and videos available to members" (124), while George Zornick attests that "all of the posters—and many of the sites patrons—appear to regard the combat photos with sadistic glee, and pathological wisecracks follow almost every post." *NTFU* soon began to attract substantial media interest as a result of these war images, and Wilson was duly arrested on obscenity charges in October 2005. Although he struck a plea bargain, and thereby managed to avoid a jail sentence, *NTFU* was shut down, and its creator was banned from working on any adult websites for five years.[2] The war images are therefore no longer accessible in their original context. However, several were archived and repurposed on the antiwar website *After Downing Street*. Indeed, in a personal interview, P. Sears (a representative of *After Downing Street*) confirmed to me that hundreds more of the *NTFU* images are currently available for viewing at Wilson's recent (and necessarily less sexually explicit) online venture, *Documenting Reality*.

NTFU, then, appears to demonstrate not only some of the less laudable possibilities of democratic forms of consumer generated media, but to represent something like the kind of disconcerting blending of material discussed in Chapter 5 in relation to *Oryx and Crake*. Here, a site established and developed to cater for a desire to see amateur sex was transformed, via the introduction of confrontational and self-consciously gory documentary images of war, into something appealing to more diverse forms of prurient interest. Within a single online venue, patrons were able to view both images of the sexualized human body and images of the wounded, suffering, and violated human body; *NTFU* allowed two varieties of spectacle that are conventionally positioned as separate—pornography and war reportage—to be brought into conversation.[3] The incidents surrounding the high-profile closure of this website can be seen to provide further evidence of a link between adult entertainment and nonsexually explicit forms of representation, as well as to demonstrate a certain understanding of this link as socially unacceptable.

With this site, however, our previous examinations of the diversified interests of adult entertainment begin to expand in new directions. It should be noted that the images of combat collected on *NTFU* do not, on the level of content, contain anything that would suggest a potential association with the realm of the conventionally pornographic. That is to say, they do not contain explicit representations of sex acts, and nor do they feature deliberately or self-consciously sexualized depictions of nudity. These pictures of the victims of war are, we might say, graphic without being pornographic; it is only the context in which Wilson and his consumer-contributors placed these images that resulted in them being positioned as adult entertainment at all. We are beginning to see evidence to back up the idea that, not only do pornography's generic interests *exceed* the sexually explicit, but those materials that might receive the designation "pornographic" do not necessarily have to *engage* with the sexually explicit at all.

It is at this point in our discussion that we turn away from pornography as a genre and look toward the contemporary pornographic as a wider reaching phenomenon. The examples of warporn that we have already discussed can justifiably be linked to the commercial realm of adult entertainment through factors such as their conditions of production and distribution. There is another side of the warporn phenomenon, however; not only is there pornographic material in existence that to some extent draws upon and interprets the political landscape, but there is also a burgeoning realm of documentary imagery of warfare that has, in some way, become attached to the category of the pornographic. The phrase "warporn" has evidently entered the contemporary cultural vocabulary as a description of a whole range of nonsexual depictions of war, as evidenced by the response to certain (particularly amateur) documentary images. In April 2012, for example, the *LA Times* acquired pictures showing US troops "grinning and mugging for photographs" besides the corpses and disembodied limbs of dead Afghans insurgents (Zucchino). The pictures are undeniably gruesome, but they could hardly be described as overtly titillating or obviously sexual; even the pair of severed male legs with which the soldiers pose are largely clothed. Speaking about these images in an interview with the television channel RT America, the ex-soldier Matthis Chiroux repeatedly referred to them (and images like them) as "warporn," without feeling the need to explain, explore, or define this term. The interview was even posted on *YouTube* with the title "US military 'War Porn' surfaces."

A lack of sexual explicitness, it would seem, does not prevent such images from being discussed as a form of porn or from being positioned as an example of the pornographic. Warporn, in other words, is one example of what we might call the nonsexual pornographic. Why might such material warrant the use of the porn suffix in this manner? How is it perceived as being linked to the pornographic as a cultural concept? As I aim to demonstrate here, it may well be that certain kinds of nonsexually explicit imagery are viewed as being particularly likely to trigger the itching, voyeuristic desire or lascivious curiosity typically associated with pornography as a visual genre, or that depictions of the violently violated body are perceived as being especially available for interpretation in a variety of transgressive ways. After all, as Susan Sontag has remarked, not all responses to images of cruelty and suffering "are under the supervision of reason and conscience. Most depictions of tormented, mutilated bodies do arouse a prurient interest" (*Regarding the Pain of Others* 85).

Perhaps the most obvious contemporary example of warporn produced outside of an adult entertainment context is the imagery that was at the center of the 2004 Abu Ghraib scandal. Many critics problematically view these images as fitting Katrien Jacobs' definition of warporn as "the hybridization of war documentation and pornography" (118), and much has been made of the *influence* of porn upon the Abu Ghraib images. Sontag suggests that many of the abuses may have been "inspired by the vast repertory of pornographic imagery available on the Internet"; imagery "which ordinary people, by sending out Webcasts of themselves, try to emulate" ("Regarding the Torture of Others"). Marita Gronnvoll, meanwhile, also has conceptualized the images as operating as a kind of re-enactment of pornographic scenarios. In reference to the now infamous photograph of simulated fellatio, for example, in which two prisoners are positioned in the foreground while two others stand by, one with both hands on his hood, Gronnvoll suggests the following:

> Were it not for the man holding his head in despair, the shot could be read as a standard pornography scene where two people have sex, while a voyeur looks on and masturbates. Whether the man holding his head is simply adjusting his hood or is on the verge of emotional breakdown, his posture of hopelessness and helplessness takes this photograph from pornography to something that is heartbreaking in its frankness. (390–91)

Although seen as transcending adult entertainment, then, this image also is viewed as referencing the language of the genre. There is a bilateral tendency here; just as *Gag Factor 15* can be seen to take inspiration from current military events, so too can these horrifying snapshots from a war zone be viewed as drawing on porn's generic conventions.

Indeed, not only do many critics view the tortures depicted in the Abu Ghraib images as being directly influenced by adult entertainment, but some also view the photos as being to some extent pornographic in and of themselves. The historian Joanna Bourke, for example, argues not only that these images "have a counterpart in the worst, non-consensual sadomasochistic pornography," but also that they themselves can be understood as "the pornography of pain," due to the fact that the "abuse is performed for the camera. It is public, theatrical, and elaborately staged." The presence of the camera and its role in determining the spectacular forms taken by the torture are seen as putting the resulting images on a par with adult entertainment; indeed, these factors appear to be enough to render the photographs pornographic in Bourke's eyes. The images do not just mirror porn in this analysis, they become it, and this further stresses the idea of hybridization at the heart of warporn.

Mary Ann Tétreault makes a similar point regarding the Abu Ghraib photographs as pornography. In the context of a wider discussion of the so-called war trophy images sometimes taken by soldiers—images, such as those unearthed by the *LA Times*, which typically feature scenes of dead and suffering bodies—she says the following:

> I would call all these photographs pornographic, if we define pornography as a record of the violation of a subject's physical and psychic integrity. However, many Abu Ghraib images also are pornographic in the conventional sense. Their subjects are naked and lewdly posed, some with clothed American women playing dominatrix roles. (34)

I dispute the assertion by Tétreault and others that the photographs that have emerged from the prisoner camp can be thought of as "pornographic in the conventional sense." Yes, some of the depicted bodies are unclothed or placed in sexualized situations and positions, but there is no unsimulated or explicit sexual activity visible in these photos, and nor is there any obvious attempt to elicit physiological states of arousal in the viewer. If we assume that Tétreault is using the phrase "pornographic in the conventional sense" to mean of or relating to pornography as it is popularly understood as a genre, then I would suggest that the Abu Ghraib photos can hardly be said to warrant such a designation.

I am not trying to suggest that the Abu Ghraib images have zero points of comparison with pornography as a contemporary visual genre. Indeed, the availability and appeal of these images for adult entertainment—their evident vulnerability to appropriation, as demonstrated by texts such as *Gag Factor 15*—would make any attempt to dismiss a link between the two realms extremely problematic. However discomforting it might be for pro-sex feminists and anti-censorship activists, and however much it might disrupt politically motivated attempts to rehabilitate porn as a genre, the documentary images *do* brush against certain elements of adult entertainment. For example, they share their apparent artlessness and "raw see-all-the details glare" with some forms of gonzo and nonprofessional porn (Krzywinska, *Sex and the Cinema* 63).[4] My point is that, despite any potential points of comparison, it is just as important to recognize points of divergence. It is imperative that we distinguish such images from the fictionalized and (one hopes) consensual output of the contemporary adult entertainment industry.

A number of critics have been quick to stress this very point. In her book *Frames of War*, for example, Judith Butler directly challenges Bourke's claims about the links between the torture images and pornography. Using an apparently conventional definition of pornography, she disputes Bourke's "presumption that pornography is fundamentally defined by a certain visual pleasure being taken at the sight of human and animal suffering and torture" (88), and expresses a concern that "the old slippage from pornography to rape reappears here in unexamined form" (88).[5] We must on no account rush to conflate the photos from the prisoner camp with adult entertainment. To do so would be profoundly uncritical for, as Anne McClintock points out, "the vast majority of the images from Abu Ghraib are not standard pornography at all, not at the descriptive level of the imagery itself nor in their conditions of production or of consumption and distribution" ("Paranoid Empire" 62). If these images are to be considered pornographic, it can and should be only as a result of the explosion of the pornographic as a concept—that is, as the result of the word "pornography" no longer being viewed as synonymous with the genre of adult entertainment.

To label these images as conventionally pornographic risks misrepresenting or inaccurately characterizing them. Indeed, such moves may even to some extent allow us to dismiss that which is most deeply troubling about these images, for, as McClintock remarks, the operations of misrepresentation that took place in the wake of the scandal "*banalized the torture*, underplaying the extremity of the atrocities slowly being divulged" ("Paranoid Empire" 62). In the "storm of moral agitation about *our* pornography and *our* loss of the moral high ground," she suggests, "the terrible sufferings of ordinary, innocent people in two occupied and devastated countries were thrown into shadow" ("Paranoid Empire" 63). In raising the sensational specter of porn's supposed negative influence on individuals and on society as a whole, then, our culture was able to redirect its moral response toward more manageable targets, and toward more familiar territory. In conflating these profoundly troubling images with a certain idea of pornography, we were able to domesticate them.⁶

In addition to this taming effect, however, there are also perhaps less immediately ethically significant consequences to the inaccurate characterization of the Abu Ghraib images. Labeling these photographs of abuse as "pornographic" also risks diluting the sense and the integrity of this word as an adjectival label. When texts that display little obvious relation to adult entertainment as a genre, or that do not even engage with the realm of the sexually explicit, start being discussed in such a manner as to be brought under the banner of the pornographic, I argue that the cultural category of pornography begins to lose its specificity, and its already-contested identity can be seen to further erode. So, why has this adjectival contortion occurred? Why is it exactly that we feel justified in applying the term *pornographic* to material that, by most standards, simply does not deserve the description? In order to answer these questions, I believe that we must look back to some historical documentary texts representing acts of torture and combat, and at the manner in which the adjective "pornographic" has been (mis)used by commentators and scholars in more recent years.

Sympathy and Titillation: The Pornographic in Abolitionist Propaganda

In his important work on British antislavery propaganda, Marcus Wood sets out to highlight and critique the functioning of a certain sexual—specifically sadomasochistic—impulse within abolitionist materials that target the man or woman of sentiment.⁷ He notes that, in the culture of the 1790s, the "ability to empathize with another's pain is set up as the supreme test of humanism, and in Burke as a true test of the 'Sublime' experience" (101). The sympathetic capacity, he argues, is "seen above any other to separate the human from the brute or the savage" (101). As a result, abolitionist texts actively seek to appeal to this ennobling capacity, and invite their audience to contemplate and identify with the depicted suffering of the slave. Wood views this invitation as problematic. Our senses, he notes:

> can never realize or communicate precisely what constituted, constitutes, or will constitute another person's traumatic suffer-

> ing under torture. Consequently, the only way of drawing near to the sufferer's experience of pain is to mimic it, to fantasize it, using imagination. This assumption is finally based on the premise that an observer's (viewer's, voyeur's, witness's) sympathetic response to another person's pain lies in a gesture of extreme psychic masochism. It is the duty of the sympathetic imagination to try to appropriate the victim's pain to such a degree that we "enter" that person's body. (102)

As such, Wood argues, works of propaganda from the period encourage the reader to appropriate the suffering of the slave victim and, through the operations of eroticism, to covertly enjoy this suffering.[8]

Sympathy, the deadening of which so haunts Atwood's *Oryx and Crake*, can therefore be positioned as in itself suspect; a surfeit of affective response, just as much as a dearth, can be seen to invite an interrogation of the subject's motives and drives. Leo Bersani and Ulysse Dutoite make some enlightening comments about this in their book *The Forms of Violence: Narrative in Assyrian Art and Modern Culture*. In this volume, they suggest that a trace of sexual pleasure inevitably makes its way into any experience of sympathy. With this in mind, they argue the following:

> there is a certain risk in all sympathetic projections: the pleasure which accompanies them promotes a secret attachment to scenes of suffering or violence. We are not, it should be stated, arguing (absurdly) "against" sympathy. Rather, we wish to suggest that the psychic mechanism which allows for what would rightly be called humane or morally liberal responses to scenes of suffering or violence is, intrinsically, somewhat dysfunctional. The very operation of sympathy partially undermines the moral solidarity which we like to think of as its primary effect. Our views of the human capacity for empathetic representations of the world should therefore take into account the possibility that a mimetic relation to violence necessarily includes a sexually induced fascination with violence. (38)

This emphasis on the interpenetration of sexuality and sympathy, and its concomitant insights into the dysfunctional operations of the sympathetic response, will inform much of this chapter's discussion of Wood's historical abolitionist examples.

What is most notable about Wood's account of covertly eroticized propaganda is, for our purposes, the wide range of material that he brings under the adjectival label "pornographic." He asserts, "There is a lot of abolition propaganda, both written and in the form of single-sheet prints and oil paintings, which treats the slave body (any gender, any age) as punishment object or fetish in directly exploitative and eroticized ways which are blatantly pornographic" (92–93). Yet the material that Wood considers to be "blatantly pornographic" is, I argue, somewhat atypical when it comes to conventional understandings of this term. Like Tétreault, his understanding of the pornographic is unusual in its decentering of sex acts, and in its eschewal of explicitness and an overt intent to arouse as significant factors. That is to say, Wood's idea of the pornographic is not a close relation to today's adult entertainment.

Wood detects the pornographic within the largely nonsexual engravings produced by William Blake and Francesco Bartolozzi to accompany John Gabriel Stedman's 1796 text *The Narrative of a Five Years Expedition against the Revolted Negroes of Surinam*. Here is Wood discussing Bartolozzi's frontispiece—an engraving that depicts the narrator-author standing over the bleeding body of a black slave: "Is the frontispiece to the *Narrative* a pornographic image? I think it is; it is certainly highly erotic, but the manner in which it both sentimentalizes, sexualizes, and trans-sexualizes the body of the black victim at the moment of death has pornographic elements" (98). There is, Wood argues, "an extraordinary tension between the two bodies: the black all vanquished, supine, feminized and available nudity, the white clothed and full of points, and pointing" (105). And yet he admits, "at no point are the actual bodies allowed to touch. The only contact the two bodies enjoy is through the barrel of the gun, the biggest phallic object of them all" (105). There is no explicit suggestion of sexual acts in this engraving, and no depictions of genitalia. It does not appear to primarily seek to stir physiological sexual arousal in the viewer, and nor does it seem intent on facilitating the viewer's sexual climax. For all the eroticism in the image, is it really justifiable to call it pornographic? Only, I would suggest, if the meaning of this adjective is not attached to pornography as a genre, but instead refers to some other phenomenon or discourse.

Wood later brings a further eccentric example under the label of the pornographic in the form of a "sheet of engravings produced to describe the implements used to torture slaves during the middle passage" (409). The anonymous copper engraving, which features in Thomas Clarkson's

History of the Abolition of the African Slave Trade (1807), depicts the devices in a clear and dispassionate fashion reminiscent of the style of instructional diagrams. This is perhaps an even less conventional example of pornography than is Bartolozzi's frontispiece. That there are no depictions of the human body in this plate would seem to suggest that the engraving shares very little territory with the generically pornographic, but this fact only leads Wood to argue that the images act as an invitation to "pure fantasy, focused on the absent flesh of the black slave body" (413). Wood admits that Clarkson's description of the functioning of these implements is "methodological and unenthusiastic" (413), rather than frenziedly sexual or overtly eroticized, but again, this fact merely prompts the suggestion that "in the very coldness and detachment of his tone there is a Sadean delight in the efficiency of the equipment and in the absolute power of the master to use it with brutal detachment" (413).

Both the frontispiece of Stedman's *Narrative* and this anonymous engraving are considered pornographic despite the absence of explicit representations of sexual acts or, in the case of the latter, the absence of corporeal beings altogether. These images are even less like adult entertainment than is the warporn of Abu Ghraib, and to label them pornographic would require a fairly substantial slippage in one's sense of what pornography is and means. Some points within Wood's discussion of Stedman's *Narrative* would appear to suggest that such a slippage in understanding is indeed at work. He remarks, for example, "Death, violence, decadence, sex, luxury, slavery, torture and bondage are constant foci in Stedman's writing about his life in Surinam. Given these fixations, the work almost inevitably shades into pornography" (97). Here, sex is given as one of a number of factors whose presence might render a text pornographic; tellingly, it is not even the first factor on Wood's list! Sex is clearly displaced in this understanding of the pornographic. The question is why and how this displacement comes to take place, and what it might be seen to suggest. Therefore, it might be helpful at this point to consider how the pornographic is conceptualized in the work of some of the critics most influential on Wood's thinking.

Wood's account is heavily influenced by the understandings of pornography propagated by anti-porn feminists, and he derives his working definition of pornography directly from the sex wars era theories of Helen E. Longino, Gloria Steinham, Andrea Dworkin, and Catherine MacKinnon. It is perhaps worth noting at this point that many of the rhetorical devices deployed by polemical anti-pornography writings can be seen to resemble, or even to borrow from, the kind of propagandist strategies that Wood examines. That is, they appeal to the sympathy of the observer by facilitating the observation and eroticized appropriation of a victim-figure's pain and suffering. B. Ruby Rich, for example, detects such operations at work within Bonnie Klein's 1981 anti-porn documentary *Not a Love Story*. Rich suggests that, in its role as propaganda, this film offers covert scopophilic pleasures, to the extent that it becomes

> an acceptable replacement for porn itself, a kind of snuff movie for an anti-snuff crowd. In this version, outrage-against replaces pleasure-in, but the object of the preposition remains the same. Cries of outrage and averted eyes replace the former clientele's silent pleasure and inverted hats; the gaze of horror substitutes the glaze of satiation. The question, though, is whether this outcry becomes itself a handmaiden to titillation, whether this all eyed look of horror is not perhaps a most sophisticated form of voyeurism. (343–44)

Not a Love Story, we might say, actively appeals to that dysfunctional psychic mechanism that Bersani and Dutoite view as smuggling certain forms of sexual arousal into the experience of sympathy. Like Wood's abolitionist examples, then, Klein's documentary targets interests that exceed the sphere of the political or the moral.[9]

Dworkin's work also provides an example of the links between the rhetorical strategies of anti-slavery propaganda and those of anti-pornography feminism. Both her fictional and nonfictional writings dwell on the suffering of victims who are, like slaves, viewed as being persecuted "as a class" ("Against the Male Flood" 260)—that is, as a result of their political or social identity rather than as random individuals.[10] Her writings also seek to target the contemporary person of sentiment, attempting, in their brutally emotive style, to affect the good liberal reader into a state of proper feminist enlightenment. Here she is, for example, commenting on the response, or lack of, to women's perceived plight:

> Instead of any so-called humanist outcry against the inhumanity of the use of women in pornography—an outcry that we might expect if dogs and cats were being treated in the same way—there has been the pervasive, self-congratulatory, indolent, male-supremacist assumption that the use of women

in pornography is the sexual will of the woman, expresses her sexuality, her character, her nature, and appropriately demonstrates a legitimate sexual function of hers. ("Pornography and Male Supremacy" 232)

Leaving aside the troubling suggestion that human females can be compared with domestic pets in terms of their sexual agency, it is clear that Dworkin is critiquing what she views as the lack of a properly sympathetic response to pornography's use of women. The wider culture is not sentimental enough about women, she seems to suggest, preferring to direct this particular type of feeling toward animals.[11]

Like the abolitionist texts Wood discusses, however, Dworkin's appeals to her readers' honorable sympathies can simultaneously be seen to provide an outlet for the functioning of less honorable and more lascivious concerns. After all, as Harriet Gilbert notes, the sexual degradations chronicled in Dworkin's polemical autobiographical novel *Mercy* frequently use the language and the conventions of pornographic fiction, engaging, on the level of literary style, "with Sade and with Réage" (227). The novel therefore exists in something of a liminal position, operating primarily as polemic, but functioning also as a site for the potential interpenetration of sexual and sympathetic impulses. Not only abolitionist texts but political propaganda of various kinds can be seen to draw quietly on a pervasive prurient interest in the sorrowful or the horrific, whilst openly addressing itself to concerns of a less denigrated kind.

Yet Wood's investigation into the covert pleasures of propaganda indicates that the incorporation of strongly eroticized elements into materials with self-conscious activist political intentions is a flawed polemical strategy. For one thing, it encourages in the reader a transgressive investment in the horrors depicted, thereby undermining the moral force of the text's affects in a sort of overly determined version of the generally dysfunctional sympathetic response. Such titillating and troubling works of propaganda can be seen to court, in a circuitous form, the very interest that the polemicist is attempting to combat, whether that be the desire to enjoy the violation of the slave's body, or the will to take pleasure in the sexual subordination of women.

This blending of titillation and activism has quite a tradition within reformist discourses. Discussing nineteenth-century American feminist-abolitionist fictions, for example, Karen Sánchez-Eppler suggests the following:

On the one hand the horrific events narrated in these tales attract precisely to the extent the buyers of these representations of slavery are fascinated by the abuses they ostensibly oppose; For despite their clear abolitionist stance, such stories are fueled by the allure of bondage, an appeal which suggests that the valuation of depictions of slavery may rest upon the same psychic ground as slaveholding itself. On the other hand, the acceptability of these tales depends upon their adherence to a feminine and domestic demeanor that softens the cruelty they describe and makes their political goals more palatable to a less politicized readership. (98–99)

Politically motivated material can be seen to both exploit and skirt around public prurience for its own specific ends. In the case of Dworkinite feminist work, of course, any erotic side effects are particularly ironic, for the sympathetic projections that such sentimental propaganda seeks to generate can, perversely, be seen to encourage the very prurient, voyeuristic interest in sexualized suffering that this material explicitly seeks to resist.

However, despite these issues, I suggest that there is something slyly pragmatic about this rhetorical strategy. Certainly, many people may partly be intrigued by these sentimental political materials out of a transgressive prurient interest in enjoying the spectacle of suffering that they provide. At the same time, however, these materials crucially provide a mechanism through which one may disavow one's lascivious or morbid fascination at the very moment that one indulges it. These are, after all, works with expressly political, rather than pornographic, intentions, that set out to address themselves to reputable and high-minded concerns. In other words, certain varieties of sentimental propaganda pander to prurient interest while simultaneously allowing the subject to deny this fact, and thereby to placate his or her superego. The subject can assuage any sense of guilt or culpability, and go some way toward concealing the full extent of the transgression from the self, by having recourse to something like the legal notion of redeeming social or political value.

What does this possibility of simultaneously entering into both prurient and wholesome forms of engagement suggest or achieve? Does an admixture of prurience always undermine political or propagandist intentions, or might it in some way work as a device to affect and manipulate the reader or viewer in desired ways? It is my contention that, although the concealed sexual undertones of political propaganda may mobilize a certain prurient interest, they also may play an unacknowledged role in the mobilization of sympathy itself. By activating the morbid, conflicted desire to witness suffering while providing a mechanism by which the presence of this desire can be roundly and robustly denied, the sentimentalizing and eroticizing depictions of suffering found within certain works of propaganda provide something of a service. Their explicit appeal to the sympathetic impulse acts as something like an indirect form of licensed transgression. Under these limited conditions, we allow ourselves to succumb to a forbidden and denigrated desire to take pleasure in accounts of suffering, precisely because we can to some extent mask the full force of this desire from the self and the other. This may prove polemically expedient, for although, as Sontag notes, "painful, stirring images supply only an initial spark" when it comes to meaningful political action (*Regarding the Pain of Others* 92), and may not necessarily prompt any form of useful reflection at all, the powerful desire to be able to disown and disavow the transgressive pleasure elicited by these texts may indeed work to promote political engagement.

This idea is in some ways reminiscent of Adam Smith's comments in *The Theory of Moral Sentiments*, first published in 1759, regarding that which is "generous" and "noble" within human nature (158). "It is not the love of our neighbor, it is not the love of mankind," he argues, "which upon many occasions prompts us to the practice of those divine virtues. It is a stronger love, a more powerful affection, which generally takes place upon such occasions; the love [. . .] of the grandeur, and dignity, and superiority of our characters" (158). We are attracted to an inflated idea of the self, then, and our attempts to behave honorably may be a byproduct of precisely this attraction. Actions of generosity, sympathy, and self-sacrifice may, by this reckoning, in fact stem from a self-interested investment in the image of our own noble characters, and this investment is therefore available to be exploited for political ends.

By facilitating the exploration and enjoyment of prurient interest within the context of propaganda, the materials that we have been looking at in this chapter may prompt both engagement and action. What better way to conceal the indulgence of an itching, morbid, or lascivious longing than by converting it into a reputable—and, indeed, admirable—impulse? Prurience may therefore prove to trigger a secondary political or ethical response, as the viewer seeks to protect a sense of his or her own grandeur, dignity, and superiority. As Wood puts it, "the enlightened man of sentiment [. . .] can have his cake and eat it" (98), and it could be that the attempt to do just this, apparently so disingenuous, may help to make certain forms of social change possible.

The Role of Violence in Understandings of the Pornographic

As I suggested in my brief discussion of *Not a Love Story* and *Mercy*, and in Chapter 1's analysis of the resemblance of Dworkin's polemical tableaux to works of pornographic flash fiction, many anti-pornography feminist tracts touch on sexual acts in ways that verge on the explicit. Their vulnerability to being labeled as pornographic is perhaps, therefore, not particularly surprising. However, as we have seen, many of the texts that Wood discusses do not even come close to sexual explicitness, and at times omit corporeal forms altogether. That Wood is able to position these texts as pornographic is in some ways a triumph of the ideas of anti-pornography feminism, and much of his discussion of British abolitionist propaganda as pornography is made possible by the theoretical maneuverings of Dworkin, MacKinnon, and their ilk. After all, despite the sporadic explicitness of their own writing, many of these thinkers work to diminish the importance of sexuality in any conceptualization of the pornographic, positioning violence, rather than sex, at the center of this contested cultural category. Dworkin, for example, claims that the "spread of pornography that uses live women, real women, is the spread of the whorehouse, the concentration camp for women, the house of sexual slaughter" ("Pornography and Male Supremacy" 234),[12] while Steinham argues that, unlike the "mutually pleasurable, sexual expression" of erotica (53), pornography is really concerned with "violence, dominance, and conquest" (53). Longino, meanwhile, makes the anti-pornography feminist decentering of sex within pornography very clear: "What is wrong with pornography, then, is its degrading and dehumanizing portrayal of women (and *not* its sexual content)" (87).

The high profile of this facet of the women's movement has resulted in the particular reconceptualization of pornography that it enacts gaining something of a toehold in the contemporary imagination. Although common-sensical understandings of adult entertainment may prioritize sexual contents and affects, the word "pornography" also now brings with it a realm of associations with violence and violation.[13] Indeed, the *Oxford English Dictionary* entry for "pornography" not only states that it is the "explicit description or exhibition of sexual subjects or activity in literature, painting, films, etc., in a manner intended to stimulate erotic rather than aesthetic feelings," but also makes reference to the word's extended use in the "pornography of violence"; for the *OED*, "pornography" is now linked to "the explicit description or depiction of violence in a manner intended to stimulate or excite." From this, we can clearly see that pornography is widely understood as being in some way associated with ideas of violence.

This linkage is not entirely the result of the sex wars, perhaps. After all, as Carolyn Dean remarks, "social commentators and analysts began to postulate a significant link between the wartime proliferation of pornography and the unprecedented violence of modern combat" in the immediate wake of World War I (61), and it was at this point, she suggests, that "pornography and violence became continuous with descriptions of assaults on the integrity of the human body, establishing a sense of continuity that remains essential to the idea that pornography is a mobile category of meaning with no fixed referents" (61). Although our sense of what constitutes pornography has long been changing to incorporate elements of violence, however, I suggest that such shifts have been cultivated, promoted, and propagated within popular understandings of the category since anti-porn feminism entered the cultural scene and proved so successful in spreading its message.

Even if it never managed to get its doctrine on pornography widely accepted, either within feminism as a whole or within the wider culture, this movement did reinforce a certain understanding of the pornographic as a realm in which violence and sexuality might be said to interpenetrate. The profile of this idea of porn as a site of such interpenetration has been significantly raised since the sex wars, and the shift toward violence appears to have become increasingly pronounced. As Kendrick notes:

> We are no longer so frightened of "sex" as we used to be; in the MacKinnon-Dworkin ordinance, for example, sex plays a surprisingly ancillary role, because the real target is violence, with sex as an enabling attribute though possibly not an essential one. The latest phase of the pornography debate seems to entail its elevation from morals to politics, the long-overdue recognition that what we have been arguing about the entire time is a matter of power, of access to the world around us, of control over our own bodies and our own minds. (236)

This shift, I argue, is reflected in various cultural sites. Williams, for example, stresses that "the hallmark of sophisticated adult sexual representations in Western cinema since the eighties has just as often been a flirtation with the taboo of violence in sex rather than with the taboo of explicit sex itself" (*Screening Sex* 221), which implies that, since the successful dissemination of the anti-pornography feminist message during the sex wars, explicitness alone has lost something of the transgressive force apparently suggested by the adjective "pornographic."

The post-sex wars decentering of sex is further reflected in the important cultural barometer provided by Western censorship regimes. Although Carolyn Dean notes that "during the years since 1920 *nonviolent* heterosexual "pornography" has gradually been exempted from obscenity prosecution in the United States and Western Europe" (61), attributing this to the "massive redefinition of pornography sparked by the Great War" (61), legal and policy shifts also have been triggered by developments in second-wave feminist theorizing. As Philip French and Julian Petley remark, the British Board of Film Classification (BBFC) is "highly exercised about films that mingle sex and violence, whether or not in an explicitly pornographic context" (26). In its Annual Report 2003, for example, the BBFC moves to justify its "robust policy on sexual violence" (14), stating that it "continues to work on the assumption that particular violent scenes with the potential to trigger sexual arousal may encourage a harmful association between sexual violence and sexual gratification" (74). Not only that, but the BBFC's 2003 report also makes explicit reference to media effects research from the sex wars era, some of which has undoubted links with the anti-pornography feminist cause: "Much of the relevant research into the effects of depictions of sexual violence was undertaken in the USA in the 1980s by researchers such as Donnerstein, Linz, Malamuth, Check, Zillman, Bryant, Berkowitz and Burt" (74). Edward Donnerstein, the first expert on the BBFC's list, is featured in Klein's *Not a Love Story* and was even one of the experts MacKinnon questioned during the Minneapolis hearings.[14]

Indeed, the influence of this feminist-inflected media effects research can be seen to continue to this day, with Donnerstein's name appearing numerous times in the recent rapid evidence assessment (REA) commissioned by the Ministry of Justice prior to the passing of the Criminal Justice and Immigration Act 2008's new extreme pornography legislation. Donnerstein's work is therefore among the research that made it possible for the REA to conclude of extreme pornographic material that the government must focus on "the damage it does to the attitudes, beliefs, fantasies, desires and behavior of those who use it" (Itzin, Taket and Kelly 29). It would appear that Dworkinite feminist understandings of pornography, having gained influence within the wider culture, have worked to further the shifts in understanding begun in the wake of the Great War; that which is most troubling or culturally visible about the pornographic is increasingly being viewed, from a number of cultural sites, as being a matter of much more than simply explicitness.

Throughout this section, we have encountered a range of examples of cultural artifacts that can be seen to intersect with the category of the pornographic in unusual or unexpected ways, and that might therefore be seen to in some ways displace or decenter the sexually explicit. These include the war images on *Now That's Fucked Up*, which feature no conventionally erotic acts, and yet are displayed within the context of an adult website; the notorious Abu Ghraib photographs, which some commentators argue are a form of pornography, despite their numerous differences from the genre of adult entertainment; and the abolitionist materials that Wood labels as pornography, regardless of the fact that they may not feature sex acts or even bodily forms. The anti-pornography feminist texts that we have been discussing, meanwhile, have been shown to incorporate some explicitly sexual elements into their own sentimentalizing political projects, and it may be that their occasional reimagining as pornographic therefore feels less surprising. At the same time, however, we also have seen that these writings work to expedite those shifts in understanding initiated by World War I in which violence becomes increasingly central to the manner in which pornography is conceptualized, with the effect that the importance of the sexual would appear to be somewhat diminished. There is evidence, then, that would suggest that the sexually explicit can be side-lined in various ways when it comes to the category of the pornographic.

And yet, I suggest, the tendency remains to consider pornography as being synonymous with adult entertainment. After all, although the examples discussed in this section seem to demonstrate a contemporary slippage when it comes to understandings of the adjective pornographic, the idea of a nonsexual pornographic remains somewhat counterintuitive. Although the pornographic is now on some level understood as a category that exceeds the mere presence of the sexually explicit, it is at the same time typically conflated with a genre whose unique selling point is in fact this very presence. This leads me to conclude that there is something of a paradigm shift occurring in contemporary understandings of the pornographic, which has not yet been fully acknowledged or which, perhaps, has simply not been sufficiently represented in the linguistic field.

Conclusion: Transgression, Prurience, Intensity

The sense attached to the adjective pornographic has, as we have seen, undergone something of a slippage in recent times. Beginning in the early twentieth century, and continuing into our own era, alterations have occurred in terms of our interpretation of this cultural category. Although the contemporary understanding of pornography as violence is undoubtedly part of the uncoupling of the pornographic from the representation of sexual acts and the sexual body—of the establishment of a nonsexually explicit dimension to the pornographic—I suggest that it is not now simply a case of violence replacing sex as the key determining factor of pornography. My discussion may have intersected with ideas of violence through its engagement with the violated bodies and subjects of warporn and the affecting representation of suffering in sentimental propaganda, but other elements of my discussion have emphasized the idea of diversification—the generalized interests at the heart of the pornographic examined in Chapter 4. Some of the representations to be found in *Hustler* or on the *Porn Jackass* website, for example, can be seen to exceed conventional notions of the violent just as much as they go beyond the typical terrain of the sexual, and this may demonstrate something of what Carolyn Dean has labeled "the now extraordinary descriptive breadth of the 'pornographic'—no longer confined to 'pornography,' a clearly identifiable category of material against which one could legislate" (69).

This all rather begs the question of how we might define the concept of the pornographic, even provisionally. If it is not to be limited by either ideas of violence or notions of sex, how might we characterize it? From what qualities might it be said to derive its specificity and identity? The work of Sarah Leonard may prove helpful in our attempts to formulate a partial answer to these questions. In an insightful analysis of obscenity, Leonard suggests that documentary images of violated bodies constitute a particularly conspicuous and significant presence within contemporary visual culture. Of the Abu Ghraib photographs, she remarks:

> Images of men forced to stand in place with electrical wires connected to their genitals raises a second understanding of

pornography as the pleasure attending the viewing of others' pain. At stake in all of it seems to be the desire to document—and by extension, to view—other people in extreme states (of excitement, fear, pain, even death).[15] (201)

Pornography is not understood as something inherently sexual here. It need not involve the display of aroused naked bodies or the representation of interacting sexual organs. Instead, it is connected to the desire to witness the vulnerable human body in exceptional circumstances. We find that the sexual frenzy can be replaced as the object of our viewing pleasure by depictions of bodies experiencing less enjoyable, but equally intense, scenarios of physical agitation, in a manner that recalls the adolescent pursuit of any form of affecting spectacle depicted in Margaret Atwood's *Oryx and Crake*.

This idea of the body in a state of intensity—that is, the body in a state during which "the organization of the self is momentarily disturbed by sensations or affective processes somehow 'beyond' those compatible with psychic organization" (Bersani 38)—seems key to me. It is not violence, we might suggest, which is positioned as central to the category of the pornographic, but a more general desire—a desire to witness the human subject suffering or enjoying extreme physical states, and, through the transgression attached to pursuing one's prurient interest in such scenes, to experience at least a ghost of this intensity for oneself. As Carol J. Clover puts it, then, "The pornographic body: this is the heart of the matter. Although our systems of censorship and our production codes concern themselves with the status of bodies 'up there' (on the photograph, on the canvas or screen), what is really at stake is the body 'down here,' the body of the viewer" (3). The embodied experience of the reader or spectator may be just as important when it comes to characterizing or identifying this cultural realm as what is depicted, and prurient interest and intense affects of any kind may prove central to the pornographic, even if the corporeal spectacle which triggers these responses would not conventionally be thought of as sexual.

This idea of a displacement of the scopo- and epistemophilic desire to see, from the sexual body and sexual acts to *any* scene of the body in a state of intensity, leads us some way toward the idea of a linguistic slippage in terms of the usage of the adjective "pornographic." Leonard herself remarks on the changing resonances of the terms *obscenity* and *pornography* in her article, noting that "It is now not uncommon to use the word 'obscene' to describe images of the mass destruction of bodies in German concentration camps during the Second World War—or, perhaps better put, the use of 'pornographic' to describe the combination of horror and pleasure with which we view such images" (200). From this, we can see once again that the word "pornographic" is no longer simply applied to the output of the adult entertainment industry but can, in fact, be applied to the manner in which a person responds to visual texts—to the particular combination of affective responses that take place under the auspices of prurient interest. The act of spectatorial engagement is paramount here, as graphic, but not explicitly sexual, depictions of the body may intersect with the concept of the pornographic precisely through the figure of the enthralled yet conflicted (in other words, the transgressing) observer.

In light of the paradigm shift in terms of understandings of the pornographic, then, I propose a provisional redefinition. The adjective "pornographic," it seems to me, now refers to something related to the body in a state of intensity, rather than to the body in a state of physiological sexual arousal. This state may certainly contain conventionally sexual elements, but need not necessarily. Repulsive, upsetting, or otherwise affecting elements are all equally as likely to warrant the label, and the adjective may apply to the qualities of a representation or to the experiences and desires of the consumer. It is the concept of a generalized state of intensity that is paramount here. We have seen this though our discussion of warporn, abolitionist propaganda and anti-porn polemics, but also through our discussion of the gross-out, stunts-and-pranks style of "trashy" or willfully transgressive forms of adult entertainment. Equally, we saw traces of this idea in the previous section's examination of disgust in Roche's *Wetlands*, and through our discussion of the novel's transformation into pornography via its engagement with generalized transgression.

Transgression, prurience, and *intensity*: These, I suggest, are key terms in helping us to understand how the pornographic is understood and how it operates as a concept within contemporary Western culture. Representations that intersect with this particular, highly loaded cluster of concepts—most of which lack a single privileged object—would seem to be more likely to be more frequently framed as examples of the pornographic, even if they lack any form of explicit genital display or any obvious intention to arouse. This would go some way toward explaining the existence of what I call the nonsexual pornographic, for certain texts would be incorporated into this cultural category as the result of the interpenetration of certain wide-ranging ideas that have somehow emerged around it. In the next section, I further test the legitimacy of this suggestion that the pornographic has been popularly redefined by examining it in relation to a set of materials apparently even further divorced from the conventionally erotic—that is, misery memoirs, known as "misery porn." Why might these decidedly nonsexual materials warrant the label of porn? Do they offer any further evidence for the claims made in this section? And what role do the ideas of authenticity and the real play in connecting these texts to contemporary understandings of the pornographic?

PART III

Pornography and the Real

So far in this book, we have used the concepts of transgression, intensity, and prurience to help theorize the manner in which certain unconventional—and at times, nonexplicit—materials have come to be viewed as pornographic. In this section, I extend my analysis of the displacement of sex within contemporary understandings of the pornographic by considering the separate but related concept of authenticity. Authenticity, I demonstrate, is central to the way in which both adult entertainment and the more capacious notion of pornography are currently characterized, and an interest in the notion of the real can be seen as one important influence when it comes to perceiving or positioning a text as pornographic. Beginning with an examination of contemporary understandings of (and anxieties about) authenticity, Chapter 7 uses the work of Linda Williams, Pasi Falk, and Tanya Krzywinska to briefly outline some of the many ways in which adult entertainment can be seen to be invested in ideas of the real. It then analyzes how particular examples of contemporary porn—including the output of the well-known adult director Rocco Siffredi—work to generate an authenticity effect, or to convey an impression of reality.

Chapter 8 focuses on a very different subset of representations that are labeled as pornographic. The key object of analysis for this chapter is the popular literary phenomenon known as "misery porn"—that is, the subgenre of autobiographical works that are based on the author's real-life experiences of physical or emotional suffering. I interrogate exactly what it is about such works that makes them available for consideration as pornography, and consider what effect the ideas of genre and authenticity have on their reception. Life writing's generic identity is heavily reliant on the idea of reality, and this—combined with an emphasis on trauma—may be one reason why memoirs of a certain kind come to be identified as a species of porn, regardless of their level of sexual explicitness. I conclude the discussion by considering literary hoaxes, such as the one perpetrated by James Frey, as examples of the centrality of the authentic text to autobiography and pornography.

In the final chapter, I discuss one particularly intriguing illustration of the intersection of the ideas of pornography, autobiography, and authenticity; that is, the work and authorial persona of JT LeRoy. Jeremiah "Terminator" LeRoy was a gender dissident street hustler from West Virginia, who spent "most of his teens with his truck-stop prostitute mother, who drew him into a nomadic life of drugs, destitution and abuse" (Crisell). However, after the publication of his novel *Sarah* in 1999, LeRoy (then still in his teens) managed to transcend these supposedly traumatic boyhood experiences in order to become a successful writer. Two books—the short story collection *The Heart is Deceitful Above All Things* (2001) and the novella *Harold's End* (2004)—followed in quick succession, and the author became involved in a number of journalistic and cinematic projects. LeRoy, however, turned out to be a hoax; articles by the journalists Stephen Beachy and Warren St. John, published in late 2005 and early 2006 respectively, revealed that LeRoy was the pseudonym of Laura Albert, a female writer and musician in her late 30s whose real life bore little in common with that of the LeRoy persona.

I focus on JT LeRoy here not because "his" work is one of the more exemplary cases of the genre—far from it—but precisely because LeRoy is a figure existing at the intersection of what I perceive to be various significant fault lines within contemporary thinking on misery memoir. As is seen in the chapter, his work straddles the already tenuous boundary between fiction and autobiography—presenting itself, in a multilayered deceit, as thinly veiled memoir *masquerading* as make-believe—and draws attention to contemporary anxieties about the viability of the distinction between the phony and the genuine. In addition to this, LeRoy's writing can be seen to trouble the distinction between misery porn and pornography proper,[1] providing as it does various explicit accounts of acts of sexual abuse or prostitution, which supposedly have some claim to extra-textual authenticity. It is the marginal position of his work—the difficulty, evident both before and after Albert's exposure, of knowing quite where to place it or how to talk about it—that makes it such a productive object for analysis in this context. After all, such instability or volatility is arguably a key characteristic of pornography itself. I conclude Chapter

9 by reflecting on alternative definitional criteria for pornography. Drawing on my discussion of the role of trauma throughout this chapter and, indeed, throughout the section as a whole, I seek to push beyond notions of authenticity to find a more nuanced way to think about pornography and the real. How, I ask, might we reframe the pornographic in relation to a dual emphasis on both reality and the Real as *jouissance*?

7

Pornography and the Appetite for Authenticity

The Contemporary Hunger for Authenticity

It may seem somewhat counterintuitive to argue for the cultural significance of authenticity in the contemporary Western world. After all, the postmodern age is more typically characterized by a move away from an ethos of authenticity. As Baudrillard famously claims, the development of information and communication technologies has rendered the conventional relationship between the authentic and the simulated somewhat tenuous and unstable, with reality being increasingly obscured due to "the accumulation of images through the increasing power of technological media" (Bewes 20). As Richard J. Lane notes, such a culture "produces a reality of its own without being based upon any particular bit of the real world" (30), and this is viewed as a typical attribute of digital cultures and of the increasing dominance of the virtual.

This move away from authenticity also has been seen as a defining characteristic of postmodern thinking and critical practice. As Timothy Bewes remarks in his book *Cynicism and Postmodernity*, the "concept 'postmodern' has reified to such an extent that any attachment to useful notions such as identity or subjective agency is dismissed as 'essentialist' by a banal sensibility for which 'irony' and 'parody' enjoy the status of perverse creeds" (47). Concepts, even the "useful notions" that facilitate certain kinds of ethical or political engagement—"the author, the subject, reality, sexual and cultural identity, the universal" (Bewes 48)—are viewed as not holding up to rigorous deconstructive scrutiny and as therefore being inauthentic cultural constructs. What role can be claimed for the real in this kind of cultural climate, then? Surely its perceived importance is now diminished (or at least complicated), and any residual focus on authenticity within contemporary society must be positioned as a mere anachronism?

I contend that such a reduction of influence has not in fact occurred and that concerns regarding the endangerment of the real can be characterized as a particularly key attribute of the postmodern condition.[1] This is something that Bewes acknowledges in his exploration of the dominant strands of postmodern theory. Although irony can certainly be positioned as one of the key contemporary modes, he argues, this does not simply reflect a disinterest in authenticity, but must be viewed as the symptom of a profound and frustrated *desire* for it. The ironic or cynical mode only becomes necessary because we are making heightened demands on authenticity and the real: "our conceptions of truthfulness, say, or authentic subjectivity, are so far in excess of those of any previous era [. . .] that any manifestations of these ideas, whether in political life or in artistic forms of representation, are likely always to fall short of our demands" (Bewes 47). As the "authenticity threshold is shifted a notch higher" (Bewes 52)—a response to contemporary anxieties regarding the validity and veracity of language, concepts, the coherent self, and so on—the postmodern subject is forced to adopt what Bewes describes as "a defensive strategy of cynical indifference" (56). As a result of impossibly high standards, we find ourselves trapped in a "mournful relationship" with authenticity (Bewes 48).

Far from reducing the importance of the real, then, it would seem that the prevalence of simulation within the contemporary world has worked to further emphasize and intensify a preoccupation with locating the authentic.[2] This is perhaps reflected within the world of the arts (as well as that of adult entertainment), where "the ubiquitous hype of virtual life—with the internet gurus claiming that we can transcend our bodies—has left artists with an absolute fascination with real bodies and body fluids" (Boyle 128). David Boyle detects this fascination in operation within much of the material produced by the Young British Artists, remarking that "Damien Hirst's work is very much concerned with authenticity. It's about the real cow, or shark. It's about the stark fact of death, just as Tracey Emin's unmade bed was about her own real life. Their success bears testament to our fascination with the immediate and the tangible" (129).

Hal Foster also remarks upon this tendency in his discussion of Western society's current "concern with trauma and abjection" (123). For

Foster, however, the interest in the body and its substances evident within the visual arts is not merely characteristic of discourses regarding the unsimulated or the extra-textual—the real cow, the real shark, or the real life. It goes beyond any simple interest in the immediate or the tangible, and intersects with what Alain Badiou identifies as the "veritable exaltation of the real, even in its horror" (*The Century* 19). It is apparent that two very different discourses of the real are at work here, each playing into and reinforcing the other. As Foster demonstrates, the preoccupation with the real body and its products is part of a wider exploration of the Lacanian real—"the source of both horror and enthusiasm, simultaneously lethal and creative" (Badiou, *The Century* 32).[3] Foster argues that much contemporary art refuses the "age-old mandate to pacify the gaze, to unite the imaginary and the symbolic against the real" (110), and suggests that "*It is as if this art wanted the gaze to shine, the object to stand, the real to exist, in all the glory (or the horror) of its pulsatile desire, or at least to evoke this sublime condition*" (110). The real, then, is positioned at the core of a particular extreme strand of contemporary artistic practice that is largely preoccupied by ideas regarding the abject, the violent, the perverse, and the visceral.[4]

Bewes also touches on the idea that violence might be important to postmodernism, suggesting that it has the ability to function as a key generator and guarantor of authenticity. In his opinion, "the prospect of violence, which delimits rather than conserves, which forecloses rather than distends, has a magnetic glamour born of its vitalism and certitude" (107), and serves as the "actualization of action in a climate in which action is pathologically resisted" (108–09); "amid the dizzying vastness, the featurelessness of the postmodern moral landscape," he writes, "manifestations of violence appear as peremptory landmarks, flashes of certainty, instants of explicitness" (108). The (actual, extra-textual) body in a state of intensity is positioned as central to discourses of the real, then, and an interest in trauma and *jouissance* can be seen as an important manifestation of the contemporary preoccupation with authenticity. As is seen later in this section, "trauma's centrality to self-representation" is evident not only in the relatively rarefied context of contemporary art (Gilmore, "Limit-Cases" 129), but also within the popular literary genre of misery memoir. These autobiographical works combine an investment in the historical, verifiable life with an interest in more disturbing or affecting currents of the real. Now, however, I turn my attention to adult entertainment—a genre that very much mirrors wider cultural anxieties about authenticity, and that is committed to demonstrating its own validity and evidential power at every opportunity. How can diverse discourses of the real be seen to play into today's commercial pornographic landscape?

Pornography and Authenticity: Adult Entertainment's Textual Strategies

Both autobiography and pornography are invested in the importance of the "real world," and can be seen to demonstrate a pervasive concern with the concept of authenticity. Adult entertainment relies on "a documentary impulse, a guarantee that we will behold 'the thing itself,' caught in the indexical grain of cinematographic sound and image" (Hansen, Needham, and Nichols 211).[5] Jean Baudrillard draws attention to this idea in *Forget Foucault*, in his typically polemical style:

> Let everything be produced, be read, become real, visible, and marked with the sign of effectiveness; let everything be transcribed into force relations, into conceptual systems or into calculable energy; let everything be said, gathered, indexed and registered: this is how sex appears in pornography, but this is more generally the project of our whole culture, whose natural condition is "obscenity." (21–22)

We have already touched on the importance of the apparently sexually authentic in relation to the generic conventions of pornography, particularly those conventions surrounding the representation of the penis. Linda Williams considers the external money shot to be "the obsessive attempt of a phallic visual economy to represent and 'fix' the exact moment of the sexual act's involuntary convulsion of pleasure" (*Hard Core* 113)—an attempt to prove that sex has really taken place, and that genuine pleasure has been achieved. In a similar vein, Pasi Falk claims that the penis in pornography "can be understood as an 'indexical sign' in Peircean sense [. . .], that is, referring to a sign wherein there is a spatio-temporal or physical connection between the sign vehicle and the entity signified" (19). The penis functions, in other words, as "something real and authentically present, something with the power of *evidence*" (Falk 19).

In addition to this fixation on the erect and ejaculating penis as proof of genuine arousal, there are a number of other obvious textual strategies deployed within adult entertainment for the purposes of foregrounding ideas of the authentic. In her discussion of low-fi lesbian porn, for example, Tanya Krzywinska suggests "the endorsement that the sex is indeed genuine is not entirely focused on the bodily feats" recorded by the camera ("Dissidence and Authenticity" 164).[6] Instead—as with some of the websites imagined in *Oryx and Crake*—factors such as poor sound and image quality, and a certain pervasive amateurishness, are seen as carrying some of the burden of generating an authenticity effect. The subgenre of gonzo porn, too, has its own textual strategies for presenting itself as an authentic discourse. In gonzo films, the camera is frequently acknowledged, not in order to foreground the theatricality of the sexual representations, but in order to reinforce the authenticity of the sex on display. As Richard Dyer has remarked, "what a porn film really is is a record of people actually having sex; it is only ever the narrative circumstances of porn, the apparent pretext for the sex, that is fictional" (109). In getting rid of this narrative pretext, gonzo pornography obviates any explicit reference to fictionality, and thereby shores up its aura of hardcore authenticity.

Authenticity—the focus on attempting to verify that a representation depicts an actual extra-textual event—is evidently a significant concern within contemporary photorealistic forms of still and moving-image pornography.[7] I contend, however, that adult entertainment's "mad obsession with the real" (Baudrillard, *Forget Foucault* 22), exceeds this interest in the extra-textual or evidential. Certain marginal currents of pornography, I argue, can be seen to explore not only the real as the unsimulated, but also the real in its more psychoanalytical sense—as an affective realm fixated on the *jouissance* of the live body in a state of intensity. Anchoring my analysis here will be the figure of Rocco Siffredi—the Italian porn director, producer and performer who has been described as one of the contemporary era's "quintessential exemplars of pornographic brute force" (Bozelka 70)—and, particularly, the third scene of his 2009 movie *Rocco Ravishes LA*.

The scene in question clocks in at a substantial 54 minutes and 54 seconds, and features some notably rough sexual action, even by Siffredi's standards. It begins with Siffredi behind the camera, interviewing the actress Jamie Elle about her expectations regarding the shoot. It then cuts to Siffredi's interview with Bobbi Starr, the second of his two female performers. During this conversation, Starr and Siffredi discuss the location of the scene (a luxurious bathroom), and address the issue of the director's controversial reputation. "I heard about you," says Starr, "and what you do with girls in toilets." This is a reference to a recurring motif in Siffredi's work involving the depiction of penetrative sex with female performers who are positioned with their heads inside a toilet bowl. Siffredi responds at some length to Starr's comment, insisting that the first time he performed this particular pornographic act (with Sidonie Lavour in 1995's *Sandy Insatiable*) it was a completely spontaneous manifestation of genuine and mutual sexual desire. He claims, "The first time was surrealistic because I did not even know that I would do that. It was surprise for me too [sic]. It was circumstance." He then further reinforces this suggestion of an unscripted eruption of unstoppable desire by stating that "I see the toilet and I go crazy. My mind completely changed." The mutuality of his encounter with Lavour also is emphasized, with Siffredi invoking that supposedly undeniable proof of sexual complementarity, the simultaneous orgasm.

The scene from *Sandy Insatiable* discussed here may be one of the key moments of controversy in Siffredi's career, not least because the moment itself is excised from the American version of the movie. In the cut of the film distributed in the United States by Evil Angel, we see Lavour on her hands and knees in front of the toilet as Siffredi penetrates her from behind. The scene and its soundtrack then separate. The spectator hears grunts and groans, a kind of ceramic clinking and the sound of water flowing, but what we see on screen both jumps and lags. The visible action cuts to a slow motion facial cum shot, with Lavour's hair suddenly lying damp and disheveled across her shoulders. The spectator is left to piece together what has happened here, as the instant when Siffredi submerges his co-star's head in the toilet bowl is left unseen. The fact that this moment was deemed transgressive enough to be cut clearly aids its reputation as illicit and controversial, and it is likely that any dedicated Siffredi fan will be aware of the importance of the scene that Starr and the director intertextually reference in their interview.

The scene in *Rocco Ravishes LA* then shifts from gonzo-style action, with Elle and Starr addressing the director and looking into the camera, to a more conventionally cinematic style where Siffredi remains silent and the performers do not indicate their awareness of the camera's presence. The women, situated on the marble tiled floor in front of an enormous elevated bathtub, engage in an extended (and at times fairly rough) lesbian scene, with Starr taking on the more active or dominant role. The male porn star Toni Ribas is then brought in to perform such typical extreme feats as irrumatio and forceful anal sex, before Starr leads him over to the toilet to engage in the sex act that she's already spent so much time discussing. Ribas spits on her, fucks her while holding her head in the toilet bowl, and ends his performance by ejaculating onto her wet face.

As with many of the examples referenced in this book, the viewer is witness to a spectacle of transgression, as the taboo against aggression toward women within a pornographic context is violated. We are a long way away from a redemptive project of sex here.

This seems like the natural end point of the scene. The action has been going on for some time, the male star has ejaculated, and rough toilet sex (implicitly promised through intertextual reference) has taken place. However, it is at this point that Siffredi's voice reasserts itself from behind the camera. As he pans over Bobbi Starr's body, curled up on the fluffy white bathmat beside the toilet, he engages her in conversation. Starr, once more acknowledging the presence of the camera and at times looking directly into the lens, then declares that she wants "the Rocco experience." Siffredi tells her that she just had it, but Starr expresses a desire for something more authentic—for a chance to perform with the infamous originator of said experience. The director seems surprised by this—"You want to experience this with me? Really? With me?"—but, of course, agrees nonetheless, and lays his camera down on the bathmat so that he can engage in the sexual action unfettered.

As with the aforementioned scene from *Sandy Insatiable*, the spectator's visual access to the scene is somewhat compromised. We hear the sounds of sexual action—loud slaps and vocalizations of pleasure—but we see only Starr's face looking into the lens of the discarded camera in front of her. The reasons for such restricted visibility are different in each case, however. In 1995, distributors censored the very brief scene with Sidonie Lavour. In 2009, however, Evil Angel is happy to show Toni Ribas performing the same type of act. As the pornography market has developed in the United States, the company apparently feels less concerned about the legal implications of disseminating representations of rough sex. So, what function does this kind of visually limited shot have in *Rocco Ravishes LA*?

Siffredi initially insists on the spontaneity of his first toilet scene with Lavour, stressing shared desire and reciprocal pleasure. In seeming to discard the camera in pursuit of unpremeditated pleasure with Starr, Siffredi finds a visual language to express this notion of authentic lust, and to communicate a desire that apparently exceeds the professionalization of pleasure associated with the porn industry. As Simon Hardy has noted of homemade, not for profit pornographies, "What the hard-core image in itself cannot prove, namely the veracity of the female performer's erotic engagement, can instead be deduced from the circumstances surrounding amateur performance, where it is known that the motive of the performers is sexual rather than financial" (9). Zabat Patterson advances a similar view on the authenticity effect associated with amateurism, writing that the "loss of control of the amateur is contrasted to the control of the professional—and it is the loss of control that guarantees the realness of the sex. It also demonstrates the type of access at issue here—[the consumer-viewer] is turned on by seeing something the girl does not necessarily want to reveal, something that goes past the performance of sex" (116). By implying that both performers are going beyond the call of duty, exceeding the agreed on set-up and sexual action, Siffredi's 2009 scene seeks to absorb some of this discourse of amateur authenticity, affirming the legitimacy of the pleasure depicted by distancing it from commercial porn's typical proficiency.

Conveniently for the viewer invested in hard core's usual standards of visual proof, however, somebody picks up the camera a few minutes into the scene, thereby allowing greater visual access to the action. We see Siffredi slapping Starr's breasts, and engaging in anal sex with his co-star as he forces the lid of the toilet seat down onto her head and neck. Throughout the performance, the dialogue returns to the theme of veracity. When Starr answers in the affirmative to questions about whether she's enjoying herself, Siffredi exclaims, "You're so real. So real." He later refers to her as "Beautiful one, so pretty and so real," and returns throughout the scene to his earlier encounter with Lavour, recalling a scene that has already been coded as authentic by Siffredi's descriptions of its impulsive, ecstatic mutuality.

Paroxysms, Fluids, and the Real

Whether or not the action between Starr and Siffredi is "real" in the way that it purports to be, the scene can be seen to create a kind of reality effect by using intertextuality and visual language to create a sense of authenticity. All of the scene's textual strategies point to and try to conjure up a sense of the fundamental veracity of the action on display. It is also notable that we see Siffredi performing energetically rough deep throat fellatio with Starr, prompting her to drool and retch, in another of the acts for which the director is best known. The act and the bodily by-products that it elicits can be related to the strategies of authentication enacted by a number of contemporary porn films, particularly those belonging to the genre of extreme post-gonzo hard core. As Tim Stüttgen remarks in his discussion of "rough sex performances" (12), "Through more body fluids like spit and tears, an attempt is made to somehow double the effect of the cum shot: any fluid seems to generate more visual authenticity, more verifications of the 'real act'" ("Before Orgasm" 12).[8] Much of the gonzo subgenre, Stüttgen argues, features the "intensification of body practices" ("Before Orgasm" 12), and it seems to me that intensity and intensification are potentially useful concepts here.

I have already touched on the idea of the bodily paroxysm as intensity, in relation to what Williams has called "the ecstatic body 'beside itself'" (*Screening Sex* 65). This paroxysm, we have seen, need not be sexual to solicit our prurient interest. Reactions of pain or disgust are just as capable of fascinating as those of pleasure, and the involuntary shudder induced by the gag reflex is capable of functioning for the viewer in ways reminiscent of the spasms of orgasm. Evidently sexual fluids, as well sexual paroxysms, can be displaced by various alternatives under the generalized interests of prurience and of being affected. Indeed, Krzywinska implicitly gestures toward this idea in her discussion of the shared textual strategies of porn and horror. Adult entertainment, she notes, "trades on its promise to show the authentic life of the sexual body—and one of the ways of generating authenticity in today's mediascape is the presence of bodily fluids. Horror films, especially body horror films, also use disgust as a means of blurring the distinction between authenticity and artifice" ("Dynamics of Squirting" 33). As different as these genres are in terms of factors such as audience, viewing conditions, and content, there is a certain point in the Venn diagram where their affects and textual strategies can be seen to intersect. It may be that it is the notion of intensity—as demonstrated by the experience of *jouissance* in the consumer-viewer—which marks this point of intersection.

Krzywinska argues that disgust is able to "break the protective shield of the representation" ("Dynamics of Squirting" 33), and thereby go beyond the mere depiction of other bodies in a state of intensity in order to provoke a state of intensity in the body of the consumer-viewer. She suggests that hard core attempts to exploit the energy of abject bodily substances—their ability to elicit powerful visceral responses—whilst at the same time protecting viewers from "the full-force of disgust" in order to facilitate arousal (38). This is a productive notion, I think. After all, although "every horror conceals a possibility of enticement" (Bataille, "The Phaedra Complex" 253), even Bataille has to admit that there are limits; "*excessive* horror paralyses [desire], shuts it off" ("The Phaedra Complex"

253). A certain amount of screening can therefore be thought of as beneficial, or even necessary, in terms of generating appeal or enticement; it may even be the case that sex itself acts as a crucial screening mechanism in certain circumstances. Most pornographic material, Krzywinska argues, "couches bodily fluids and the organs that produce them within the framework of sexual transgression so that the substances can be secret(e)ly experienced in a pleasurable way" (38). In porn, then, *jouissance* is filtered through (and screened by) the presence of sex. The specificity of adult entertainment, in terms of its engagement with intensity, might therefore be said to stem more from the manner in which it frames its affects than from the character of those affects themselves.

Pornography, like many other discourses, is preoccupied by various forms of the frenzy of the visible, and the affects that it produces can, as we have seen throughout *Beyond Explicit*, be seen to be accordingly diverse. However, porn is distinct in that its identity is largely founded on offering at least the possibility of genital sexual arousal. Adult entertainment, unlike, say, war documentation, political propaganda, or contemporary art, is obliged to frame its material *as if* it is courting the viewer's arousal, no matter what other varieties of affective response it may solicit. Whether genital arousal is always or necessarily at the heart of the pornographic project is another matter. Indeed, just as Krzywinska maintains that the abject is smuggled into adult entertainment in order to facilitate an illicit enjoyment of disgust, so a sexualized context may itself be created to provide a forum for other interests. Could it not be that the pornographic context is *grafted on* to a more diverse set of prurient interests in order to provide a kind of perverse rationale? Perhaps sex, in the form of pornography, has become a Trojan horse for a range of other prurient interests and unwholesome representations which have been unable to find an appropriate vehicle (or a degree of cultural visibility) elsewhere.

At any rate, the sexual action and textual strategies on display in *Rocco Ravishes LA* can arguably be seen to intersect with ideas of the real in terms of both their insistence on their own spontaneity or nonprofessionalism, and their engagement with *jouissance* and intensity. Like the majority of contemporary hard-core pornographic materials, Siffredi's work is evidently interested in generating an authenticity effect. This preoccupation with authenticity is not a generic trope limited to adult entertainment, of course; a "pornographic" interest in representing the real also manifests itself in other cultural forms, including various reality genres. Falk, for example, notes the similarity between the episodic structure of many contemporary gonzo porn releases and a "genre of disaster-aesthetics, in which the most spectacular accidents—including the fatal ones—which have taken place in motor sports, are serialized into a repetitive sequence" (34). For Falk, "The pornographic pursuit of evidential explicitness—ending up with the representation of presence—is repeated, and even multiplied, in these documentary genres" (34-35). Something similar might be said of misery memoir.

In fact, it may be that this subset of autobiographical texts receives the title of misery porn precisely because it is so invested in seeming to represent the authentic. Its links with pornography as a genre are certainly far from self-evident; as with the idea of warporn, the application of the porn suffix apparently does not function to designate an overt attempt to generate genital sexual arousal in the consumer. There must, then, be some other facet of these autobiographies which prompts their consideration as porn—something that links them to an expanded concept of the pornographic—and this may well be rooted in the kinds of ideas regarding authenticity and the real that I have been sketching out here. After all, the "conventional expectation about auto/biography is, of course, that in the process of documenting an individual's life, something approaching the truth about that individual will be told" (Evans 2), and the genre often is seen as being linked to "the confession, a form in which telling the truth or not telling the truth can meet with dramatic and occasionally fatal results" (Gilmore, "Policing Truth" 59). This generic obsession with depicting events that have some claim to evidential power and to historical extra-textual reality provides an obvious point of intersection with porn.

Of course, written confession and autobiography have strong links with certain currents of pornography. Foucault discusses the Victorian sexual autobiography *My Secret Life* as a particularly loaded example of nineteenth-century confessional discourse; in his eyes, its author is the era's "most direct [. . .] representative of a plurisecular injunction to talk about sex" (*Will to Knowledge* 22). More recent examples of this kind of blending of autobiography and pornography can be found in the letters pages of porn magazines (Jenkins 133-53), as well as in the trend for women's sexual autobiographies; Catherine Millet's *The Sexual Life of Catherine M.* (2002), for example, or Belle de Jour's *The Intimate Adventures of a London Call Girl* (2005). This link between the confession and the pornographic is worth exploring, I think, but it is important not to obscure the differences between misery porn and texts that are pornographic in a more conventional sense. There is an additional element at play in the case of misery lit that we would do well not to overlook, and that is the notion of ordeal or suffering. In the next chapter, I think further about the real as reality and—crucially—about the Real as *jouissance*, this time in the form of trauma.

8

Autobiography and/as the Real

Reality in Representational Forms and Practices

The contemporary hunger for the real can be seen to manifest itself via the cultural visibility currently associated with reality-based forms of representation. With increasing frequency, it seems, we are incorporating the real into the sphere of entertainment for, as Misha Kavka remarks, the ongoing tabloidization of culture means that "information is increasingly harnessed for purposes of spectacle, and entertainment is more spectacular when based in actuality" (8). There are numerous important examples of this phenomenon from the realm of visual culture, not only in the form of those pornographic texts that emphasize "real sex," but in the myriad subgenres of a still-booming reality television industry.[1] The popularity of television talk shows is relevant here, for despite the heavily mediated nature of much of their content, their appeal can be seen to lie squarely in their claim to offer the viewer some kind of access to the real. As Linda Martín Alcoff and Laura Gray-Rosendale note in their discussion of televised depictions of survivors of sexual abuse:

> In a culture where audience sensations are dulled by graphic depictions of violence (both real and fictional) on television and in which mass sensibilities have atrophied under conditions of late capitalism, these shows provide a moment in which real, raw, and intense feelings can be observed, and in some cases remembered. This emotional "shock value" is their use value as a media commodity. (211)

The contemporary preoccupation with authenticity feeds audience interest as TV shows of this kind give their viewers access to intense and moving stories of abuse that are, crucially, anchored in a historical and extra-textual reality.

Within the realm of literary culture, meanwhile, various forms of life writing have come to the fore as a response to this same wave of contemporary interest in the authentic. As David Shields points out in relation to the habits of contemporary readers, the "illusion of reality—the idea that something really happened—is providing us with [a] thrill right now. We're riveted by the (seeming) rawness of something that appears to be direct from the source" (82). Sam Leith, meanwhile, makes a similar point in his discussion of misery memoir, commenting, "The idea that you're close to real suffering is the selling point, not the writing." From these remarks, we can again detect something of an investment in the dual meanings of the real discussed in the previous chapter; the evidential qualities of life writing combined with a fixation on affecting states of intensity.

These kinds of depictions of "real suffering" form the primary object of analysis here, as I explore the uncritical conflation of porn and misery memoir. Misery memoir is the name given to the literary subgenre that, according to one commentator, was initiated by Dave Pelzer's best-selling *A Child Called It* in 1995 and that "reached its zenith (or nadir) in 2006" with the publication of Stuart Howarth's memoir of abuse *Please, Daddy, No: A Boy Betrayed* (Flood). It has by all accounts proved hugely popular with readers in the first decades of the twenty-first century, with reports stating that "As much as 30% of the non-fiction paperback chart on any given week is made up of accounts of [. . .] grinding childhood misery" (Addley). According to research cited in *The Times* in November 2008, at the height of their popularity misery memoirs accounted for as much as 9% of the British market, equating to £24 million in sales (Sanghera).[2]

It is notable, I think, that these books should often be described as "misery porn"; that is, in such a manner as to align them with pornography as a representational genre. Admittedly, many misery memoirs do touch on issues such as child abuse and sexual violence, but others stage little or no engagement with adult entertainment's primary territory of depictions of eroticized bodies and genital contact. Memoirs of mental health problems, or substance abuse, or body image issues need not mention sexual acts at all; James Frey's *A Million Little Pieces* features very little in the way of graphic sexual content, for example, despite a rather conventional boy-meets-girl subplot. And yet this kind of text finds itself receiving a descriptive suffix that positions it as a species of porn. Once more, therefore, we encounter what appears to be an expanded understanding of the concept of the pornographic, and find ourselves prompted to question why, in the absence of sexually explicit content and of any kind of purposive attempt to arouse, these representations come to be associated with porn.

What's Pornographic About Misery Porn?

One reason for this association might be the fact that pornography is not averse to using elements of misery porn as a kind of sexual intensifier. As we have seen, some forms of pornography deliberately set out to exploit the affective charge associated with transgressing cultural norms. Within certain marginal currents of the genre, this can manifest itself as an interest in the kind of taboos associated with misery memoir, including violence, incest, and child abuse. Sade is a key historical example, of course; his *120 Days of Sodom* famously exploits the deliberate subversion of kinship and the narrative spectacle of the sexual torture of children. More recent examples include the works of Max Hardcore, which are often "fraught with pedophilia themes, beginning when he stumbles upon his subjects in playgrounds" (Breslin),[3] as well as those works of pornographic genre fiction that touch on incest themes. Jeffrey Masson argues (albeit without reference to any hard data) that there are "literally hundreds" of works of literary incest pornography in existence (143), many of which further engage with misery memoir via their presentation of themselves as "taken from psychiatric testimony or from a tape recorder" (143); these texts engage with the idea of the autobiographical confession by encouraging the reader to believe that they "are 'real' cases, not inventions" (144). Susanna Paasonen, meanwhile, remarks on the frequent inclusion of incest themes in submissions to the amateur erotic story site *Literotica*, noting that "the incest taboo is a source of considerable anxiety and an object of emotional investment. Literotica stories are galvanized by the taboo and acts of transgressing it" (*Carnal Resonance* 109). It may be that this cross-over of content—this sharing of certain transgressive tropes between misery memoir and more extreme forms of adult entertainment—helps to facilitate the transformation of misery memoir into misery porn.

As Masson admits, however, works of literary incest pornography are very obviously functioning within a realm of fiction and fantasy, and are highly unlikely to be taken as authentic accounts of historical trauma.

Instead, in both Max Hardcore's output (in which postpubescent actresses perform a role for the camera) and literary incest pornography (where context and generic language typically code the narratives as fictional) it is the *idea* of horrific transgression that is engaged in an attempt to elicit an intense affective response. The traumatic *reality* is kept somewhat at bay. As with Krzywinska's analysis of the abject within visual pornographies, then, we find that that which is most unsettling about the material is at least partially screened via its presentation as sexually enjoyable. In the cases of these particular examples, consumers are encouraged to enjoy transgression in a manner that protects them from the full-force of horror, trauma, and disgust. The mobilization of ideas of fantasy facilitated by an overtly pornographic context cannot occur in the case of true-to-life memoirs, however. Without recourse to the screening effect of fictionality, fantasy, and consensual professional performance, the idea of misery memoir as a kind of pornography becomes more complicated. These texts do not work to enable the kind of genital arousal associated with adult entertainment as a genre. The specter of real children and real suffering renders the *jouissance* of the sexual representations atypically raw. Is there something else about the misery memoir (or its consumers) that might link it with porn?

Perhaps the generic association of pornography with certain kinds of autobiography can be linked to the idea of prurient interest that we explored in detail in Part II. As with contemporary anxieties regarding abolitionist propaganda, there is a noticeable focus on the motives of those reading and engaging with these kinds of texts. Carol Sarler, for example, states that misery memoir readers "probably have all sorts of excuses why they read them: that they seek "greater understanding." [. . .] That they are interested in the psychology or the sociology or some other ology of the human spirit" ("I'll tell you what's Ugly"), but she emphatically dismisses any such attempts at justification. She claims, "textbooks are for the schoolroom or the college library [while] these books are pored over on beaches and buses and trains, with an enthusiasm that veers between the dangerously obsessive and the plain grubby" ("I'll tell you what's Ugly"). Leith expresses similar reticence about these autobiographical works, arguing that "the genre offers a fig leaf to prurience in the form of self-help," while Esther Addley writes that the "authors of these books may feel they are revealing important truths about the situations of some children today, but can they be certain that there isn't a degree of uncomfortable prurience, or worse, in the relish with which such tales are whisked off the shelves?"

Such remarks indicate a certain anxiety on the part of cultural commentators about the pleasures of these texts; specifically, an anxiety that the appearance of sympathetic concern or social consciousness may in fact mask a distinctly unwholesome (and unhelpful) enjoyment of the spectacle of suffering. Unlike antislavery polemics, which explicitly position themselves as a call to action, many contemporary examples of misery porn offer no obvious incitement to political intervention. As Aarti Iyer notes of films such as 2009's *Precious*—misery memoir's cinematic counterparts, which relate stories of real life abuse and survival—the characters' "misery is our pleasure, and our pleasure comes with no obligations." An apparent concern (be that intellectual or sentimental) regarding the treatment of society's most vulnerable people is viewed here as in fact concealing a politically disengaged pleasure in encountering genuine accounts of human suffering.

To a certain extent, it is precisely this idea of a passive and prurient interest on the part of the reader that allows nonsexually explicit autobiographies to be linked with the pornographic. Remarks by Frank Furedi, for example, clearly illustrate this perceived link. In a highly disparaging look at misery memoir, Furedi claims the following:

> This is the pornography of emotional hurt. Book publishers often claim that misery memoirs are popular because they provide life-affirming stories of survival. In truth, the reason why they sell in millions is because they give permission to the reader to enter into a supposedly private world of intense degradation, appalling cruelty and pain. These memoirs confess to so much that they take on the character of a literary striptease. They provide titillating and very graphic accounts of traumatic pain which actually turn readers into voyeurs.

Sex is again displaced in this understanding of the pornographic, as misery memoirs become the "pornography of emotional hurt" not because they court genital sexual arousal but because they facilitate a somehow unwholesome enjoyment of accounts of suffering and precarious lives. As with Marcus Wood's analysis of abolitionist propaganda, we find that a certain type of text comes to be positioned as pornographic because it can be seen to provide, in a veiled and deniable fashion, experiences of titillation and prurient pleasure.

An interest in covertly enjoying representations of abuse is seen to cloak itself in condemnation of the enjoyment of abuse itself.[4] This acts as a kind of prophylactic for the superego, which allows the reader to take pleasure in representations of violence whilst protecting her from the taint of a too-significant transgression. The idea of disavowal is central here, I think, not only in terms of reader engagement, but also in terms of media censure. It might appear that the application of the porn suffix acts a short hand for the expression of derision primarily because it links misery memoir to pornography as a culturally "bad object." As Paasonen suggests, when deemed "disgusting, lowly, or sleazy porn facilitates acts of distinction" (*Carnal Resonance* 55). However, as we have seen throughout this text, the explicit representation of sexual activity is no longer necessarily understood in these moralizing terms, and the consumption of nonmarginal adult entertainment can just as easily be framed within neoliberal discourses of sexual liberation and individual choice. It may in fact be the "misery" in "misery porn" that is most crucial for theorizing journalistic criticism of the genre, because it reflects what is seen as the inappropriate diversion of certain impulses away from pornography. Prurient interest in the representation of sex in mainstream porno is one thing, but prurient interest in less standard forms of *jouissance*-inducing psychic and bodily intensity is quite another.

Indeed, although distaste at pornography can no doubt be detected in the response to misery porn, I believe that the moral judgments involved go beyond the demonization of the genre. It is perhaps as much a dislike of mendacious disavowal as it is an aversion to pornography that renders the consumers of misery memoir so disreputable in the eyes of many commentators. It is not just that the subject matter is seen as an inappropriate object for unwholesome curiosity; the attempted concealment of this curiosity within claims of empathetic and ethical modes of engagement is itself positioned as a particularly dubious affront. This is made clear in the hostile journalistic response to readers' attempts at self-justification—the use of some "ology of the human spirit" (Sarler, "I'll tell you what's Ugly") as a "fig leaf for prurience" (Leith). This perceived hypocrisy is seen as somehow augmenting the genre's unseemliness, and as rendering the memoirs and their readership even more distasteful.

Consumers are left in a somewhat difficult position here, of course. Their enjoyment of representations of suffering and violence is framed as being ethically suspect, whilst their disavowal of this enjoyment is viewed as being duplicitous, hypocritical, and therefore similarly problematic. As with the abolitionist materials discussed in Part II, we are again faced with some pressing ethico-political questions regarding the intersection of morbid curiosity and the task of thinking the suffering of the other. Does prurience invalidate compassion? I'm inclined to think not. If we accept the idea that a pure and wholly disinterested mode of engagement is a fallacy, then it is necessary to accept that prurient affect might be a fairly standard by-product when it comes to the experience of sympathy. A far more urgent concern in terms of the possibilities of misery memoir would in fact be related to the limited usefulness of individual responses of compassion. As discussed, the genre typically does little to encourage direct action or intervention on the part of the reader; the generation of sympathy appears to be the full extent of its "activist" aims. Compassion can make us tremblingly alive to the sufferings of the individual while leaving us blind to wider, more significant, but less personalized or immediately heart-wrenching structural inequalities. The kind of sympathetic and empathetic feeling—feeling *for* or *with* the other—encouraged by these texts cannot, to my mind, compete with rationally driven collective action when it comes to effecting social change.

Too Real, Not Real Enough

It is worth noting at this point that it is not only misery memoir's critics or detractors who highlight its links with pornography. That is to say, it is not only those who find the genre distasteful and its readers' motives questionable who deploy ideas of the pornographic in the course of theorizing memoir. In her introduction to the collection *Close to the Bone: Memoirs of Hurt, Rage, and Desire*, for example, editor and contributor Laurie Stone remarks upon what she perceives to be a growing culture of no-holds-barred self-disclosure. She states that, when preparing the collection, she "solicited writers energized by the new wave of candor and willing to cut as deep. As far as specific subject matter was concerned, I didn't want to be prescriptive. *Everyone's pornography is their own*" (xix, italics added). If a critic as enthused by the genre as Stone feels comfortable discussing it in the same breath as pornography—indeed, discussing it *as* pornography—then it would seem that the association needs to be attributed to more than anxieties about a "grubby" and ethically suspect interest in others' pain. What else might motivate the transformation of misery memoir into misery porn? As I have suggested, there is an obvious point at which autobiography and pornography can be seen to intersect, and that is via a certain insistence on the real—that is, on the centrality of both the extra-textual event and the subject in a state of self-shattering intensity.

Life writing generates an aura of authenticity via the deployment of a number of textual conventions, many of which are derived from other culturally recognized forms of truth telling. As Leigh Gilmore remarks, "Authority in autobiography springs from its proximity to the truth claim of the confession" ("Policing Truth" 55), and in order to "stand as an authoritative producer of "truth," one must successfully position oneself as a confessing subject whose account adequately fulfills enough of the requirements of confession" (55).[5] These perceived links with the various forms of confessional speech are central to conceptualizations of autobiography, as they arguably play a powerful role in shaping the expectations of the genre's readership. Unlike fiction, life writing is tied into certain elements of the history and traditions of self-disclosure, for "the confession imports not only the spiritual but also the legal constraints of truth telling and potential punishment for error into the genre. The story of the self is constructed as one that must be sworn to and will be subject to verification" (Gilmore, "Policing Truth" 57).

It is not only religious and juridical traditions that inform popular perceptions of autobiography; contemporary narratives of the self have now come to be almost unavoidably associated with that other site of confession and self-revelation, the psychoanalyst's couch. Stone describes the authors gathered in *Close to the Bone* as working in "a literary genre I call the post-therapeutic memoir" (xv), linking their writing to the intimate statements of self extracted during psychoanalysis. The label "post-therapeutic" suggests a link between particular kinds of life writing and the need to process one's experiences, but Stone suggests that there is more than psychic healing at stake here:

> Though post-therapeutic memoirists are devoted to truth, self-display is part of their incentive, the frisson of going public with secrets, shameful emotions, all the linty unmentionables stuffed in the back of the sock drawer. Perhaps every story worth telling—whether fiction or autobiography—is a dare, a kind of pornography, composed of whatever we think we're not supposed to say, for fear of being drummed out, found out, pointed at. (xvii)

In these texts, Stone suggests, the emphasis is less on healing than on what Foucault refers to as "pleasure in the truth of pleasure, the pleasure of knowing that truth, of discovering and exposing it, the fascination of seeing it and telling it, of captivating and capturing others by it, of confiding it in secret, of luring it out in the open—the specific pleasure of the true discourse on pleasure" (*The Will to Knowledge* 71).

This disclosure of truth is part of the rationale behind Stone's linking of memoir with porn. Autobiography is presented as "a kind of pornography" not only because of the role of prurience (in the form of the interpenetration of pleasure and shame), but also via the thrill of the authentic; via the frank and open confession that reveals the truth of that alleged "source of mystery, intelligence, and inscrutable will that is concealed from everydayness" that we might call the "real" self (Guignon 82). Both pornography and autobiography are, as we can see, linked to the frisson provoked by the real. In the absence of conventional porn's explicit sex scenes and solicitation of the consumer's genital sexual response, misery memoir may be linked to ideas of the pornographic via this frisson.

With these connections between autobiography and authenticity, I argue, comes a concomitant preoccupation with ideas of the counterfeit, and with texts that transgress the category to which they seem (and profess) to belong. This is particularly evident in the recent interest in falsified true-life tales. As the journalist Polly Vernon notes:

> The Noughties have been an outstanding time for literary hoaxes. In 2006, James Frey was exposed as inventing parts of *A Million Little Pieces*, his memoir of a lifetime of drug addiction. This year, it transpired that *Love and Consequences*, Margaret B. Jones's memoir of growing up as a mixed race, drug-running foster child in South Central Los Angeles, was the fabricated work of private-school-educated, all-white Margaret Seltzer. Stephen Glass turned his multiple journalistic hoaxes into a professional identity; his story became the subject of a 2004 film, his 2003 autobiographical account of the hoaxing having done very nicely indeed, thank you.

And we can add to this list the case of JT LeRoy—the subject of our next chapter.[6] Indeed, just as Glass ended up with an autobiography and a biopic documenting his adventures in deceit, so Savannah Knoop—Laura Albert's sister-in-law, who "bound her breasts, and wore a preposterous blonde wig and sunglasses" to appear as LeRoy whenever a "physical boy was needed" (Vernon)—had her own autobiography published in 2008, providing an account of her role in the hoax. The proliferation of such stories in their own right surely can be seen as testament to the reading public's preoccupation with such cases.[7]

Much of this fixation on the fake can be seen to link in with wider concerns about authenticity in the genre; that is, with certain anxieties surrounding the question of whether autobiography can ever really be truthful. By weaving together ideas of truth and memoir, I suggest, we not only help to shore up an identity for the genre, but inevitably raise the possibility that this identity is incomplete, insufficient, and fragile. A great deal of critical work on autobiography makes mention of this precarious position in terms of generic identity. Life writing is discussed as being especially difficult to position in terms of other literary forms and modes, particularly in terms of its relationship to fiction.[8] Paul de Man, for example, stresses the centrality of issues of generic instability to any attempt to conceptualize autobiography. 'Empirically as well as theoretically,' he argues,

> autobiography lends itself poorly to generic definitions; each specific instance seems to be an exception to the norm; the works themselves always seem to shade off into neighboring or even incompatible genres and, perhaps most revealingly of all, generic discussions, which can have such powerful heuristic value in the case of tragedy or of the novel, remain distressingly sterile when autobiography is at stake. (920)

For him, "any book with a readable title-page is, to some extent, autobiographical" (922), and yet, "by the same token, none of them is or can be. The difficulties of generic definition that affect the study of autobiography repeat an inherent instability that undoes the model as soon as it is established" (922). Autobiography as a genre, then, is characterized as much by its porous boundaries with other forms and by its lack of a readily discernible identity as it is by any perceived qualities of its own.[9]

These prevalent issues of generic instability, along with contemporary preoccupations regarding (in)authenticity, suggests a further point of confluence between autobiography and pornography—that is, a further potential rationale for the development of a counterintuitive understanding of the pornographic that to some extent displaces or de-emphasizes sexuality. Both porn and life writing can be seen to exist at a sort of crossroads of the real—at a disturbing point between the supposedly incommensurate terms of reality and fiction. Gilmore, for example, notes:

> autobiography has often been seen as insufficiently objective because the eye-witness may be simultaneously the most sought after and the most suspect interpreter of events. At the same time, autobiography has been spurned as insufficiently subjective (or imaginative) because it relies too much on the constraints of the real to be taken as art. Thus autobiography has fallen outside both fiction and history. ("The Mark of Autobiography" 6)

Such texts can be thought of neither as a reliable historical record, nor as a work of imaginative or artistic genius. They are neither real nor fake enough to fit within these more privileged cultural categories.

Gilmore's comments on the liminal position of autobiography offer interesting parallels with Falk's response to what he calls the anti-aesthetics of pornography. Falk argues that "from an 'orthodox' psychoanalytical perspective, the sexual stimulation by visual (or, generally, representational) means is turned into a perversion if it does not lead into an actual realization of the sexual act. Thus pornography is not *real enough*" (1). Conversely, however, he argues, "the aesthetic discourses condemn pornography precisely because it is *too real*, abolishing the reflective distance" (1). Porn is another discourse at the limit of conventional categories, then, and is seen as both insufficiently real and insufficiently artful. As in the case of autobiography, the genre's products exist somewhere between the concepts of the recorded and the invented, and this shared trait may contribute to an association between misery literature and pornography, even in the absence of any conventionally or generically pornographic features.

There are numerous elements of pornography that evidence this liminality. Falk particularly picks up on the genre's sporadic use of a narrative register—the fact that it deploys invented storylines that are in some sense incompatible with its focus on the extra-textual real. I add to this the genre's vampiric relationship with more overtly fictional forms. As shown in Chapters 4 and 6, for example, pornography at times puts aside its interest in generating the appearance of authenticity so that it can engage with and exploit the conventions of other body genres, such as horror. We might also consider here adult entertainment's pervasive fascination with parody as a mode for presenting hard-core sex acts. For example, there are live-action pornographic versions of those most unreal of moving-image texts, *Avatar* and *The Simpsons*. Entitled *This Ain't Avatar XXX* (2010) and *Simpsons: The XXX Parody* (2011), both were produced and distributed by branches of Larry Flynt Publications. The real and the fantastical appear to exist in a strange kind of tension here, with the genre's focus on generating an authenticity effect coexisting with the use of characters best known as animated entities. This is clearly represented by one of the taglines used on the *Simpsons: The XXX Parody* web page: "Ever Wonder What The Simpsons Would Look Like In Real Life? Or Better Yet . . . If They Were FUCKING???"

Authenticity Anxiety

Bearing in mind this mutual generic history of precariousness in relation to the real, it is perhaps no coincidence that both pornography and autobiography have to work overtime to produce the convincing appearance of authenticity. Skepticism about both genres is certainly evident in Furedi's comments about misery porn; "as in real porn, there is a lot of faking going on." Indeed, the possibility of faking it—"it" being the female orgasm—is arguably at the heart of the development of the external cum shot as perhaps the most significant generic convention of still and moving-image photorealistic pornographies. As we have seen throughout *Beyond Explicit*, Williams argues that, in heterosexual porn, this particular trope works as compensation for the less visually spectacular female orgasm, which cannot be offered as proof of authentic pleasure. She suggests the following:

> Hard core desires assurance that it is witnessing not the voluntary performance of feminine pleasure, but its involuntary confession. The woman's ability to fake the orgasm that the man can never fake (at least according to certain standards of evidence) seems to be at the root of all the genre's attempts to solicit what it can never be sure of: the out-of-control confession of pleasure, a hard-core "frenzy of the visible." (*Hard Core* 50)

As I mentioned, Falk takes a similar position on the role of the male body in pornography, relating it to the genre's "insistence on the primacy of the evidential presentness" (28), and stressing its importance in terms of providing the viewer with proof of the reality of the sex depicted. Falk argues that, unlike the female performance of pleasure, "the phallic system

[. . .] does not fit into the realm of representation: it is presentation, an actual presence of (sufficient) sexual arousal" (18), and he thus positions it at the epicenter of adult entertainment's authenticity effect; how drugs such as Viagra fit into such arguments is unclear.

There is, as I have already suggested, a similar preoccupation with veracity in the case of nonfictional forms of life writing, to which issues of generic instability and the rash of recent hoaxes have surely contributed. Although critics such as Shields argue that "The memoir rightly belongs to the imaginative world, and once writers and readers make their peace with this, there will be less argument over the questions regarding the memoir's relation to the 'facts' and 'truth'" (133), many continue to fixate on the genre as a vehicle for the extra-textual real. As Jason Roush puts it in his review of Matty Lee's prostitution memoir *35 Cents*, "In the wake of the recent scandal surrounding the popular yet fraudulent gay author JT LeRoy—not to mention the Oprah Winfrey-fueled outrage over James Frey's fabricated tale of drug addiction, *A Million Little Pieces* (2005)—the question of truth and authenticity in a nonfiction literary work has acquired a new urgency" (45). Although he acknowledges that the book could never be a perfect record, and recognizes that questions surrounding the moral responsibility of autobiographical writers remain unresolved, Roush nevertheless praises Lee's "no-nonsense" and "straightforwardly gritty" style, displaying an obvious (if self-reflexive) investment in the genre's claim to authenticity. This is, after all, one of the primary sources of the genre's appeal in the contemporary era.

The visibility of literary hoaxes within the cultural landscape cannot, therefore, be seen to prompt a dismissal or wholesale reassessment of the genre, or of the reading protocols that surround it. Instead, these hoaxes can be seen to further foreground issues of truthfulness in relation to life writing—a fact that may stem in part from ideas about authenticity itself. After all, as Jacob Golomb, following the work of Sartre, suggests, "authenticity is a negative term. Its presence is discerned in its absence, in the passionate search for it, in inauthenticity and in various acts of 'bad faith' (*mauvaise foi*)" (7). As well as this idea of a negatively derived definition—an idea that (post)structuralism suggests could be applied to all concepts and to the entirety of language—we should also remark on the fact that this proven unreliability in relation to the truth claim seems to be simultaneously the engine *and* the outcome of anxieties surrounding authenticity. In circular and self-perpetuating fashion, it would seem, the claim of the genre to be defined by a certain degree of authenticity begets a pervasive anxiety about its relation to the real, and this anxiety (supported by explicit disputations and the uncovering of hoaxes) in turn begets an insistence on the genre's need for authenticity.

As I have stressed throughout this section, the focus on the extra-textual is not the sole example of the real within such works, for a mundane idea of the unsimulated can frequently be seen to intersect with a different and more disturbing set of currents surrounding the real. That is to say, the generic identity of misery porn is founded on an investment not only in the reality of the lives under discussion, but also on the extreme and precarious nature of these lives. These books are preoccupied with trauma, and with the real as *jouissance*. As Gilmore notes, "Trauma, from the Greek meaning "wound," refers to the self-altering, even self-shattering, experience of violence, injury, and harm" ("Limit-Cases" 132); it is interesting to note how similar her language is to that utilized by Bersani in his discussion of intensity—of "the self-shattering mechanisms of masochistic *jouissance*" that characterize all sexuality (*The Freudian Body* 41), and of the idea that the subject is "shattered into sexuality" via sensation and affective processes (38).

Evidence for the prevalence of an interest in the real can be found in the key themes of many recent autobiographies—Gilmore suggests, in relation to the memoir boom that began in the 1990s, that "the defining subject has been trauma" ("Limit-Cases" 128)—as well as in the academic work that has emerged around life writing. Although the surge of misery memoirs may well be abating, scholarly interest in the ideas of auto/biography and ordeal certainly isn't. In the journal *Biography*'s extensive "Annual Bibliography of Works about Life Writing, 2009—2010," compiled by Phyllis E. Wachter, there are more than fifty separate works engaging with trauma, in addition to another nine unique works dealing with abuse.[10] We also might consider the evidence provided by the *nature* of the hoaxes that have emerged within the realm of misery memoir. Susanna Egan argues that such "impostures are topical and timing is key to their success. Particular times and places are sensitive to particular identity performances" (133). Today's phony memoirists, in other words, can be seen to exploit those issues and concerns about which mainstream society is currently most sensitive. In this sense, the hoaxes provide something of a road map to contemporary cultural preoccupations. As Egan notes, particularly in relation to faked accounts of torture in the Middle East, "imposters play back to their readers the assumptions with which readings begin, tapping into cultural anxieties, mapping a psychological shift between white or Western dominance and its Other suffering through a time of crisis or need" (136).[11] Beyond this specific context, however, it seems that it is a fascination with trauma, and the horror of the real in general, which is being most persistently tapped. Recent authenticity scandals seem to cluster around a few particular sources of distress or anxiety, including the holocaust (Wilkomirski; Defonseca; Herman Rosenblat's unpublished concentration camp "memoir"), the violence of the racial other (Khouri; Margaret B. Jones), and dissident sexualities and sexual abuse (Johnson; Albert/LeRoy).

At this point, I think, it is useful to ground our discussion in the concrete example of the writing and identity of JT LeRoy. How does his work endeavor to create an authenticity effect, and where does it subvert or complicate this effect? How do theories of autobiography and authorship play into this, and how do they undergird the reactions to both LeRoy's work and the hoax itself? In addition to exploring these questions, the next chapter looks at how the LeRoy case can help to further our understanding of misery memoir's relationship with the real as both the extra-textual and as *jouissance*-inducing trauma, and continues our exploration of how these characteristics have become entangled with ideas regarding the pornographic.

9

Sex, Trauma, and the Authenticity Effect

The Author Is Deceitful Above All Things?

The scandal surrounding the unveiling of JT LeRoy—which I outlined in the introduction to this section—is intriguing for a number of diverse reasons. First, the strength of feeling provoked by the hoax, within the literary and intellectual community as well as within fan cultures, is perhaps somewhat remarkable. Figures such as the contemporary avant-garde writer Dennis Cooper, the novelist Joel Rose, and the radical pro-sex activist Susie Bright, for example, displayed evident irritation in response to the hustle, with Bright announcing that if "you've read *Sarah*, and *The Heart is Deceitful*, go unveil Dennis Cooper's *The Sluts* and view the original source. Dennis is writing fiction, masterful fiction, which Leroy [sic] churned into an autobiographical persona and fan-imitation."[1] In the article that broke the scandal, Rose is reported as viewing the hoax as "a betrayal" (Beachy), whereas Cooper is said to "express anger [. . .] about how these revelations might affect JT's fans" (Beachy).

That this hoax should be capable of eliciting such intensity of feeling may seem remarkable considering twentieth-century developments in thinking about the concept of the author. After all, the importance of this figure has been widely questioned and steadily undermined by theoretical discourse for many decades now. As early as 1946, the New Critics were asserting that, as William K. Wimsatt and Monroe C. Beardsley put it, "the design or intention of the author is neither available nor desirable as a standard for judging the success of a work of literary art" (1374–1375). Roland Barthes' later claims that "the author is never more than the instance writing" (145), and that "a text is not a line of words releasing a single 'theological' meaning (the 'message' of the Author-God) but a multidimensional space in which a variety of writings, none of them original, blend and clash" (146), are by now largely familiar to almost everyone with a basic undergraduate training in literary theory. The prominence of the author, her centrality and relevance to understandings of the text, has been challenged for many years, so why should the revelations about LeRoy's identity provoke such a reaction? Why should a hoax that is founded on a simple disjunction between the actual author behind and the assumed authorial persona of a particular set of texts prove capable of stirring up so much controversy and fascination?

In addition to these cultural shifts regarding the role of the author, it is worth remembering that the (related) cultural frameworks provided by postmodernism can further complicate understandings of authorial identity. Indeed, the notion of identity itself can be problematized by certain postmodern positions, as we see the possibility of the real or the authentic being increasingly questioned in relation to all areas of human existence, even as its importance is emphasized. As Neville Wakefield remarks, the postmodern world "is a world in which the gravitational pull of the 'real' has been thrown into crisis, as simulation increasingly corrodes any chance of spontaneous or unreflexive faith in any ability to 'situate' ourselves within a new landscape of instability and flux" (116). The self, and its relationship with the world, is rendered increasingly unstable and complex, and the notion of the true or deep self is positioned as naïve and largely untenable in the face of postmodernism's impossibly inflated standards of the authentic.

Many postmodern thinkers view the self as being as mediated and unreal as the rest of the contemporary social world. Daniel Albright, for example, challenges the idea that the self is authentic, stressing the importance of the conscious and unconscious operations of mediation when it comes to shaping the self:

> We suppress extraneous parts of our being in order to show some lithe, smooth, shapely, consistent mask to the outer world—and perhaps to ourselves as well. How much of our remembered self is carefully, scrupulously edited in order to conform to some vision of how we would like our self to appear? If we speak of a remembered self, we should also speak of an editorial self that consciously or unconsciously selects the memories that wrap us round with the sense of our dig-

nity, our erotic power, our nonchalance, our good will toward mankind, all those pleasures that our self-consideration craves. (32–33)

He argues that our sense of our own identity is "everywhere informed by and dependent on literary concoctions, sometimes quite flimsy and absurd literary concoctions" (33), and that we may therefore find ourselves unsure of "the exact boundaries of our affective systems—just where our own memories end and literary pseudomemories begin" (33). The "true" self, by this rationale, is obscure and unknowable, as the self we encounter is always already the product of various literary (not to mention photographic, cinematic, and televisual) simulations of selfhood.

Such attempts to problematize the self have obvious ramifications for thinking on autobiography—a genre that many perceive as being dedicated to the articulation of selfhood. Indeed, Evans remarks:

The form of auto/biography carries with it some considerable responsibility for allowing authors to convey the impression that lives are lived in orderly and coherent ways. Thus what has to be recognized in any account of auto/biography is the collusion, whether conscious or not, between writers of auto/biography and the deep desire of late twentieth-century society for order and stability. (134)

The idea of the self as an unknowable, and simultaneously fictional, entity does more than render life writing a performative discourse on the illusionary coherent self, however. It also seems to promote a rethinking of autobiography as a genre grounded in the authentic or the extra-textual real. Evans, for example, states that life writing's "search for the 'real' person is doomed to disappointment" (138), attributing this to the fact that "no 'real' person actually exists, and cannot be contained, let alone represented, in print" (138).

Other postmodern approaches to autobiography similarly challenge the authenticity of the genre, rejecting the possibility of any correspondence between memory and a historical event on the grounds that "there is no single valid interpretation of the original event against which to attempt a match. By this view, past realities are always being constructed anew and any match is illusory" (Winograd 243). Autobiography (and the selves it represents) can never, by this analysis, hope to be truthful, and should not be read as a genre with any particular or privileged basis in authenticity. Given this intellectual context, we might be prompted to question why the JT LeRoy affair should have proven itself to be so powerfully affecting, even to readers as sophisticated and theoretically literate as Bright, Rose, and Cooper. If it is understood that, as Gilmore expresses it, "the telling of lies is inextricable from the writing of memories" ("Policing Truth" 71), then why did LeRoy's lies elicit the reactions that they did?

Much of the anger at LeRoy's literary hustle might be attributed to the fact that, as we have seen, there are certain expectations at work when it comes to autobiographical writing. It continues to be seen, rightly or wrongly, as a genre with compelling links to the extra-textually real, and readers expect it to comply with the widely accepted idea that an autobiography is properly authentic. As Philippe Lejeune argues in his influential analysis, autobiographical texts "entail what I will call a 'referential pact,' implicit or explicit, in which are included a definition of the field of the real that is involved and a statement of the modes and degree of resemblance to which the text lays claim" (22). This pact is central to the manner in which readers engage with autobiography, and many commentators viewed this idea of a referential pact as crucial to the reception and interpretation of LeRoy's literary output.

Anthony Lane touches on this idea, remarking, "On no page of *The Heart is Deceitful*, a necklace of loosely linked stories published in 2001, did [LeRoy] claim that they were rooted in fact, but he was trading on the earnest pity of his readers" (95).[2] In fact, although LeRoy's later works might have been billed as fiction (a label that, as is seen later, LeRoy's persona frequently complicated), he did actually begin his career as a life writer, making his debut in Laurie Stone's collection *Close to the Bone: Memoirs of Hurt, Rage, and Desire*. In contributing the story "Baby Doll" to this collection, LeRoy invited readers to understand his work as memoir. Indeed, "Baby Doll"—the story of a young boy wearing his mother's lingerie in a successful attempt to seduce her male lover—later appeared within the author's ostensibly fictional collection *The Heart is Deceitful Above All Things*, thereby inviting readers with knowledge of the story's original publication context to read the entire collection as a work of veiled autobiography.

In publishing his work as memoir, LeRoy might be seen as implicitly agreeing to write in accordance with the rules of the genre. After all, as Kenneth J. Gergen remarks, "to 'do memory' is essentially to engage in a cultural practice. Instances of self-memory, then, take place within and are shaped by social process" (89), and "that which counts as legitimate memory is [. . .] a culturally fashioned production. To remember oneself is to join in a public ritual" (94). Like all other social subjects, the authors of autobiographical texts are not "free to report on [their] past lives in any way [they] wish. [They] are importantly constrained by cultural rules for self-accounting" (90). LeRoy automatically signed up to a shared code when he published his fake real-life account in Stone's collection, and in so doing, he undoubtedly flouted cultural rules and violated shared understandings about genre and authenticity. Certainly, he duped the anthology's editor, who claims in the introduction that the authors of the collected post-therapeutic memoirs "aren't playing games with illusion and reality" (Stone xv).[3]

However, most people come to "Baby Doll," and to LeRoy's writing more generally, not via a relatively obscure volume of post-therapeutic life writing, but through LeRoy's singly authored works. All of these books are presented as fiction—a genre that, as Claudia Mills notes, "lacks memoir's accountability, its public declaration that it offers at least an attempt at the truth" (116). Surely the fact that the vast majority of LeRoy's writing is packaged and encountered as being fictional works to render the scandal even more out of step with contemporary thinking about authorship. Kira Cochrane certainly seems to think so, claiming, "The writing really wasn't a hoax. The books that Albert created retain their literary merit and there's something sad and sick that, for some, the work's value has plummeted just because its author wasn't actually pimped out as a child." But, I would contend, even in the cases of those works that are presented as being fictional, the reader is encouraged to read through the fantasy to access an underlying layer of autobiographical real. That is to say, LeRoy's novels and short stories seem deliberately crafted to generate the appearance of authenticity via the implication that his writings, although ostensibly fictional, are in fact autobiographical works of misery porn.

The note about the author included at the back of *Sarah* is short and uninformative, stating only that "J.T. LeRoy lives in California and enjoys playing whiffle ball. He writes for *NY Press*, *Nerve* magazine, and *The Stranger*. His e-mail address is Le_terminator@hotmail.com. His homepage is http://www.jtleroy.com" (168). Despite this apparent disinterest in sharing explicitly biographical details within the context of the books themselves, there is a great deal of paratextual information orbiting around LeRoy's writing that appears expressly designed to encourage biographical interpretations. In interviews given before the hoax was uncovered, LeRoy repeatedly suggested that the origins of his fiction lay in his personal history and his attempts to process and come to terms with that history via therapy. In conversation with Kevin Sampsell, for example, he claimed, "I have my obsessions. For novels I still have stuff to vomit, so to speak. When I run out, maybe I'll have to tell the love story on the banks of a snowy lake in Minnesota or whatever, but in the meantime, I'm still not done." Speaking to Litsa Dremousis, meanwhile, he stated:

> [my psychiatrist] felt I had a problem with continuity and he kept asking me to write. He taught at the University of San Francisco, which he still does, and he was teaching these social workers, or people who wanted to be social workers. So he said, why don't you write about the real deal on the street, because he knew I hated social workers because so many of them had fucked me over and they had no idea what they were doing. ("An Interview with JT LeRoy")

In LeRoy's case, then, we see that the writing of fictional texts is repeatedly linked to issues of personal history and to individual obsession. As Meghan O'Rourke puts it, LeRoy's "foregrounding of his 'autobiography' turned his fiction into a therapeutic object rather than a purely literary one from the start. While some writers might have been bothered by this, LeRoy actively invited this confusion."

Indeed, a substantial portion of the interest in LeRoy's work appears to come from this confusion. Reviewers and commentators, at least, are quite insistent when it comes to accentuating the idea that much of his writing can be seen as covert autobiography. Chris Sullivan, for example, describes the books as "eminently controversial and largely autobiographical," whereas Sampsell states that *The Heart is Deceitful* is "being billed as fiction, but is obviously autobiography" (interview with LeRoy). Luke Crisell is even more emphatic, writing, "LeRoy always denies that the books are autobiographical. But you had a pet snail! The book [*Harold's End*] is about the snail. You have told me about experiences with your mother, and the same things happen to Cherry Vanilla [in *Sarah*]." But, I suggest, it is not just the idea that LeRoy's writing stems from and reflects his life that taps into the recent interest in the real, but also the apparent nature of that life itself—precarious, troubled, and itinerant. A particular aura of authenticity was created by Albert's development of the LeRoy persona as a masochistic, transgendered, white-trash ex-hustler, who had endured a childhood of physical and sexual abuse. By making LeRoy's life the stuff of misery memoir, Albert succeeded in making him more compelling and more real. As Anthony Lane puts it, LeRoy "punched all the right buttons, telling of losers, abusers, cross-dressers and crackpots, enabling eager readers to feel doubly validated in their response" (95). He was fascinating, in other words, because his story was extreme, extraordinary, and traumatic.

The contemporary interest in such marginal voices is perhaps associated with the cultural politics of canon formation. Betty Bergland, for example, has remarked on the fact that "Institutionalized efforts to incorporate literatures of the cultural other, and efforts to expand the canon, have meant that autobiographies of women and ethnics receive particular attention in the academy, as scholars become more receptive to cultural diversity and complexity" (130), and the same might be said of work by gender dissidents and sexual minorities. Claire Lynch makes a similar point when she suggests that, in current academic work on life writing, "approaches familiar in feminist criticism and postcolonialism are invoked in which texts of the 'oppressed and displaced' are recovered" (216), adding that it is now common within scholarly circles "to think of autobiography in exactly this way, not as the preserve of the lives of great men, but as active in the promotion of untold life stories" (216). An investment in making space for the myriad forms of non-normativity arguably creates an environment that is particularly conducive to writers with LeRoy's back story and ex-centricity, and Albert can be viewed as—consciously or unconsciously—exploiting this fact.

But I also suggest that there is a wider tendency to assume that voices from the cultural margins are somehow able to achieve a greater degree of authenticity. After all, as Charles Guignon remarks, "To be authentic is to be in touch with something that is concealed to the people who accept the outlook of society. At some level, to be authentic is already to be asocial. What is more, being authentic involves having a personal 'take' on reality that is 'Other' to the social, a deeper reality that is masked by social customs" (76). In depicting the disenfranchised way of life of underage prostitutes, drug addicts, and abuse victims—and by implying that this was also the author's own story, grounded in both the real of trauma and the real of the extra-textual—LeRoy appeared to give his readers access to this alternative point of view, a perspective unpolluted by conventionality and by acceptance of and capitulation to dominant social norms. In so doing, he (and his creator) briefly managed to tap into the contemporary hunger for the authentic, and to generate the kind of prurient thrill that puts the "porn" in "misery porn."

In the case of LeRoy, the emphasis on the biography of the author was sufficient to render the (supposed) life at least as prominent as the work, to the point where the literary product was seen as merely an extension of LeRoy's persona. This process of effacing the work by foregrounding the life is one that, before LeRoy's unmasking, many journalists appeared to lament even as they perpetuated it. Crisell, for example, suggested, "What is known about LeRoy's life has become a sort of layered narrative, which is now threatening to overshadow his work. This is a shame, because his writing is brutally immediate, and compulsive." At the same time, however, Crisell can be seen to be particularly insistent on the books' autobiographical elements, claiming, "Of course, while he'd like us to believe his books are fiction and that being JT LeRoy is an act, he also relies on that disputed and painful past to feed his writing."

Even after the hoax was revealed, commentators stressed the vital significance of LeRoy's life and personal history to the success of his writing. For many, without the extra-textual real provided by his purported past, LeRoy's fictional works lacked validity. Dennis Cooper, for example, wrote about LeRoy on his blog, just as the scandal was breaking. He began by asking whether a writer's work can ever be separated from his or her identity:

> In most cases, I think it's possible, even when it's a persona-heavy writer like Rimbaud or Hemingway or Burroughs or Acker, as long as the writing is strong and sufficiently complete in and of itself that the biography of person [sic] who wrote it is an optional pleasure or additional source of information. In the cases I mentioned, I think that's true. With JT Leroy, I think it's a different situation. JT Leroy's work has always been completely attached to the presentation of the author as a teenaged boy whose difficult life occasioned the subjects of his work. The work was fiction, but its legitimacy came through the understanding that his stories' subject matter resembled the content of his real life, and JT Leroy forced this reading from the very moment "he" appeared.

Cooper goes on to add that "The fact that his books had serious weaknesses—rampant sentimentality, clichéd characters and storylines, uneven writing, etc.—was forgiven due to 'his' youth, the fact that 'he' supposedly had never attended school in 'his' life, 'his' emotional problems, 'his' precarious health, and so on." Clearly, for Cooper (admittedly not an unbiased observer, considering the patronage he offered LeRoy early in his career), the removal of the claim to an autobiographical real renders LeRoy's work invalid. Without the claim to authenticity, the books are no longer seen as deserving of serious attention.

With LeRoy, however, it is not just that the life validates or achieves the same profile as the work. In many ways, what is intriguing about the hoax is the way in which the authorial persona and the literary product begin to intersect. That is, LeRoy and his fiction exist on the same register of (un)reality. Jannah Loontjens, in one of the very few academic articles addressing Albert and LeRoy, comments on this fact:

> That the fictitious speaker and the author of a novel are not one and the same seems obvious to most theorists. Yet, in LeRoy's case it is difficult to separate author from narrator. As a result of the unmasking, we know that LeRoy is none other than the fictitious speaker in his book. In the telephone interviews, in which Albert pretends to be LeRoy—using street slang and imitating a boyish voice—he speaks about his life; a life that Albert made up. Leroy [sic] functions as a narrator of the author; a narrator outside the work.

For Loontjens, the hoax is a symptom of a wider cultural tendency in which "the boundaries between (fictional) biographical information about the author, and the author's oeuvre are becoming porous and interdependent," because, contra Barthes, the writer is increasingly being viewed as part of the literary product. The author is now as much of a commodity as his or her books, and the lives of writers are becoming as available for scrutiny as "the lives of citizens in reality soaps and talk shows" (Loontjens). This current of popular thinking about the author—this sense that one is buying into the author just as much as one is buying a particular volume of poetry or prose—perhaps provides a counter-point to twentieth-century theories that seek to depose the author, and may go some way toward explaining the hostile reaction to the LeRoy hoax, and to other hoaxes of this kind.

Staging the Real:
Corporeal and Psychic Intensity in JT LeRoy

As we have seen, an incessant foregrounding of the real—the author's "genuine" trauma, which supposedly undergirds the writing process—encourages the reader to interpret LeRoy's texts largely according to the generic codes associated with autobiography, rather than with fiction. However, it is worth noting that it is not just the implicit codes of genre that work to foreground issues of the real in relation to LeRoy's work. Even in the material that is overtly billed as fiction, and that cannot therefore be held to the same standards of authenticity expected of autobiography, we encounter numerous familiar images associated with misery memoir and with contemporary understandings of the real more generally. Deeply personal experiences of states of corporeal and psychic intensity, as well as themes of social marginality, for example, are frequently emphasized throughout LeRoy's work.

In LeRoy's novella *Harold's End*, this takes the form of scenes of drug addiction and its negative effects. The narrator, a teenaged rent boy who tries "to catch a few tricks for enough cash" to score drugs (15), finds precarious refuge in the home of a wealthy older trick, who supplies him with take-away meals and "balloons filled with [. . .] clean colorless powder" (46). The abuse of narcotics similarly permeates *The Heart is Deceitful Above All Things*. In the story "Coal," the protagonist, Jeremiah, lives in a "$75-a-month shack on the outskirts of a small town in West Virginia" (188), in which his mother, Sarah, and her lover manufacture crystal meth. He reports that his mother's eyes "are ringed red like someone drew marker circles around them" (170), and that she "scratches at her face constantly and chomps her jaw back and forth even though there's nothing in her mouth" (170–71). After an explosion at the meth lab, Sarah suffers a psychic break and, believing that coal is now bleeding and that the "sky has black fire coming" (163), she decides to take her young son on the road: "You and I will be the only survivors. Everyone and everything else will be burned, crushed, poisoned" (197). As with *Harold's End*, this scenario allows LeRoy to engage with culturally established sources of the real such as the unruly and demanding addicted body, intense and disturbed psychic states, and experiences of socioeconomic marginality.

The Heart is Deceitful also incorporates other tropes common to misery porn, such as physical child abuse. Taken into the custody of his Christian zealot grandparents, Jeremiah is bathed in scalding hot water and scrubbed until he's "a bright pinkish red with blood pinpricks and scratches marking [his] skin" (64). He is also regularly beaten by his grandfather: "when I fall, when I displease him, I pay, [. . .] leaning over the desk, breathing in the rich lemony wood polish, and waiting for him to rest his hand on my head for a minute. I cry, and I'm cleansed. I'm with him, my grandfather, just me and him and the rod of correction, restoring me" (78–79). Sarah, too, is depicted violently abusing the narrator, at one point burning his penis with a car's cigarette lighter. Describing the incident, Jeremiah states, "I see the coils, red and glowing, disappear down to where her fingers hold my thing. I dig my hands, sweaty and cold, under my thighs. I watch the tip of my thing disappear into the lighter. I don't move, I don't scream, I don't cry. I've learned the hard way that lessons are repeated until learned properly, and silently" (126).

Sexual abuse is also a feature of LeRoy's work, whether skirted over as in *Sarah*—where we learn that the narrator, an underage lot lizard (or truck-stop prostitute), has "been with enough of [his mother's] boyfriends and husbands, that if they had paid me I could buy a gator farm" (14)—or described in explicit detail in *The Heart is Deceitful*. In that text, we see not only Jeremiah's 'seduction' of one of Sarah's lovers in "Baby Doll," but also his rape (and first experience of penetrative anal sex) at the hands of his stepfather:

> I wake up screaming; the crows' red wings flash over my eyes as he pulls my legs apart, his hot breath against my neck, claws push my face down into the pillow. And for the first time they peck at me, and it's worse than I ever imagined. It's a drill blade twisting and hollowing me out between my legs, and he cries her name again and again in my ear until it bleeds. (47)

He reports that the "towel under me is turning crimson and soggy like tomato bread soup" (47), before his stepfather abandons him and he wakes up in a hospital.

This combined history of sexual and physical abuse results, the book suggests, in Jeremiah's (and, by extension, LeRoy's) sexual identity as a masochist. In "Natoma Street," the final piece in the collection, Jeremiah pays a man $100 to physically dominate him, his narrative voice reporting that the "belt is slamming into me all over, my back, ass, and thighs, and the tears are streaming, and confessions of every sin and every evil thought or action I ever did or almost did pour out of my mouth" (246). It is not only the placement of this story within the collection that denotes that it is a culmination of Jeremiah's experiences of abuse, but also the repeated suggestion that the feelings evoked by the masochistic sexual acts recall ambiguous feelings from childhood. At one point, the narrator states that "It's all coming back, like being lost in waves of wheat" (238), and as he is being beaten, he describes "the familiar sound of air being thrashed" (240). "Natoma Street" is even interrupted by an extended passage of analepsis (243–46), in which we see Jeremiah, as a boy, being beaten by a shop security guard at his mother's request, and attempting to conceal his erection, which he describes as "a gleaming badge of guilt, waiting to be discovered and ripped from me" (246).

We might link these kinds of scenes—coded as they are, via both paratextual information and the use of personal names, as autobiographical—with the conventional subject matter of misery porn. For example, we might suggest that much of the affective power of *The Heart is Deceitful* stems (or rather, originally stemmed) from the idea that we are encountering, in a mediated but nonetheless recognizable form, a confession of pleasure and of suffering that is grounded in historical experience. There is, it is suggested, a truth to the events depicted; a boy actually did endure something resembling these events, and it really did shape his sexual identity. As we have previously suggested, it is partly through this emphasis on authenticity that such scenes come to intersect with porn as it is more conventionally understood—that is, as a genre of sexually explicit representations. To put it another way, it is not only the depiction of genital contact, sexual awakenings, and "perverse" acts that links LeRoy's work to the pornographic as it is currently understood, but also the affective charge attached to ideas of the extra-textual, especially as it relates to trauma and suffering.

LeRoy's work exploits the idea that there is a singular, extra-textually real body behind the text, which, like Jeremiah's, is marked by scars—"the little gullies and streams" left by a boyhood of abuse (236). As Hansen, Needham, and Nichols suggest, adult entertainment relies on similar ideas, using "the singular body of the individual performer for authentication. (Orgy scenes, such as the ones that conclude *Behind the Green Door, II* and the bisexual videotape, *Innocence Lost*, may sacrifice identification with specific individuals, but dependence on singular bodies for purposes of authentication remains total)" (216). Porn requires a certain degree of individuation to help generate the impression that the sexual feats enacted are authentic. Photorealistic forms of pornography anchor viewers by presenting us with the same face and the same body, so that we know that a single real person is experiencing the corporeal intensities of various forms of sexual contact.

Similarly, the focus upon the experiences of a single concrete historical subject permeates the response to LeRoy's work. It is real (and therefore, interesting) because it supposedly happened to LeRoy himself. Shields picks up on this in the course of his discussion of faked life writing, arguing that a "frankly fictional account would rob the memoir/counterfeiter, his or her publishers, and the audience of the opportunity to attach a face to the angst" (36). Just as pornography relies on the authenticating powers of the singular body, so too does misery porn. In her account of her role in the hoax, Laura Albert emphasizes the importance not only of the idea of a single author—as indicated by a proper name and an imagined case history—but also of a single legitimating body. In an interview with Nathaniel Rich, for example, she states that as LeRoy's reputation grew, "there were starting to be rumors that he was not real, so I knew I needed to supply a body." She refers to this idea again a little later in the interview, noting, "When *Sarah* was published and it got fabulous reviews, magazines wanted to run articles about JT with their own photos. They didn't want to use the author photo. So again I realized I had to produce a body."

Indeed, this narrow focus on the individuated and authenticating body is arguably reflected in some of *Sarah*'s thematic content; particularly, it's interest in the idea of the holy body. In the novel, the 12-year-old male protagonist—known variously as Cherry Vanilla, She-ra, and Sarah—is mistaken for the reincarnation of the Biblical figure of Sarah, and is set up as a saint by the inhabitants of "the roughest, toughest truck stop in all of West Virginia" (28). The narrator, at the peak of his saintly career, notes that the customers of the truck stop's female prostitutes

> would overhear the other truckers attesting to the miracles their visits with me had wrought, and they'd drop to their knees. The large tips [. . .] were quickly placed on the collection plate with an extra fifty dollars or so along with an attached prayer that they too might have the blessing of being able to haul overloaded rigs through weigh stations without nary a blink from an inspector. (64)

The narrator's body, then, becomes invested with phenomenal, even supernatural, importance in the novel, as his flesh becomes a site of pilgrimage. Only those prepared to pay an inflated rate are permitted to touch Saint Sarah (65), whereas the rest hope that merely being in the presence of a holy body will grant them the luck that they need. Indeed, saints are often associated with the corporeal as well as the spiritual or ineffable. As Charles Lindholm puts it, "Relics are transitional between totem and artwork: personal, yet not created; they gain their spiritual authority solely by virtue of their degree of closeness to the saint or martyr, with the holiest being the actual body parts" (14). Through the depiction of "divine" corporeality, the importance of the seemingly authentic body is woven into the fabric of LeRoy's work. Both the fiction and the hoax to some extent revolve around the legitimating and authenticating qualities of the body, that key contemporary vehicle of the real.

And it is not just the content of LeRoy's work that stages an engagement with ideas of the real. Its form, too, can be seen as part of the writing's "authenticity work" (Gubrium and Holstein 123)—that is, as part of the constructive activity by which the appearance of authenticity is produced. I am thinking here particularly of LeRoy's somewhat inarticulate prose, and of the critical response to it. Before his unmasking, several commentators mention the amateurish feel of LeRoy's work. Sullivan, for example, touches on this. He remarks that LeRoy is "concentrating on honing his craft," and quotes the author as saying that "My commitment is to become better. If [my writing] is good, it shouldn't matter who I am or what I look like, it should just live on its own merit." Crisell, too, notes the imperfection of LeRoy's prose, and suggests that "He writes almost like someone new to the discipline, structuring sentences so precariously that they shouldn't work," and that his similes are "delicate and awkward."

Such comments, I suggest, offer further evidence of journalistic and critical interest in the authenticity of LeRoy's work. It is not just, as Cooper seems to think, that the low quality of the prose is overlooked by generous readers who sympathize with LeRoy's backstory. Rather, LeRoy's lack of eloquence is valued as further "proof" of authorial identity and realness. Baudrillard's comments in the essay "Dust Breeding" are illuminating here:

> Foucault used to refer to self-expression as the ultimate form of confession. Keeping no secret. Speaking, talking, endlessly communicating. This is a form of violence which targets the singular being and his secrecy. It is also a form of violence against language. In this mode of communicability, language loses its originality. Language simply becomes a medium, an operator of visibility. It has lost its symbolic and ironic qualities, those which make language more important than what it conveys.

The confessional mode seeks to strip language of any and all qualities that detract from its communicative function; it seeks, in other words, to make language seem transparent. A lack of finesse only serves to make LeRoy's writing seem more real. It is not literature, but something more immediate, less contemplative and less artful. Its rough and ready qualities function as apparent proof of its authenticity.

This links back, of course, to the idea that LeRoy's oeuvre is in fact a thinly camouflaged form of therapy.[4] As O'Rourke suggests, LeRoy relies on "the drama of descent and recovery to attract attention to his persona—and thereby endow his novels with the culturally very marketable status of 'real' artifact, not just art." A concern with and an interest in authenticity, I have demonstrated, pervade not only the response to the scandal, but also reactions to LeRoy's fiction and, indeed, the very content of that fiction. That is to say, the texts themselves can in some ways be seen to invite the reader to look for authenticity, despite their outward claims to fictionality, and this might help to explain the sense of betrayal evident in some responses to LeRoy's exposure as a character, rather than an author.

Destabilizing the Authenticity Effect

Having sketched out some of the strategies via which LeRoy stages the real, however, I now adopt a slightly different perspective. I highlight some of the ways in which the writing, as well as Albert's JT LeRoy persona, undermines this seemingly dominant trend toward authenticity. Certainly, there are elements of the LeRoy case that are anomalous in terms of my provisional thesis that the author, his work, and the critical investment in it all demonstrate a preoccupation with generating an authenticity effect. It is clear that some elements of the hoax—both textual and paratextual—do not invite the reader to view the books through the prism of the author's real life. For example, the books contain many non-naturalistic, even surreal or magical realist, moments. In *Harold's End*, for example, the vulnerable street kids with whom the narrator socializes all seem strangely other-worldly. This is an effect accentuated by Cherry Hood's delicate and ethereally beautiful illustrations of the characters, and by the fact that these drug-addicted hustlers all have their own pets, ranging from a "pedigree Colby dog" (13), to a "seal-point Siamese breed" rat (14), to a "Columbian/Surinamese mix" boa constrictor (13). The oddness of the idea of an underage homeless girl traveling with a snake—"she unwinds the boa snake from her neck and stuffs it in her backpack" (10)—complicates any attempt to read purely for the extra-textually real.

There are further, more pronounced moments of weirdness in LeRoy's *Sarah*, the narrative of which is infused with folklore, superstition, and supernatural occurrences. At one point, for example, Cherry

Vanilla visits "the patron saint of lot lizards: Holy Jack's Jackalope" (25), in the hopes of becoming the most world's most talented gender-ambiguous truck-stop rent boy. He reports that, as rumor has it,

> it was Highway Patrol that hit and killed this Jackalope and a pack of renegade lot lizards held the wild run-over beast in their arms, cradling its bleeding head next to their exposed bosoms, warming its paws under their skirts and in their privates, and sucking on its once tiny antlers with their painted mouths. And when the Jackalope passed, the lizards not only had the first real orgasms of their lives, but they suddenly were transformed into the most desired lot lizards at any truck stop ever. (32–33)

In a further example of the novel's interest in the authentic saintly body, the corpse of this mythical animal is now bolted to the wall of Holy Jack's bar, where lot lizard pilgrims come to visit it. According to the narrator, the Jackalope's antlers have continued to grow even after its death: "I've heard it said the roof has had to be raised five times just to accommodate the miracle. I can even make out the phosphorescent buds of new antler" (33).

Although much of the lore of the Jackalope is presented as a tall story—"I've heard it said," "It's been said" (32)—Cherry Vanilla's visit to Holy Jack's is shown to have actual effects in the narrative. Both the narrator and Pooh, the young female prostitute that he meets at the shrine, miraculously develop a specifically sexual form of second sight, allowing them to psychically ascertain the preferences of their johns. As the narrator puts it, "It comes to me in a hazy sensation, like trying to recall a particular scent from childhood. I sense what position they favor, whether they like to be spanked or chastised for being naughty, or what nasty words they are partial to having moaned into their ear" (67). At one point, these psychic powers even allow Pooh to prevent her own murder, and the narrator to access the assailant's memories of the attack. Cherry Vanilla lays her hands upon the attacker, one of Pooh's customers, and is able to visualize the attempt on her life. He reports that Pooh

> saw me staring at the thick finger marks around her neck and the blue pallor her face still carried. Pooh had anticipated what he would do to her. She had used her second sight to know that it was the lack of surprise in her eyes, the lack of struggle

on her part that would cause him to lose interest and loosen his grip. She was the first not to end up face-down in a ditch at the side of the road. (67)

Pooh's psychic gift later leads her to fame and fortune, after she services a "famous Hollywood agent" (126). She tells the narrator that she used her "second sight to know all he wanted was to be wrapped in diapers, nursed with a bottle, and burped like an armbaby. He had never told a being in this world, bless his poor tortured soul" (127).

Although it might be said that these events work to reinforce certain key tropes of the contemporary real—namely, the idea that there is a "truth" of sex, even if it can only be uncovered by supernatural means—there is no denying that LeRoy disturbs his own attempts to establish an aura of reality. The surreal qualities of the narrative mark the novel off from conventional autobiographical writing, distancing the text both from misery memoir and, indeed, from any straightforward claim for a basis in the historical or extra-textual real.[5] The books are, as Cochrane states, "highly imaginative, bizarre, evocative works of fiction." Even *The Heart is Deceitful*—the work with the strongest links to ideas of the post-therapeutic memoir—has a somewhat other-worldly, hyperreal quality to it. As Loontjens notes in her discussion of the blurb on the back of the Bloomsbury edition of the text:

> Although it is suggested that his stories are based on real experiences, the adjectives that are used to describe LeRoy's style of writing all seem closer to fiction than reality. First his "fantastical imagination and lyricism" are mentioned, which evoke fantasy rather than reality, and furthermore his past is considered "utterly strange and magical." *After* the unmasking these descriptions perhaps seem to betray the deceit of the author JT LeRoy, just as the title itself *The Heart is Deceitful Above All Things* does.

Indeed, as Loontjens suggests here, deceit is itself a central theme in LeRoy's work. That is to say, the books can be seen to enact a perpetual complication of identity, and to issue repeated warnings about taking personas at face value. Characters frequently are not what they appear to be. Cherry Vanilla, for example, passes as a girl (and a holy one at that) for much of *Sarah*, only to be exposed by a pedophile abuser who attempts to molest him while he is sedated. The abuser shakes him awake, asking,

"Where's your other hole at?" (102), before exclaiming, "You are not a little girl!" and running for help (103). Jeremiah similarly passes as a girl at various points in the stories of *The Heart is Deceitful*. Sometimes Sarah presents him as her brother, but more frequently he finds himself cast as her sister because Sarah thinks, "Men like girls, not boys" (44). And in addition to these false identities and incidents of role playing, the reader is presented with various scams and cons, from Sarah throwing rocks at her son in an attempt to convince a park ranger that they have been hit by a meteor ("Meteors," *The Heart is Deceitful* 209–28), to an exploitative pimp claiming that Cherry Vanilla can "walk on water" to extract money from some well-off Yankee tourists (*Sarah* 68).

In fact, LeRoy's deliberate foregrounding of the slipperiness of appearances also can be detected within the paratextual material surrounding his fiction. As Beachy puts it, "in both his interviews and his books he seems always to be suggesting that nothing he says should be believed." That is to say, it is not just the fictional material that stages an explicit engagement with ideas regarding the deceptiveness of outward identity, but also the supposedly nonfictional material in which LeRoy talks about himself. In conversation with Crisell, for example, he says that "if people want to say that I don't fucking exist then they can do that. Because in a way I don't. I have a different name that I use in the world, and maybe JT LeRoy doesn't really exist." As previously suggested, however, Crisell is quite emphatic when it comes to foregrounding the role of the autobiographical real in LeRoy's work, and resists this kind of identity play in favor of arguing that "while he'd like us to believe his books are fiction and that being JT LeRoy is an act, he [. . .] relies on that disputed and painful past to feed his writing." In an interview with Dremousis, too, we see LeRoy distancing himself from idea that his books are a truthful representation of the past. He declares that he believes that "there's no such thing as autobiographical writing" ("An Interview with Fiction Writer JT Leroy"), and goes on to add, "everything I publish will always be fiction."

Of course, all of this might be a clever play upon reader preconceptions. There is perhaps a pervasive tendency to want to read the negated other of the fiction/nonfiction binary into a text, and, in attempting to foreground ideas of fictionality, Albert may well be working to circuitously channel readers' responses back toward a more biographical interpretation. In seeming to disavow the role of autobiography in the novel, in other words, the author generates a sense of the hidden or the covert, and makes biographical readings particularly appealing to the contrary minds of a contemporary readership. Having said this, however, it is clear that ideas regarding the extra-textual real are complicated within LeRoy's discourse. Unlike conventional misery porn, autobiographical authenticity is not overtly attested to, and readers are perpetually encouraged to be skeptical about the identities of both the author and his characters.

The LeRoy scandal represents a complex nexus of numerous currents of thinking about issues of genre and authorship. It also taps into those features that, I have suggested, link certain strands of contemporary adult entertainment to the realm of misery porn—that is, prurience, authenticity, and the real. There is a sense in which the exposure of LeRoy represents also the exposure of his reading public. I suggest that, without the idea of an extra-textual body and a concrete historical past, the books appear as pure manifestations of contemporary readers' prurient interest in suffering. To return again to Anthony Lane's comments, LeRoy can be seen as "just the hoax that the rage for confessional writing has been asking for. He, or she, has punched all the right buttons, telling of losers, abusers, cross-dressers and crackpots, enabling eager readers to feel doubly validated in their response" (95). Without a real victim of abuse behind the texts to give them their claim to authenticity, readers cannot feel validated, and much of LeRoy's work suddenly appears to be deliberately pandering to an appetite for exploitation and suffering. The texts come to seem like a symptom and a materialization of an unsettling (and perhaps unethical) hunger for the real.

I suggest that there is a certain tension at play here, however, when it comes to the description of autobiographical accounts of suffering as porn; specifically, there seems to be a discrepancy between adult entertainment's apparent attitudes toward authenticity and those of misery porn. As seen in the discussion of misery porn in Chapter 8, the presence of an apparently real story of trauma and survival is one of the primary factors allowing readers to dispute accusations of a prurient motive for reading such texts. Ideas of the autobiographical real work to, at least partially, prevent these kinds of literary works from being seen as pornographic. In other words, the real as the extra-textual provides a gateway to, and a justification for, representations of the real as it is manifested in trauma. It is this element of the authentic that renders a misery memoir a testimony or a historical record, rather than simply a market-driven fantasy.

As we have seen, however, adult entertainment as a still or moving-image genre is largely defined by precisely such claims to authenticity. That is to say, regardless of the role played by fantasy, texts are seen as belonging to the genre because they show actual bodies, real sex acts, and seemingly irrefutable scenes of genuine pleasure. Indeed, the perceived centrality of authenticity to an expanded understanding of porn is confirmed by the fact that certain texts that eschew graphic depictions of sexual activity come to be seen as pornographic partially as a result of their investment in the real. It is (at least partially) a shared emphasis on authenticity that links memoir to pornography, and that helps to make misery memoir available for the application of the "porn" suffix. And yet, rather paradoxically, it is this very claim to authenticity that is used to absolve autobiographical texts from accusations that they are pornographic. Elements of the extra-textually real can therefore be seen to both prompt and prevent people from perceiving these texts as pornographic. The operations of authenticity are evidently complex and multifaceted, and we would do well to be aware of the nuanced manner in which the concept informs understandings of different genres, rather than to simply accept the obfuscation of specificity invited by the explosion of the pornographic.

Conclusion: Misery Porn's Money Shots

In the case of JT LeRoy, and of misery memoir in general, one of the chief sources of audience fascination is encountering, through the operations of constructed unmediation, the appearance of authenticity—of experiencing the sensation of finding out what actually happened to various extra-textual bodies. As with the majority of photorealistic pornography, it is the depiction of actual experiences of concrete, corporeal, individuated subjects that gives the genre much of its unique appeal. And the huge importance placed on authenticity within the genre contributes to a pervasive concern about and fascination with scandal, dispute, and hoaxes. Indeed, the reading public appears almost as invested in moments of deceit and revelation as it is in the memoirs themselves. David Shields remarks upon this in a chapter of *Reality Hunger* entitled "Trial by Google":

> This chapter used to be named after James Frey, but along came (at pretty much the same time) JT LeRoy, then Misha Defonseca, Margaret Seltzer, Herman Rosenblatt. Similar phenomena keep arriving again and again, like the next scheduled train. That million-dollar, career-exploding, trick-tease train of these so-called "misery lit" (also called "misery porn") memoirs, first praised, then shamed, each taking its turn on the

double-crested rollercoaster of celebrity and infamy. This just in: Oprah Winfrey duped again! It's become a national tradition, each fallout more engrossing than the book itself. (32–33)

Gilmore makes a similar point, aligning the interest taken in the scandals surrounding misery memoirs with the sentimental narratives of redemption that such works contain. As she puts it, when an author is "lifted out of obscurity, the same audience that embraced his memoir consume his celebrity, which recreates the conditions for another cycle of redemption to be played out as public scandal brings him low, but may yet enable him to rise anew" ("American Neoconfessional" 656). Readers may, therefore, find an alternative source of pleasure—once again founded on the key misery memoir trope of triumph over adversity—in the hoaxes and scandals to which the realm of autobiography has found itself so prone.

This idea of the engrossing scandal is born out not only by the flurry of articles and angry comment that accompanied the exposure of Frey, LeRoy, and others, but also by misery memoirs themselves. It is telling that the front cover of recent editions of Constance Briscoe's misery memoir *Ugly* bear the slogan "Now including the sensational trial." Pages 299 to 431 of the book are dedicated to Briscoe detailing the experience of being sued for defamation in the British High Court by her mother, as a result of the unflattering depiction of her cruel and neglectful parenting. The proceedings were unsuccessful, and Briscoe cleared her name and maintained her reputation, but it seems that the publishers felt that the public's interest would be piqued by the family drama and by the whiff of scandal. It is not only the autobiography itself that is appealing, then, but also its "sensational" aftermath.

In many ways, these moments of dispute and scandal are as ensnared within ideas about authenticity and prurience as the memoirs which trigger them. Indeed, if one thinks of these scandals as extra-textual events that endeavor to establish and pin down the real—an idea that is particularly evident in the performative manufacture of truth in a legal context, but that also applies to the revelations enacted by investigative journalism—then surely one can argue that they are themselves to some extent pornographic. That is to say, if the fallout from a misery memoir revolves around a prurient interest in establishing authenticity, then it shares some key characteristics with the expanded notion of the pornographic that we have been discussing here, including an obsession with generating an authenticity effect. The court cases and exposés are, in some sense, misery porn's money shots; they are the seemingly verifiable proof that something really happened. In Briscoe's case, events that took place after the memoir's publication act as reassurance that the narrative is authentic. It has been legally decreed that the text represents reality.

Even in cases where the truthfulness of a literary work is challenged, there seems to be a similar authenticity imperative at work. Interest in an account of supposedly real suffering does not necessarily dissipate in response to its being exposed as a fake. Indeed, the hurt feelings, the arguments and the indignation that such a scandal provokes all provide material for a new kind of pseudo-voyeuristic or prurient interest. We see this in relation to the LeRoy scandal; the 2006 interview with Laura Albert in the *Paris Review*, for example, suggests an ongoing curiosity about the hoax, as does Savannah Knoop's 2008 memoir about her involvement with the affair. There is, I would suggest, a sense in which even evidence of the inauthenticity of a piece of autobiographical writing gets drawn into a pornographic logic of and fixation with the extra-textual real. After all, when an autobiography is exposed as a fake, the revelation itself has the status of a real event, uncovering the actual story behind the fabrications. When Beachy revealed the evidence that JT LeRoy was in fact Laura Albert, he reintroduced a sense of authenticity into the case, even as he was stripping the books of their claim to represent the extra-textual real; the fake truth was instantaneously replaced with the "real" truth, the hoax was revealed, and an aura of authenticity was achieved.

What I'm trying to suggest here is that the scandals surrounding fake memoirs play into our hunger for authenticity—a hunger that also informs an interest in the pornographic. As Baudrillard puts it, we "want to reach the extreme, attain the paroxysm of exhibition, achieve total nudity, find absolute reality, consume live and raw violence (*au direct et à l'écorché vif*)" ("Dust Breeding"), and the exposure of fakes allows us to feel that something has been ultimately unveiled. We experience the illusionary sensation that we have finally reached the elusive truth. In some ways, this is the pay-off for having had one's prurience exposed: Yes, the misery memoir was inauthentic, and was faked largely in accordance with the ethically questionable demand of the reading public for increasingly harrowing depictions of suffering and the real as trauma; however, not only can the discomfort of this realization be displaced onto the dishonest author, but some of the lost authenticity can be recuperated through the final unveiling of the truth. The misery memoir reader is brought into contact with the extra-textual real, if not through the text itself, then through the scandal that surrounds it. Either way, the pornographic pleasure of the appearance of authenticity persists.

But, I suggest, even after the apparent proving or disproving of autobiographical accounts—even after the genre's money shot—something remains obscure. Authors like Albert and Frey will never truly cease to be defined by their involvements in such scandals, because readers and commentators alike fail to settle the issue to their satisfaction. There always seems to be a final veil, screening a deeper truth, which cannot be removed. Any ambitions to rend this veil, Baudrillard suggest, are misguided:

> how sad is the idea of demonstrating sexuality through the sexual act! As if displacements, deviations, transfers, and metaphors had nothing to do with sex. Everything is in the filter of seduction, in *détournement*. Not the seduction in sex and desire, but the seduction of playing with sex and desire (*le jeu avec the sexe et le désir*). This is exactly what makes impossible the idea of "live sex." The concepts of live death or live news are just as naively naturalist. They are all linked to the pretentious claim that everything can happen in the real world, that everything craves to find its place inside an all-encompassing reality.[6] ("Dust Breeding")

There is always a sense that some elements of the extra-textually real escape representation, if not comprehension, and that neither autobiography nor pornography, despite their incessant attempts to achieve an authenticity effect, can ever finally succeed in appearing absolutely authentic. This is of course especially obvious when the subject matter is the real as intensity or *jouissance*. As Griselda Pollock notes,

> trauma is the radical and irreducible other of representation, the other of the subject and, as Thing, cannot thus become something. We try to think it as an effect, a condition, even a shadow that will never be identical to that which might be its displaced and displacing narration or representation, both always being a passage away from trauma, a transformation— a working in Freud's sense of *Arbeit* (dream work, mourning work, working through)—into a memory, as a part of the psychic apparatus. (42–43)

In works that deal with trauma, we encounter a struggle to represent that which resists narrativization, and that persistently exceeds the grasp of structuring discourses. It appears only as a kind of shadow. No account of trauma can ever seem real enough; the "fortress of obscenity cannot be brought down" (Baudrillard, "Dust Breeding"). Of course, the inevitable failure to achieve pure pornographic explicitness does not spell unmitigated disaster for either adult entertainment or misery porn. In fact, "such a lost quest helps to resurrect the basic rule of the game: the rule of the sublime, the rule of secrecy, of seduction (always tracked down through the endless lifting of covers)" (Baudrillard, "Dust Breeding").[7] As with the insatiable operations of desire, the pornographic pleasure of being brought near to the real can never truly be achieved or realized, but nor can it ever be exhausted.

In this section, I have considered the points of confluence between adult entertainment and so-called misery porn in an attempt to better understand the configuration of the explosion of the pornographic. Once again, we have seen that sex can be sidelined when it comes to contemporary characterizations of porn. The notions of the real and the authentic can now be added to transgression, intensity, and prurience as contributing factors when it comes to perceptions of the pornographic and to the usage of the porn suffix. I conclude this volume by considering some of the limitations and problems that might emerge as a result of my analysis, and by attempting to disentangle my arguments from those regarding "pornographication."

10

Conclusion

*Pornographication and the
Explosion of the Pornographic*

In this book, I have explored a somewhat counterintuitive idea; the idea that sex has, to a certain extent, been displaced within contemporary perceptions of the pornographic. That which is signified by the word "porn" has, I have demonstrated, undergone something of a slippage.[1] It is not simply a matter of adult entertainment having achieved a greater degree of visibility or having expanded into new cultural territories, but is in fact a matter of a more profound and perverse adjustment in popular understanding, whereby transgression, intense affect, prurient interest, and the real are rendered sufficiently central to conceptualizations of porn that they are seen as capable of displacing—or even *re*placing—the seemingly crucial element of sexual explicitness.

The arguments advanced in *Beyond Explicit* may arouse certain issues, however. Widened understandings of the pornographic may not simply effect the usefulness or meaningfulness of the concept within popular discourse,[2] but may prove dangerous if incorporated into a legal context. As Laurence O'Toole notes in his discussion of attempts to reform the United Kingdom's Obscene Publications Act, certain anti-censorship activists have come to believe that "fuzzy legislation founded on open-ended definitions is actually preferred, to make it a catch-all kind of prohibition. Thus considerable extensions in the activities of the police, trading officers and Customs are apportioned" (147). The broad, indistinct usage of "porn"—at both the linguistic and the conceptual levels—may therefore risk playing into the hands of those who would restrict the circulation of certain forms of representation; if sexually explicit material has long been at risk for being positioned as obscene, then to align other types of representation with the idea of pornography may risk rendering a great swathe of material more vulnerable to attempts at censorship. To be loose in our definition of porn may also be to invite or to make possible the emergence of "catch-all" legislation.

A key issue with the explosion of the pornographic is that cultural objects that are not works of adult entertainment get dragged into the genre's orbit in a manner that can result in unwelcome political and social side effects. This was demonstrated in Chapter 6 in relation to the so-called "pornographic" images at the center of 2004's Abu Ghraib scandal. In the case of these images, it may not simply be that sex is displaced, but that other cultural anxieties are also displaced *onto* sex. As per Anne McClintock's remarks, in the "storm of moral agitation about *our* pornography and *our* loss of the moral high ground" ("Paranoid Empire" 63), the torture was to some extent domesticated and rendered banal. Clarissa Smith makes a similar point, suggesting that to label the tortures pornographic "reduces the very real harms done to prisoners by US soldiers to individuals acting under the supposed influence of sexually explicit representations" ("Pornographication" 107).

In the essay just cited, Smith also raises a number of points about the idea of *pornographication*—a term that applies to the seemingly increased influence and visibility of adult entertainment in contemporary society. She argues that the discourse surrounding pornographication is too "saturated in the languages and references of concern and regulation" to be a useful critical tool ("Pornographication" 104), and suggests that the term frequently exploits "the condemnatory potential of the associations with pornography" ("Pornographication" 104). She asserts the following:

> Those who use the term pornographication do so precisely so that they can avoid any of the particularities of sexually explicit media. The obviousness of the term should alert us to the ways in which pornographication is not something that can be "discovered," "uncovered" and "challenged," but instead it is a means of ensuring that behaviors, practices and actions can be labeled and assessed as problematic without addressing specific issues relating to their history, production and consumption; and that can suggest "solutions" which are both

intensely political and denuded of real politics at the same time. ("Pornographication" 106)

What Smith suggests in this essay is that pornographication's usefulness as a concept is dramatically limited by the negative connotations attached to the idea of pornography itself. Even if one does not employ the term *pornographication* expressly in order to denounce the increased visibility of sex, the associations of the term make it a particularly useful discourse for the censorious. For those hostile toward adult entertainment, porn is self-evidently problematic, and its spread through culture via pornographication is viewed as being necessarily a bad thing. The history of porn, including the high-profile anti-pornography feminist activism surrounding the genre, may mean that many people jump to conclusions about the harmfulness, violence, and undesirability of porn without stopping to question their assumptions. Pornographication and pornification have been "widely taken up as descriptions and explanations of cultural shifts and worrying experiences" (Smith, "Pornographication" 104), including everything from actual sexual practices to personal grooming regimes. We might therefore view these ideas as engaging with a different strand of the explosion of the pornographic—that is, as relating to the topics addressed throughout *Beyond Explicit*.

Smith rejects the expansion of the concept of pornography that occurs in the case of some critical work on porn cultures, suggesting that it too often manifests itself as an eschewal of detailed analysis in favor of loose generalizations, and that it facilitates an uncritical understanding of the visibility of adult entertainment as "a cause for concern" and "a cause of bad behaviours" ("Pornographication" 106). Considering that *Beyond Explicit* is precisely about the broadening out of contemporary understandings of the pornographic, it is important to address some of the potential implications of Smith's analysis here. In discussing various forms of unpleasant or "unwholesome" material—from gross-out entertainment to representations of war and suffering—in relation to the pornographic, it might be said that we risk reinforcing the reductive idea that porn is itself inherently unpleasant or unwholesome. The explosion of the pornographic examined here does seem to use some of the stigma attached to pornography for its meaningfulness and specificity. Not only are nonsexually explicit representations cast in a negative light via their alignment with the pornographic, but (in circular fashion) adult entertainment is similarly positioned as something sordid and objectionable via its association with such representations.[3] Perhaps, in drawing attention to the extended deployment and understanding of the concept of porn, my work could be seen to go too far in the pursuit of its original aim of contributing to a more probing and scholarly form of Porn Studies. I agree with Elizabeth Wilson that "Sexually explicit representations, images and texts are neither reactionary nor liberating in and of themselves" (27), but if we consider this book in relation to Smith's discussion of pornographication, then my work is arguably at risk of contributing to an uncritical condemnation of porn.

I do not believe this to be the case, however, and my response to Smith's argument is threefold. First, it should be obvious that I am not invested in and nor do I endorse the extended sense in which the words "porn" and "pornographic" currently are being used. I am not suggesting that the explosion of these concepts is necessarily a positive thing, or that using the terms in this more expansive way says anything radically novel or enlightening about adult entertainment. As I see it, *Beyond Explicit* is simply attempting to account for a conceptual and terminological slippage that has taken place within contemporary cultural discourse: It is charting (and not celebrating) an existing phenomenon. Perhaps the association of pornography with war imagery or misery memoir *does* foreground some of the negative associations attached to the idea of adult entertainment, but I do not think that this necessarily invalidates my analysis. In fact, as I discussed in my introduction, I think that scholars do Porn Studies a disservice when we let a desire to celebrate or to apologize for porn dictate everything we allow ourselves to think and write about the genre. To be clear, I am not suggesting that Smith's work plays into this celebration, and nor am I attempting characterize her argument as an uncritical attempt to distance pornography from culturally denigrated media texts. Rather, I am trying to set my work apart from some of the more problematic elements of "pornographication" that she so rightly identifies.

My second point is that adult entertainment and the pornographic should not be viewed as one and the same thing. For all its diversity, adult entertainment largely retains a strong generic identity in terms of its contexts of production, its marketing and distribution, its viewers' expectations, and so on. For all the anomalous examples of the genre discussed in Part II, many consumers would no doubt still agree with O'Toole's claim that "arousal is porn's main event" (298), and with Linda Williams' suggestion that, when it comes to hard core, "masturbation is the very point of the human–screen interface" (*Screening Sex* 312). This is indicative of one of the key differences between my argument and that advanced by certain discourses of pornographication; although pornographication tends to *collapse* the disparities between various cultural artifacts, reducing all kinds of phenomena to a certain conceptualization of adult entertainment, I have been attempting to *tease out* and to distinguish elements that have become uncritically entangled within contemporary understandings of the pornographic. Adult entertainment is not, to my mind, a sordid hotbed of trauma, prurience, and heinous transgression; indeed, as Matteo Pasquinelli remarks, "there has been a notable rise in politically-correct pornography and the emergence of a new spectrum of subcultural flavors (the so-called *indie porn* or *alt porn*) have the effect of neutralizing its obscenity potential" (*Animal Spirits* 200). My own experience of the genre would suggest that it can, at times, seem positively wholesome, especially when compared with the genuinely horrific images that emerged from the Abu Ghraib prisoner camp. To call these torture images pornographic, however, is just not the same thing as labeling them works of adult entertainment.

In her discussion of the Abu Ghraib scandal, Smith writes of these photographs:

> their circulation as "pornography" insists on an understanding of the ways in which those images were consumed—the presumption is that any viewer encountered them as sexual first and foremost. There may be many ways of engaging with these images but surely the most prominent possible engagement indicates the redundancy of the use of the term pornography—many viewers of these images understood them as confirmation of the skewed politics, ethics and morals of the so-called War on Terror.[4] ("Pornographication" 107)

To call these images pornographic is, according to Smith, to suggest that they provoke and solicit a sexual response. I argue that this is not necessarily the case. There is now a shared perception of the concept of the pornographic that, as this text repeatedly demonstrates, does not always or inevitably conflate it with consumer arousal or sexually explicit forms of representation. Porn cannot be characterized as merely "a sex thing" (O'Toole 342), even if adult entertainment can; it is not preoccupied with eliciting a genitally sexual response but with provoking more general forms of queasy *jouissance*—horror, anger, sorrow, and a certain nauseated fascination.[5] This kind of response is not a symptom of categorical moral bankruptcy, but part of a dysfunctional sympathetic impulse and a persistent (if perhaps regrettable) facet of our interaction with certain images and texts.

The pornographic, then, is currently understood in relation to a range of nonsexually explicit texts that bear little resemblance to adult entertainment. When Marcus Wood describes as *pornographic* the engravings of inanimate objects accompanying Thomas Clarkson's history of abolition, for example, he is obviously not suggesting that they are works of *adult entertainment*. Something of a schism has taken place between these two terms. Indeed, it might be expedient in terms of anti-censorship activism to emphasize and exploit this schism. That is to say, those who are invested in demonstrating the positive and progressive elements of sexually explicit representations would do well to distance themselves from the pornographic—a term that is not only overly burdened with negative associations, but that is increasingly de-emphasizing the role of sex within its conceptual identity. This may well be a partial answer to Smith's question about how, in the wake of the explosion of the pornographic, "we" (presumably anti-censorship academics) can "address the specificities of the production, consumption and textual forms of those materials which actually do include purposively sexually explicit content and graphic representations of sexual activity" ("Pornographication" 107). Perhaps such activists need to cease talking about porn and start talking about adult entertainment; not only do these terms often signify different things, but such a move would function as a rebranding exercise, the importance of which the sex industry itself has long understood.

As I mentioned in my introduction, "adult entertainment" is not a phrase that I myself find particularly appealing, because it is both oblique and disingenuous. For the purposes of activism, however, "adult entertainment" might prove a particularly useful term. It not only makes it clear that the topic under discussion is a specific set of materials and practices (rather than anything more nebulous), but its euphemistic qualities lend themselves well to those arguments that seek to protect the genre from censorship and government intervention. "Adult entertainment" lacks the threatening and confrontational power of "pornography"; it is "pornography" declawed. The explosion of the pornographic outlined in this book, then, is only tangentially related to adult entertainment. It is important to recognize that calling something pornographic is not necessarily an attempt to conflate it with adult entertainment, and it may serve pro-sex feminists well to strategically emphasize this fact.

My final answer to the issues raised by Smith's account of pornographication relates to the perceived stigmatization of adult entertainment in the extension of porn's conceptual identity. It is important to note that not all of the pleasures associated with the broader understanding of porn are quite as dubious or unsettling as those I have outlined here. When it comes to the post-sexual pornographic, it's not all grief, poverty, torture, war, or misery. Less offensive materials and affects also are currently being brought under the rubric of the pornographic, and the porn suffix has become attached to certain ideas regarding lifestyle and luxury without any apparent attempt to mobilize responses such as horror or disgust. We now have the idea of *property porn*, for example, which the *Collins English Dictionary* defines as "a genre of escapist TV programmes, magazine features etc., showing desirable properties for sale" ("Asbo" and "chav" make dictionary"). The term *travel porn* also has emerged to designate "material produced for the sole purpose of creating excitement or arousal to visit a cosmopolitan city, far flung destination, exotic country, five star hotel resort, tropical island or other location" (Lowe),[6] whereas the phrase *food porn* has come to reflect the idea that, as Elspeth Probyn puts it, "the food pages of newspapers have replaced the personals as the site of titillation and innuendo" (219).[7]

These expressions have entered into circulation in relation to texts that evidently have little or no connection to adult entertainment as a genre. In these cases, the porn suffix seems to function to draw attention to a kind of harmless voyeuristic pleasure taken in representations of desirable items and covetable experiences. Therefore, one could argue that the implied relationship with pornography goes beyond expressing or generating the kind of intense aversion that Smith associates with pornographication, and gestures toward a less objectionable realm of connections and correlations. When one considers this alternative realm, it may seem that I have been selective in my analysis, lingering only on the discomforting qualities related to the pornographic; I certainly agree that there is scope for further research on the link between these lifestyle texts and the idea of porn. The fact remains, however, that the labeling of such representations as pornographic demonstrates the explosion of the concept, albeit with a different focus and in a different form.

Indeed, despite the less troubling nature of these lifestyle pornographies, I think certain ideas regarding distaste remain in play. The influence of cultural condemnation is not so easy to dismiss, I suggest, and there is more to this idea of stigma and the explosion of the pornographic that we need to consider before we conclude. As the engagement with Smith demonstrated, the term *pornographication* is widely (if problematically) used to refer to the increased visibility of the perceived qualities of adult entertainment. The genre's aesthetics, attitudes, and sexual content have, theorists of pornographication argue, been broadly accepted and mainstreamed. This argument often is somewhat lacking in nuance, and presents a partial image of what adult entertainment is and can be at this historical juncture, but I am more or less in agreement with the point about visibility. I would contend that certain kinds of adult entertainment—along with the idea of pornography itself—should not be characterized as the repressed other of Anglo-American cultures, and that viewing such texts through a lens of transgression, dissidence, or rebellion is not always helpful in terms of furthering our critical understanding.

The fact that mainstream adult entertainment is not widely stigmatized within Western cultures may be at least partially responsible for shifts in contemporary understanding. Although pornography as a genre is increasingly tolerated, the idea of the pornographic (as expressed via the porn suffix) has attached itself to an expanded range of viscerally moving and culturally disparaged materials. The pornographic as a designation retains more than a suggestion of disgust and disapproval, even if adult entertainment as a genre does not always or necessarily provoke these kinds of affect. As such, we might argue that the concept of the pornographic has migrated away from adult entertainment and become attached to other, less rehabilitated forms of prurience—a lascivious curiosity regarding war, for example, or abuse, or torture, or any other type of representation that depicts authentic scenes of psychic or bodily intensity in a culturally denigrated fashion.

This notion of the migration of the pornographic away from its traditional cultural territory in the pursuit of stigma applies equally to those seemingly less "negative" nonsexual pornographies described previously—the apparently more innocent examples of food porn, travel porn, and so on. These lifestyle pornographies are not interpretable as sources of social stigma in the same way as the other examples focused on throughout this book. However, although they may not stage an engagement with suffering or violence, these pornographies retain the taint of stigma that their labeling as porn suggests. To engage with lifestyle pornographies is, the porn suffix implies, to become simultaneously passive and obsessive before representations—to scroll through image after image, our critical faculties numbed, submitting to a consumerist spectacle. These texts are positioned as unworthy of our attention; we engage with them despite ourselves and (on some level) we should apologize for our interest in them.

Porn may remain shameful and stigmatized even in its exploded form, then; that which Clarissa Smith refers to as the "condemnatory potential of the associations with pornography" continues to prove influential ("Pornographication" 104). Where Smith and I differ most noticeably here, however, is in terms of the emphasis we place on the centrality of sex to the operations of condemnation. As this volume has endeavored to demonstrate, shame and stigma can no longer be firmly tethered to sexual explicitness or genital activity. The nonsexual pornographic suggests a new cartography of stigma—a cartography that charts a cultural landscape in which sex has been largely displaced as the primary locus of transgression.

Notes

Introduction: Critical Voices in Porn Studies

1. Anne McClintock, for example, emphasizes the fact that "So much has been written on the question of pornography (as if it were one thing), and so little on the myriad types, texts and subgenres that make up porn's kaleidoscopic variorum" ("Gonad the Barbarian" 115). In drawing attention to this, she encourages the emergence of a more sophisticated type of analysis.

2. However, with the exception of Daniel Bernardi's article on racism and pornography ("Interracial Joysticks," mentioned later in this introduction), I suggest that the essays in Lehman's anthology do not vary significantly in tone from those collected in *Porn Studies*.

3. Matteo Pasquinelli refers to these kinds of adult entertainment as "the *radically correct* commercial subcultures of *alt porn*" (*Animal Spirits* 172).

4. Julian Petley links this concern to the development of new technologies, arguing that "Unable to control the flow of information across the Internet, governments of certain democratic states are seeking instead to control their users by implanting them with the fear that if they visit websites containing material which their own government has deemed illegal, their online activity will be tracked and they will be liable for prosecution" ("Pornography, Panopticism and the Criminal Justice and Immigration Act 2008" 419).

5. Paasonen, Nikunen, and Saarenmaa draw on a similar argument: "Public displays of sexuality, including non-normative intimacies, entail the possibility of reorganizing the boundaries of respectability and normalcy. Making sex public, pornography confronts tendencies to silence or demonize sexualities—and queer sexualities in particular" (14).

6. Bernardi explicitly questions the extent of the pro-sex feminist approach's critical rigor when it comes to issues of race, in an analysis that also might be applied to Porn Studies: "Radical sex feminists seem unwilling to address the facts of racism, and in fact ignore or excuse racism in favor of arguing against positions held by their antiporn counterparts. [. . .] I find it problematic that their argument about the genre's aesthetic and subversive elements comes at the expense of its hegemonic articulations" ("Interracial Joysticks" 222).

7. Indeed, it seems that this may soon go beyond the odd marginal critic and individual article as scholars agitate for new methodologies and approaches to pornography. Lisa Downing, for example, is currently popularizing the term *sex critical*, as she resists the prevalence of "rigidly dichotomous lines of response" to the topic of sexuality. For Downing, the first principle of a sex-critical perspective is that "All forms of sexuality and all sexual representations should be equally susceptible to critical thinking and interrogation about the normative or otherwise ideologies they uphold."

8. Juffer discusses the physical and figurative accessibility of erotic fiction for women in her well-regarded analysis *At Home With Pornography* (1998); Henry Jenkins writes engagingly about the construction of illicit same-sex desire in "print-based pornography" aimed at a mainstream male audience (134); and Clarissa Smith works on linguistic texts and has commented on the manner in which the works of short fiction in pornographic magazines allow "readers to experiment with various types of feeling" (28); but contemporary theorists have otherwise remained largely silent on the matter of written narratives.

9. Chuck Kleinhans raises a similar point, suggesting, "over the past thirty years, discourse around sexuality at many social levels has focused more and more on visual representations," and adding, "although images often provoke protest and legal/political efforts at restraint, in an unremarked way, verbal descriptions of sex have become more and more common and frank in the mass media" (71).

10. For example, *Skin Two*, the popular print magazine dedicated to the world of fetish, has an online presence that has previously sold not only pornographic DVDs and magazines, but also works of pornographic fiction in paperback form (see *Skin Two Magazine*).

11. Gerry Mooney and Lynn Hancock give such examples as the British reality series *Jeremy Kyle*, *Trisha*, *Secret Millionaire*, and *Saints and Scroungers*, whereas the journalists Iain McDowall and Jane Graham of the *Guardian* have both separately discussed whether BBC Scotland's *The Scheme*—a documentary series set on a housing estate—should be viewed as an example of poverty porn.

Part I

Feminism, Pornography, Transgression

1. Peter Stallybrass and Allon White make this point in relation to carnival, noting that it "often violently abuses and demonizes *weaker*, not stronger, social groups—women, ethnic and religious minorities, those who 'don't belong'—in a process of *displaced abjection*" (19).

2. Williams suggests, for example, that it is in "the proliferation of different pornographies [. . .] that opposition to the dominant representation of pleasure

can emerge," and that it is "in the profusion rather than the censoring of pornographies that one important resistance can be found to what many feminists have objected to in the dominance of the heterosexual masculine pornographic imagination" ("Pornographies On/scene" 262).

1. The Sex Wars: Transgressive Politics and the Politics of Transgression

1. Juffer is particularly interesting on the need to separate adult entertainment from ideas of transgression in order to make the genre more accessible to women. See 233–37 of *At Home With Pornography: Women, Sex, and Everyday Life*.

2. Stephan Geene makes a similar point, suggesting that, from a pro-sex viewpoint, "Sex/porn, as it can be found in particular milieus as well as in society as a whole, is [. . .] not necessarily sex as it ought to be; sexual practices as they are to be found in the world, as they are ordinarily practiced, are not necessarily the ones to be defended; it is not the best of all possible sex-worlds that we are living in. Sex, therefore, is supposed to be altered" (64).

3. Chris Jenks makes a related comment about Bataille, writing that the conflation of violence and the erotic in his work "does not always claim a sympathetic audience. One might imagine that a range of feminists would decry such a standpoint while at the same time mobilizing the concept of transgression as a weapon in identity politics" (98).

4. Dworkin is predictably unimpressed by this argument, labeling Carter a "pseudofeminist" and stating that she occupies "a realm of literary affectation heretofore reserved for the boys" (*Pornography* 84).

5. It is also worth noting here that other forms of "inappropriate" material have been co-opted by certain forms of adult entertainment. Linda Martín Alcoff and Laura Gray-Rosendale note that there is a "market among pornographers for survivors; for example, *Penthouse* magazine paid Jessica Hahn—a rape survivor from a highly publicized case involving television evangelist Jim Bakker—large sums of money to pose, and has tried to entice other publicly known survivors to appear in the magazine as well" (221). See also my discussion of the recent controversy over *Hustler*'s attempts to obtain crime scene photographs (Chapter 4).

2. Rethinking Transgression

1. Predictably, the controversy did little to diminish the public's interest in the novel, and it went on to sell "well over half a million copies," thereby becoming "the first German book to top Amazon's global bestseller list" (Aitkenhead,

interview with Roche). It has even been adapted for the German stage, and a recent theatrical run "sold out for weeks in the respectable market town of Halle" (Caesar, interview with Roche).

2. If mere proximity to porn is enough to evoke the specter of a rebellious violation of taboos, then porn itself is surely viewed as a willfully renegade realm at the margins of culture—a domain of illicit pleasures and subversive affronts to bourgeois sensibilities. I argue that this conceptualization of pornography is an inaccurate, or at least incomplete, reflection of a contemporary pornographic landscape which, as a PBS *Frontline* documentary recently noted, is now associated with big businesses such as AT&T—the communications company ranked eighth in the Fortune 500 for 2009 (Birger).

3. Ed Caesar, for example, remarks that one particular "episode concerning an incident of hemoglobin-rich cunnilingus reversed [his] breakfast," whereas Sophie Harrison notes that the passage in which Helen "rips open her own wound to prolong her stay in hospital is [. . .] challenging for the weak-stomached reader."

4. The linkage of sex with transgression also may result from the exhilarating and pseudo-erotic thrill that attaches itself to the idea of violating taboos. This is discussed in Chapter 1.

5. Tim Dean also is aware that even non-normative sexualities are no longer inherently or necessarily taboo-busting, and states that "lesbian and gay sexualities have no essential or privileged relation to transgression. There is nothing necessarily revolutionary or, indeed, politically progressive about same-sex desires, practices, identities and representations today" (68).

6. See Part II for further analysis of this slippage of contemporary understandings of the pornographic, and for a discussion of the complex issues that arise from the troubling intersection of sex, violence, and disgust within certain types of commercial adult entertainment.

3. Sex and Disgust in Popular Culture

1. For a potted history of the video, see the "2 Girls 1 Cup" entry on the *Know Your Meme* website (Dubs 2009).

2. Although aversion may of course appear to paradoxically enhance erotic desire at times—for "it often seems that, by overcoming a resistance, desire becomes more meaningful" (Bataille, "The Phaedra Complex" 253)—it is not the sexual that is most immediately or obviously at stake here.

3. To some extent, we might argue that shock sites seem to enhance or exacerbate certain tendencies present within Internet culture more generally; the idea of unwelcome and intrusive imagery is common not only to these extreme materials but to pop-up adverts, mislabeled links, banner adverts, and so on.

4. As Linda Williams notes in *Screening Sex*, there has been "a significant escalation in the expectation of what pornography delivers" in recent decades

(312). Rather than merely being expected to trigger arousal, "there is now an assumption that masturbation is the very point of the human–screen interface" (312).

5. After all, as Kristeva remarks, abjection attracts as well as repulses: "many victims of the abject are its fascinated victims" (9).

Part II

4. "Not All of It Will Get Your Dick Hard": Pornography and Displacement

1. Maddison notes that the actress Jewel DeNyle is slapped sixty-six times during the opening sex scene, whereas porn star Taylor St Claire, playing a pregnant victim, is slapped and punched more than two-hundred times during the course of her scene (45–46).

2. Sade's perceived links with politics, in the form of his role in the French Revolution, is arguably part of the reason for the resurgence of interest in his work during that other period of perceived political upheaval, the 1960s. In "Liberating Sade," James A. Steintrager argues that "Sade's status in the 1960s was underwritten by the fact that the man and his writings seemed to confirm already existing and increasingly disseminated theories that posed sexual liberation as the key to liberation *tout court*" (362). See Part I for a critique of this take on transgression, politics, and sexuality.

3. This is interesting when one considers the focus on hard-core pornography as a "pure example of obscenity" without redeeming social value (Williams, *Screening Sex* 16). The serious political value that the *Miller* test for obscenity—established in the 1973 Supreme Court case of *Miller v. California*—views as a protection against accusations of obscenity can in fact be viewed as a central part of the genre's genealogy.

4. Gilles Deleuze also links this element of Freud's thinking to masochism: "Freud suggested the hypothesis of 'libidinal sympathetic coexcitation,' according to which processes and excitations over-stepping certain quantitative limits become erotically charged. Such a hypothesis recognizes the existence of an irreducible masochistic basis" (105).

5. In a 2004 essay on "the growing vogue for shock tactics in French cinema over the past decade," James Quandt discusses contemporary avant-garde cinema as representing a kind of blending of vitality and nihility, where "rivers of viscera and spumes of sperm" become interchangeable, and where it no longer matters whether flesh is "nubile or gnarled," just so long as it's exposed, prised open, and tested by the visceral forces of sex and violence.

6. Indeed, the eighteenth-century thinker Adam Smith suggests that pain "is a more pungent sensation than pleasure" (53), and may therefore be easier to

communicate and to discern. If "our sympathy with pain, though it falls greatly short of what is naturally felt by the sufferer, is generally a more lively and distinct perception than our sympathy with pleasure" (53), then suffering may be a more efficient and successful vehicle for a generalized frenzy of the visible.

    7. See the introduction to Part I for an analysis of Flynt's corporate persona.

    8. See Shannon McCaffrey's article for the *Huffington Post*.

    9. As Sarah Leonard notes, "Fascination with images of tortured or mutilated bodies makes us uneasy about the integrity of our own culture as well as the 'progress' attending technological development. Even more fundamentally, this provokes debates about the contemporary subject, who is often suspected of passivity (vis-à-vis images) coupled with an insatiable appetite for shock and novelty" (200). More on this throughout the section.

    10. The first printed instance of the use of this phrase that I have been able to find occurs in Peter Maas' account of the war in Bosnia, *Love Thy Neighbour: A Story of War* (1996). Maas talks about the sight of corpses and wounded bodies as "war porn" (133), and suggests that "War porn holds a strange attraction; most people want to look and don't want to look, but, in the end, there's a bit of the voyeur in most of us" (134).

    11. Matteo Pasquinelli explains that, although "English-speaking journalism defines as war porn the popular tabloids and government talk-shows [sic] fascination with super-sized weapons and well-polished uniforms, hi-tech tanks and infrared-controlled bombs" ("WARPORN WARPUNK!"), the term also can refer to a subgenre of adult entertainment that "simulates violent sex scenes between soldiers or the rape of civilians" ("WARPORN WARPUNK!"). As seen here, a range of other material also can be brought under this rubric.

    12. The Private First Class Lynndie England character is shown up as being white trash, with all the classist connotations of ignorance, bigotry, and racism that that brings with it, saying that she wants to go back home to her "trailer." This is hardly sufficient to suggest any meaningful attempt at satire, however.

    13. I intended to include a screen grab from *Gag Factor 15* at this point, but the copyright holder refused permission to use the image. I also wanted to include images depicting the positioning of this opening scene and *Gag Factor* DVD box covers but, again, permission to use the images was refused. As it is, I have done my best to describe these visuals in as accurate a fashion as possible. Elements of my descriptions inevitably are somewhat subjective, however.

    14. Like the "2 Girls 1 Cup" reaction videos discussed in Chapter 3, the involuntary shudder produced by an overstimulated gag reflex is central to the aesthetics of this series. Tim Stüttgen commented on the rise of irrumatio in hard-core pornography: "Gagging is a popular act in contemporary porn and an intensification of the blowjob, a deep penetration of the mouth, an obvious staging of male power in sex performance" ("Disidentification in the Center of Power" 52).

    15. And vice versa. The concepts of intensity, sexuality, and transgression coalesce in too many ways to permit of a simple hierarchy or cause-and-effect narrative.

5. Prurience and Postmodernism

1. See Jameson's *Postmodernism, or the Logic of Late Capitalism.*
2. Coincidentally, Žižek links this contemporary preoccupation to the work of Bataille, suggesting that it is an "urge to 'go to the very end,' to the extreme experience of the Impossible as the only way of being authentic, which makes Bataille *the* philosopher of the passion for the Real" (*The Puppet and the Dwarf* 55).
3. The same may be said of those who seek out so-called "mondo" movies that, since 1963's *Mondo Cane*, have "combined authentic and faked footage of a variety of bizarre and repulsive scenes" (Schaefer 289), including scenes of death.
4. The irony is, of course, that although the body is free to indulge itself virtually (so long as it has access to a valid credit card or is still on good enough terms with the mind to persuade it to hack into a network), it actually faces rather stringent physical limitations. In the world of *Oryx and Crake*, the scientific elite and their children live in guarded compounds, access in and out of which is strictly policed by a private corporate security force.

6. Violence, Sympathy, Titillation: The Body in a State of Intensity

1. Spectacle is a useful concept for our purposes, in that its range is wide and its objects diverse. Indeed—unlike transgression and prurience, which tend to be particularly associated with the sexual—the term *spectacle* is not commonly understand as belonging to one particular sphere or affective realm. As Eric Schaefer suggests, it can refer to "something that is presented to fascinate the eye of the spectator," "can be beautiful or hideous, the familiar presented in a unique way or the uncommon," and "invariably exerts an immediate, affective response in the spectator: loathing or lust, anxiety or amazement" (76).
2. See Dana Willhoit, "Wilson Will Avoid Jail In Plea Deal."
3. Susan Sontag's thought-provoking (if problematic) comments regarding the Abu Ghraib images seem relevant here: "An erotic life is, for more and more people, that which can be captured in digital photographs and on video. And perhaps the torture is more attractive, as something to record, when it has a sexual component. It is surely revealing, as more and more Abu Ghraib photographs enter public view, that torture photographs are interleaved with pornographic images of American soldiers having sex with one another" ("Regarding the Torture of Others").
4. But, of course, this link is not in itself sufficient to position the images as linked to the porn industry, for although amateur pornography's familiar quality of "flash-lit messiness" pervades many of the pictures from the prisoner camp (Campbell 67), this low-tech aesthetic is also familiar to us from casual snapshots and the personal image archives of Facebook and MySpace. As Peter Campbell

notes, the images of torture feel uncannily like "cousins to those that sit in our own digital cameras" (67).

5. Butler even feels compelled to remind the reader that "Pornography, after all, has many non-violent versions and several genres that are clearly 'vanilla' at best, and whose worst crime seems to be the failure to supply an innovative plot" (91). However, much of her argument in this text centers on the idea of framing—a way of presenting or re-presenting a deed that "implicitly guides the interpretation" of that deed (8). This is a mobile process, for "Although the image surely lands in new contexts, it also creates new contexts by virtue of that landing, becoming a part of the very process through which new contexts are delimited and formed" (9). If, as Butler suggests in *Frames of War*, images are perpetually available for recontextualizing, then they also are perpetually available for pornographic appropriation. Butler's objection to Bourke can be little more than strategic, for her own argument allows for flexibility in terms of contexts of reception, from which the experience of prurience, titillation, or even arousal cannot justifiably be excluded.

6. This may in fact point to wider problems with the designation "warporn," which may potentially generate or foreground concerns about pornography at the expense of concerns regarding war. See the conclusion.

7. We might think of the person of sentiment here as an individual invested with a quality akin to Adam Smith's idea of humanity, which consists of "the exquisite fellow-feeling which the spectator entertains with the sentiments of the persons principally concerned, so as to grieve for their sufferings, to resent their injuries, and to rejoice at their good fortune" (223). It is telling, when one considers the gendered implications of the idea of sentimentality, that Smith should attribute these qualities primarily to women (223).

8. Eve Kosofsky Sedgwick raises a related point: "The sacralising contagion of tears was the much re-enacted primal scene of the sentimental in the eighteenth century. If its early celebrants found it relatively (only relatively) easy to take for granted the disinterestedness and beneficence of the process by which a viewer 'sympathized' with the sufferings of a person viewed, however, every psychological and philosophic project of the same period gave new facilities for questioning or even discrediting that increasingly unsimple-looking bond [. . .] Most obviously, the position of sentimental spectatorship seemed to offer coverture for differences in material wealth (the bourgeois weeping over the spectacle of poverty) or sexual entitlement (the man swooning over the spectacle of female virtue under siege)—material or sexual exploitations that might even be perpetuated or accelerated by the nonaccountable viewer satisfactions that made the point of their rehearsal" (215). We engage with these kinds of ideas throughout the current chapter.

9. A related point might be made about Catherine MacKinnon's activist writings. Parveen Adams and Mark Cousins, for example, suggest that the collapsing of representation and event within MacKinnon's work "seeks to bind the reader to the moral intention of her discourse while deriving all the secret plea-

sures of 'shocking' the reader that are the perverse prerogative of the moralist down the ages" (66).

10. Indeed, the political causes of feminism and abolitionism have a long history of linkage. After all, as Karen Sánchez-Eppler remarks, "it is the problems of having, representing, or interpreting a body that structure both feminist and abolitionist discourses, since the rhetorics of the two reforms share the recognition that, for both women and blacks, it is their physical difference from the cultural norms of white masculinity that obstructs their claim to personhood" (93).

11. Sentiment is arguably a key tool for some varieties of feminism. As Lauren Berlant notes, sentimentality has played a role within women's discourse for many decades, and has been important in enabling certain forms of female community in the West. She argues that, in the nineteenth century, "sentimental ideology served as a structure of consent in which domestically atomized women found in the consumption of popular texts the experience of intimate collective identity, a feminine counterpublic sphere whose values remained fundamentally private" (270).

12. Such dehistoricizing comments indicate some of the problems with feminist activism's attempt to align women with any and all cultural victims; they can elide the particularities of oppression and can attempt to absorb other forms of subjugation. This was a tendency, too, within nineteenth-century feminist political agitation, where the sufferings of women and slaves were frequently conflated. See Sánchez-Eppler (95).

13. This may go some way toward explaining the particular popularity of one usage of the porn suffix: "torture porn."

14. It should be noted, however, that Donnerstein and his fellow media effects researchers Linz and Penrod "now, rather disingenuously, criticize the uses to which their research has been put by Dworkin and MacKinnon in submissions to the US Meese Commission on Pornography of 1986" (Segal 37).

15. I must confess to having come across no such images in the "Abu Ghraib files" so carefully archived on the *Salon* website, and wonder if Leonard may, as a woman of feeling, be to some extent inadvertently staging a sentimental fantasy of her own regarding the tortures at the prisoner camp, projecting herself into the body of the other in the style invited by certain abolitionist texts.

Part III

Pornography and the Real

1. This is not unique to LeRoy's work. As Carol Sarler notes, "Sometimes misery porn comes pretty close to common porn. In a single week last year, the top ten paperbacks invited you to enter the world of *Don't Tell Mummy* (a number one bestseller), *Betrayed* ('a memoir of child abuse,' in which a girl accuses both

her parents of sexual assault) and *Silent Sisters* (siblings on surviving abuse)" ("I'll tell you what's Ugly").

7. Pornography and the Appetite for Authenticity

1. Philip Lewin and J. Patrick Williams argue that "individuals celebrate authenticity in order to balance the extreme dislocation that characterizes life in the postmodern world, in which traditional concepts of self, community and space have collapsed. This collapse has led to a widespread internalization of doubt and an obsession with distinguishing the real from the fake" (66).

2. It is perhaps worth noting here that there are other currents within contemporary culture that seek to resist authenticity. Dollimore, for example, notes that camp "delights in the selfsame artifice which others distrust" (228), staging a resistance to the ideal of authenticity: "The hollowing-out of the deep self is pure pleasure, a release from the subjective correlatives of dominant morality (normality, authenticity, etc.)—one reason why camp also mocks the *Angst*-ridden spiritual emptiness which characterizes the existential lament" (224). Such attempts to transgress authenticity as an ideal, of course, can be seen to shore up the concept as a norm. See Chapter 1.

3. As Benjamin Noys has noted, however, Badiou's concept of the real has wider implications than those suggested by the contemporary investment in trauma and abjection. The twentieth century's passion for the real is "instantiated in art in the violent subtraction of the 'real' through destroying the conventions of realist representation; in politics by the production of the 'new man' through the violent reworking of mass subjectivities; in science by the destabilization of reality to reveal the formalisable 'real'; and in love by the pursuit of *amour fou* that breaks open the constraints of socially sanctioned sexuality for the radical real of *jouissance*" ("Monumental Construction" 385). As Noys remarks, these wide-ranging concerns have largely been allowed to fall by the wayside in favor of a more limited "valorization of the material residues of the body" ("Monumental Construction" 386); "The 'real' is reduced to the real of suffering, extremity, anguish; incarnating a bodily version of the Sartrean practico-inert" ("Monumental Construction" 386).

4. This is perhaps related to Charles Guignon's suggestion that there is "a sort of counter-culture to the dominant culture of authenticity in contemporary society. This counter-culture encourages us to accept the fact that what lies within is characterized by aggression, cruelty and violence, and holds that authenticity is precisely a matter of getting in touch with and expressing those dark impulses and cravings" (104–05).

5. Not all pornographies, it should be noted, seek to cultivate an authenticity effect. Sadomasochistic texts are a key example here. Anne McClintock draws our attention to "the theatrical paraphernalia of S/M: boots, chains, leather, whips,

masks, costumes and scripts," and argues that "with its exaggerated emphasis on costume and scene S/M performs social power as scripted, and hence as permanently subject to change" ("Maid to Order" 237). Linda Williams, meanwhile, suggests that the acts displayed in sadomasochistic porn are precisely "problematic *as acts*: they move us by their sensationalism even more than 'hard-core' genital sex acts, and there is every reason to believe that they can really affect the bodies of their participants; yet they can also be acts in the theatrical sense of shows performed for oneself or others" (*Hard Core* 195). Exactly what such sexual performances achieve in terms of shaping sexual and gender politics is unclear, but such theatricality appears to be a key part of how the BDSM community understands itself and its representations, over and above any commitment to authenticity.

6. For a useful queer theoretical problematization of the focus on authenticity within subcultural pornographies, see Russo.

7. Indeed, pornography's links with ideas of authenticity apparently go back some time; Paula Findlen notes, "Renaissance pornographers often presented their work as the end of metaphor, a negation of the eloquence and erudition that defined humanist culture. They loudly proclaimed that their works laid bare the truth, stripped of all the metaphorical witticisms and allegories that characterized the contemporary culture of learning" (77). Like the pornographers of today, then, they sought to "unveil 'the thing' itself" (Findlen 77).

8. Krzywinska makes a similar point about the authenticating properties of diverse types of bodily by-product in her essay "The Dynamics of Squirting: Female Ejaculation and Lactation in Hardcore Film," arguing that "Within hardcore the male come-shot is an undeniable sign of authentic sexual pleasure and [. . .] lactation is subject to the same paradigm (this is of course a male genital paradigm)" (36).

8. Autobiography and/as the Real

1. The continuing prominence of reality television is demonstrated by some elements of the 2007 to 2008 Writer's Guild of America strike. The strike action included a focus on, among other things, the fact that the role of writers in shaping and narrativizing the raw material of reality TV shows was not appropriately recognized and not covered by the Guild's agreement with the Alliance of Motion Picture and Television Producers regarding minimum basic compensation (see Staruch).

2. The market has decreased more recently, with *The Bookseller* quoting research from Nielsen Bookscan (the retail monitoring service for English-language books) showing that at the start of 2008 sales of the top 10 bestselling misery memoirs in the United Kingdom dropped by 27% compared with the same period in 2007 (Page and Neill). However, interest in this type of material

remains. At the time of writing, there were two misery memoirs in the top 20 chart of bestselling nonfiction paperbacks ("Non Fiction PB"), and Kate McCann's account of the unsolved kidnapping of her daughter Madeline was the bestselling title overall ("Official UK Top 50").

3. As with the output of Extreme Associates, this material has drawn condemnation even from those close to the porn industry. The review of *Max Extreme 4* on the *Rog Reviews* website expresses discomfort at the depiction of underage sex, triggered by the dialogue between Hardcore and his co-star Regan Starr: ""You can' tell anyone Max, cuz I'm only twelve and a half years old." God damn it, Max the fuck is that about? [. . .] Challenge the law all you want, but that shit has no fucking place in any tape you expect me to jerk off to. (Note, after this, I ff scanned, but did manage to catch Regan telling Max how her teacher fucked her in a broom closet and how her uncle liked fucking her) [*sic*]" (Pipe).

4. The representation and the reality of abuse should not be conflated, of course. Some of the least convincing (and most hyperbolic) anti-porn theories seek to position the recording and consuming of acts of atrocity and violence as a perpetration of violence and atrocity, which works to overstate the effect of such representations while simultaneously downplaying the magnitude of the original crimes. If the transgression of consuming and engaging in acts of violence are positioned as being on a par, the perceived effect of consumption is not only unduly amplified, but the significance of perpetration is unjustifiably downgraded. Linda Williams makes this point with typical verve and intelligence in her introduction to *Porn Studies*: "Such an argument encourages us to shift attention from the real crime [. . .] to the supposedly more heinous crime of filming it" (11), and misdirects our energies towards combating representations rather than addressing the violations represented.

5. Claire Lynch makes a similar point: "Readers look to autobiography with an assumption that (some) truth will be told and that the text is essentially different from other genres because its origin is confession" (211).

6. Other recent notable examples of fake memoirs include Anthony Godby Johnson's *A Rock and A Hard Place: One Boy's Triumphant Story* (1993), Binjamin Wilkomirski's *Fragments: Memories of a Wartime Childhood* (1995), Misha Defonseca's *Misha: A Mémoire of the Holocaust Years* (1997), Norma Khouri's *Honor Lost: Love and Death in Modern-Day Jordan* (2003), and Herman Rosenblat's *Angel at the Fence: The True Story of a Love That Survived*, which was due to be published in 2009, but which was exposed as a fake before it hit the shelves.

7. Writers, too, have found these peculiar stories of literary fakery appealing and inspirational. Percival Everett's novel *Erasure*, for instance, recalls such scandals in its depiction of a high-brow literary novelist who submits a parody of a "black" memoir—an account of misogyny, crime, and poverty—to a publisher, only to have it accepted and lauded as masterpiece. Attracted by the substantial advance, but ashamed of the work itself, he finds himself drawn into a farcical hoax in which he is forced to masquerade as an ex-con. Armistead Maupin's

The Night Listener, too, is highly reminiscent of both the LeRoy case and the Vicki Johnson/Anthony Godby Johnson scandal in that it depicts a man seemingly being duped by an older woman posing as an abused and HIV-positive adolescent boy.

8. This difficulty is reflected in the development of neologisms such as "autofiction" to describe texts that disturb the fiction/life writing binary. This term, as E. H. Jones notes, refers to writings in which the "author and protagonist bear the same name, but in which there is an overt attempt to fictionalize" (175). There is, however, "little consensus about the term's real meaning or its validity" (Jones, "Autofiction" 174). The idea of autofiction has some relevance in terms of the LeRoy case, but the fact that it can be seen as either "one of autobiography's many variants" (Jones, "Autofiction" 178) or as "a recent development within the long-standing but critically neglected tradition of the autobiographical novel" (Jones, "Autofiction" 179) means that it is not always especially useful as a critical term.

9. Laura Marcus shares the view that "autobiography is important as the most conspicuous example of a 'genre' that exposes the heterogeneity of all literary productions" (14), and suggests that much contemporary interest in autobiographical writing stems precisely from its "instability in terms of the postulated opposites between self and world, literature and history, fact and fiction, subject and object" (14).

10. This refers to individual works containing the words "trauma" or "traumatic," or "abuse" or "abused," in their titles or in the complier's description of them. In the case of trauma, there are two dedicated books, forty-seven articles, and two theses, making a total of fifty-one unique works. The nine separate entries on abuse are all articles (see Wachter).

11. We might consider the recent *A Gay Girl in Damascus* blog hoax in relation to these comments. See Addley and Quinn.

9. Sex, Trauma, and the Authenticity Effect

1. The issues of identity raised by the LeRoy hoax seem to be reflected in a pervasive uncertainty about how to spell his name. Is it J.T. or JT; LeRoy, Le Roy, or Leroy? There are differences evident even in his books themselves, but I favor the form deployed in his later works, *The Heart is Deceitful Above All Things* and *Harold's End*. I therefore use the spelling "JT LeRoy" throughout this chapter. I also predominantly refer to LeRoy as if he was male, treating the authorial persona as a kind of character in an attempt to avoid awkwardness and confusion.

2. Lane has little sympathy with LeRoy's readers, however, writing, "He is just the hoax that the rage for confessional writing has been asking for" (95).

3. One key reason for the credulous response to LeRoy's work may well be the politics surrounding survivors' discourse, and anxieties regarding the idea of the vulnerable and helpless being disbelieved. As Gilmore puts it, "When the

contest is waged over who can tell the truth, the risk of being accused of lying (or malingering, or inflating, or whining) threatens the writer into continued silence" ("Limit-Cases" 129).

4. Even the materiality of LeRoy's work has been linked to ideas of self-disclosure and therapeutic endeavor. In his review of *Harold's End* for the *Gay and Lesbian Review*, for example, James Withers remarks that the work "has the shape and feel of a personal diary or journal. Small in size and squarish in shape, the book sports a black cover (under the desk jacket) and, inside, the text is illustrated throughout with drawings of the story's characters by Australian artist Cherry Hood" (45). All of this makes perfect sense, Withers suggests, because "the story the narrator shares is the type of tale diaries are meant for: unabashedly intimate and filled with discoveries most of us would keep to ourselves" (45).

5. In this sense, *Sarah* is reminiscent of Jeanette Winterson's novel *Oranges are Not the Only Fruit* (1985), which tells a tale inspired by real events in a manner that, rather a-typically, uses fantastical or magical episodes and imagery.

6. See also Baudrillard's comments on production, seduction, and pornography in *Forget Foucault* (21).

7. This recalls Žižek's discussion of the Real in *The Puppet and the Dwarf*, in which he asks "what if this very notion that delusive everyday reality is a veil concealing the Horror of the unbearable Thing is false, what if the ultimate veil concealing the Real is the very notion of the horrible Thing behind the veil?" (67)

10. Conclusion: Pornographication and the Explosion of the Pornographic

1. This is reflected in the slippage occurring around the word "sex," too. As Feona Attwood notes in her introduction to *Mainstreaming Sex: The Sexualization of Western Culture*, "As sex appears to become more and more important to contemporary cultures, permeating every aspect of our existence and providing a language for talking about all kinds of things, its meaning becomes more elusive and more ambiguous; politicians and their dossiers can be 'sexed up,' and the term 'sexy' may simply indicate something that is noteworthy" (xv).

2. See my discussion of the dilution of "pornographic" as an adjectival label in Chapter 6.

3. As McClintock puts it in her discussion of the Abu Ghraib scandal, conflating the images of abuse with porn not only "*banalized the torture*" but also "*monsterized pornography* as an ahistorical, unchanging, universal realm of inherent violence and torture, which it demonstrably is not" ("Paranoid Empire" 62).

4. Of course, as shown in Chapter 4, pornography and political critique have not historically been seen as mutually exclusive.

5. It is for this reason that Pasquinelli can claim that a certain right-on variety of "contemporary porn is less 'pornographic'" (*Animal Spirits* 200); it

may be sexually explicit, but it is also somehow sanitized by its own politically progressive intentions.

6. The extent of the circulation of this term is revealed by a simple Google search; as of 15 June 2011, a search for the exact phrase "travel porn" generated more than 25,000 results.

7. This idea of "food porn" has achieved a sufficient degree of cultural visibility to warrant its own Wikipedia entry.

Works Cited

Books

Arcand, Bernard. *The Jaguar and the Anteater: Pornography Degree Zero*. Trans. Wayne Grady. London: Verso, 1993. Print.
Attwood, Feona, ed. *Porn.com*. New York: Peter Lang, 2010. Print.
Atwood, Margaret. *Oryx and Crake*. London: Bloomsbury, 2003. Print.
Badiou, Alain. *The Century*. Trans. Alberto Toscano. Cambridge: Polity Press, 2007. Print.
———. *Saint Paul: The Foundation of Universalism*. Trans. Ray Brassier. Stanford: Stanford University Press, 2003. Print.
Ballard, J. G. *The Atrocity Exhibition*. London: Harper Perennial, 2006. Print.
Barry, Peter. *Beginning Theory: An Introduction to Literary and Cultural Theory*. Manchester: Manchester University Press, 2002. Print.
Bataille, Georges. *Eroticism*. Trans. Mary Dalwood. London: Marion Boyars, 1987. Print.
———. *The Tears of Eros*. Trans. Peter Connor. San Francisco: City Lights, 1989. Print.
Baudrillard, Jean. *Forget Foucault*. Trans. Phil Beitchman, Lee Hildreth, and Mark Polizzoti. New York: Semiotext(e), 1987. Print.
———. *Simulations*. Trans. Paul Foss, Paul Patton, and Philip Beitchman. New York: Semiotext(e), 1983. Print.
Bersani, Leo. *The Freudian Body: Psychoanalysis and Art*. New York: Columbia University Press, 1986. Print.
Bersani, Leo, and Ulysse Dutoit. *The Forms of Violence: Narrative in Assyrian Art and Modern Culture*. New York: Schocken Books, 1985. Print.
Bewes, Timothy. *Cynicism and Postmodernity*. London: Verso, 1997. Print.
Boyle, David. *Authenticity: Brands, Fakes, Spin and the Lust for Real Life*. London: Harper Perennial, 2004. Print.
Briscoe, Constance. *Ugly*. London: Hodder and Stoughton, 2009. Print.
Butler, Judith. *Frames of War: When is Life Grievable?* London: Verso, 2009. Print.
Carter, Angela. *The Sadeian Woman: An Exercise in Cultural History*. London: Virago, 1979. Print.

Defonseca, Misha. *Misha: A Mémoire of the Holocaust Years*. Gloucester, MA: Mount Ivy Press, 1997. Print.
Douglas, Mary. *Purity and Danger: An Analysis of the Concept of Pollution and Taboo*. London: Routledge, 2002. Print.
Dworkin, Andrea. *Pornography: Men Possessing Women*. London: The Women's Press, 1981. Print.
Evans, Mary. *Missing Persons: The Impossibility of Auto/biography*. London: Routledge, 1999. Print.
Everett, Percival. *Erasure*. London: Faber and Faber, 2003. Print.
Feminists Against Censorship. *Pornography and Feminism: The Case Against Censorship*. Ed. Gillian Rodgerson and Elizabeth Wilson. London: Lawrence and Wishart, 1991. Print.
Foucault, Michel. *The Will to Knowledge: The History of Sexuality: Volume 1*. Trans. Robert Hurley. London: Penguin, 1998. Print.
French, Philip, and Julian Petley. *Censoring the Moving Image*. London: Seagull Books, 2007. Print.
Freud, Sigmund. *The Pelican Freud Library, Volume 7: On Sexuality: Three Essays on the Theory of Sexuality and Other Works*. Trans. James Strachey. Ed. Angela Richards. Harmondsworth: Penguin, 1983. Print.
Frey, James. *A Million Little Pieces*. London: John Murray, 2003. Print.
Gibson, Pamela Church, ed. *More Dirty Looks: Gender, Pornography and Power*. London: British Film Institute, 2004. Print.
Golomb, Jacob. *In Search of Authenticity: From Kierkegaard to Camus*. Abingdon: Routledge, 1995. Print.
Guignon, Charles. *On Being Authentic*. London: Routledge, 2004. Print.
Hunt, Lynn, ed. *The Invention of Pornography: Obscenity and the Origins of Modernity, 1500–1800*. New York: Zone Books, 1996. Print.
Jacobs, Katrien. *Netporn: DIY Web Culture and Sexual Politics*. Lanham, MD: Rowman and Littlefield, 2007. Print.
Jameson, Fredric. *Postmodernism: or, the Cultural Logic of Late Capitalism*. London: Verso, 1992. Print.
Jenks, Chris. *Transgression*. London: Routledge, 2003. Print.
Jensen, Robert. *Getting Off: Pornography and the End of Masculinity*. Cambridge, MA: South End Press, 2007. Print.
Johnson, Anthony Godby. *A Rock and a Hard Place: One Boy's Triumphant Story*. New York: Signet, 1994. Print.
Jones, Margaret B. *Love and Consequences: A Memoir of Hope and Survival*. New York: Riverhead, 2008. Print.
Jour, Belle de. *The Intimate Adventures of a London Call Girl*. London: Weidenfeld and Nicolson, 2005. Print.
Juffer, Jane. *At Home With Pornography: Women, Sex, and Everyday Life*. New York: New York University Press, 1998. Print.
Kauffman, Linda S. *Bad Girls and Sick Boys: Fantasies in Contemporary Art and Culture*. Berkeley: University of California Press, 1998. Print.

Kavka, Misha. *Reality Television, Affect and Intimacy: Reality Matters*. Basingstoke: Palgrave Macmillan, 2008. Print.
Kendrick, Walter. *The Secret Museum: Pornography in Modern Culture*. Berkeley: University of California Press, 1996. Print.
Khouri, Norma. *Honor Lost: Love and Death in Modern-Day Jordan*. New York: Simon and Schuster, 2003. Print.
Klossowski, Pierre. *Sade my Neighbour*. Trans. Alphonso Lingis. London: Quartet Books, 1992. Print.
Knoop, Savannah. *Girl Boy Girl: How I Became JT LeRoy*. New York: Seven Stories Press, 2008. Print.
Kristeva, Julia. *Powers of Horror: An Essay on Abjection*. Trans. Leon S. Roudiez. New York: Columbia University Press, 1982. Print.
Krzywinska, Tanya. *Sex and the Cinema*. London: Wallflower Press, 2006. Print.
Lane, Richard J. *Jean Baudrillard*. Abingdon: Routledge, 2009. Print.
Lehman, Peter, ed. *Pornography: Film and Culture*. New Brunswick: Rutgers University Press, 2006. Print.
Lejeune, Phillipe. *On Autobiography*. Trans. Katherine Leary. Minneapolis: University of Minnesota Press, 1989. Print.
LeRoy, JT. *Harold's End*. San Francisco: Last Gasp, 2004. Print.
———. *The Heart is Deceitful Above All Things*. London: Bloomsbury, 2001. Print.
———. *Sarah*. London: Bloomsbury, 2000. Print.
Lindholm, Charles. *Culture and Authenticity*. Oxford: Blackwell, 2008. Print.
Lyotard, Jean-François. *Libidinal Economy*. Trans. Iain Hamilton Grant. Bloomington: Indiana University Press, 1993. Print.
Maas, Peter. *Love Thy Neighbour: A Story of War*. London: Papermac, 1996. Print.
Marcus, Steven. *The Other Victorians: A Study of Sexuality and Pornography in Mid-Nineteenth Century England*. London: Corgi, 1969. Print.
Massumi, Brian. *Parables for the Virtual: Movement, Affect, Sensation*. Durham, NC: Duke University Press, 2002. Print.
Maupin, Armistead. *The Night Listener*. London: Black Swan, 2001. Print.
Miller, William Ian. *The Anatomy of Disgust*. Cambridge, MA: Harvard University Press, 1997. Print.
Millet, Catherine. *The Sexual Life of Catherine M*. Trans. Adriana Hunter. London: Corgi, 2003. Print.
Noys, Benjamin. *Georges Bataille: A Critical Introduction*. London: Pluto Press, 2000. Print.
Nussbaum, Martha C. *Hiding from Humanity: Disgust, Shame, and the Law*. Princeton: Princeton University Press, 2004. Print.
O'Toole, Laurence. *Pornocopia: Porn, Sex, Technology and Desire*. London: Serpent's Tail, 1999. Print.
Pasquinelli, Matteo. *Animal Spirits: A Bestiary of the Commons*. Rotterdam: NAi Publishers, 2008. Print.

Paasonen, Susanna. *Carnal Resonance: Affect and Online Pornography*. Cambridge, MA: MIT Press, 2011. Print.
Roche, Charlotte. *Wetlands*. Trans. Tim Mohr. London: Fourth Estate, 2009. Print.
Sade, Marquis de. *The 120 Days of Sodom and Other Writings*. Trans. Austryn Wainhouse and Richard Seaver. London: Arrow Books, 1990. Print.
Sanders, E. P. *Paul: A Very Short Introduction*. Oxford: Oxford University Press, 2001. Print.
Schaefer, Eric. *"Bold! Daring! Shocking! True!" A History of Exploitation Films, 1919–1959*. Durham, NC: Duke University Press, 1999. Print.
Shields, David. *Reality Hunger: A Manifesto*. London: Hamish Hamilton, 2010. Print.
Smith, Adam. *The Theory of Moral Sentiments*. Cambridge: Cambridge University Press, 2004. Print.
Sontag, Susan. *Regarding the Pain of Others*. London: Penguin, 2004. Print.
Stallybrass, Peter and Allon White. *The Politics and Poetics of Transgression*. Ithaca: Cornell University Press, 1986. Print.
Wakefield, Neville. *Postmodernism: The Twilight of the Real*. London: Pluto Press, 1990. Print.
Wilkomirski, Binjamin. *Fragments: Memories of a Wartime Childhood*. Trans. Carol Brown Janeway. New York: Schocken, 1997. Print.
Williams, Linda. *Hard Core: Power, Pleasure, and the "Frenzy of the Visible."* Berkeley: University of California Press, 1999. Print.
———, ed. *Porn Studies*. Durham, NC: Duke University Press, 2004. Print.
———. *Screening Sex*. Durham, NC: Duke University Press, 2008. Print.
Winterson, Jeanette. *Oranges Are Not the Only Fruit*. London: Vintage, 2001. Print.
Wood, Marcus. *Slavery, Empathy, and Pornography*. Oxford: Oxford University Press, 2002. Print.
Žižek, Slavoj. *The Puppet and the Dwarf: The Perverse Core of Christianity*. Cambridge, MA: MIT Press, 2003. Print.
———. *Welcome to the Desert of the Real! Five Essays on September 11 and Related Dates*. London: Verso, 2002. Print.

Articles and Interviews

"2 Girls 1 Cup: The Real Poop." *The Smoking Gun*. Turner Sports and Entertainment Digital Network, 2007. Web. 10 May 2011. <http://www.thesmokinggun.com/documents/revolting/2-girls-1-cup-real-poop>.
"The Abu Ghraib Files: Chapter 2." *Salon*. 14 March 2006. Web. 01 Oct. 2009. <http://www.salon.com/news/abu_ghraib/2006/03/14/chapter_2/2.html>.
"The Abu Ghraib Files: Chapter 6." *Salon*. 14 March 2006. Web. 01 Oct. 2009. <http://www.salon.com/news/abu_ghraib/2006/03/14/chapter_6/25.html>.
Adams, Parveen, and Mark Cousins. "The truth on assault." *The Emptiness of the Image: Psychoanalysis and Sexual Differences*. By Adams. London: Routledge, 1996. 57–69. Print.

Addley, Esther. "So bad it's good." *Guardian Unlimited*. 15 June 2007. Web. 27 Jan. 2011. <http://www.guardian.co.uk/society/2007/jun/15/childrensservices.biography>.

Addley, Esther, and Ben Quinn. "Second lesbian blogger exposed as a man." *Guardian Unlimited*. 14 June 2011. Web. 05 July 2011. <http://www.guardian.co.uk/media/2011/jun/14/second-lesbian-blogger-exposed-paula-brooks?intcmp=239>.

Albert, Laura. Interview with Nathaniel Rich. "Being JT LeRoy." *The Paris Review* 178 (2006). Web. 07 Dec. 2010. <http://www.theparisreview.org/miscellaneous/ 5664/being-jt-leroy-nathaniel-rich>.

Albright, Daniel. "Literary and psychological models of the self." *The Remembering Self: Construction and Accuracy in the Self-narrative*. Ed. Ulric Neisser and Robyn Fivush. Cambridge: Cambridge University Press, 1994. 19-40. Print.

Alcoff, Linda Martín, and Laura Gray-Rosendale. "Survivor Discourse: Transgression or Recuperation?" *Getting a Life: Everyday Uses of Autobiography*. Ed. Sidonie Smith and Julia Watson. Minneapolis: University of Minnesota Press, 1996. 198-225. Print.

"Arrests in abduction of American worker." *NBC News*. 21 May 2004. Web. 02 Aug. 2010. <http://www.msnbc.msn.com/id/4953015/>.

"'Asbo' and 'chav' make dictionary." *BBC News*. 08 June 2005. Web. 22 June 2011. <http://news.bbc.co.uk/1/hi/uk/4074760.stm>.

Attwood, Feona. "Introduction: The Sexualization of Culture." *Mainstreaming Sex: The Sexualization of Western Culture*." Ed. Attwood. London: I. B. Tauris, 2009. xiii-xxiv. Print.

———. "'Other' or 'One of Us'?: The Porn User in Public and Academic Discourse." *Participations: Journal of Audience and Reception Studies* 4:1. May 2007. Web. 16 Feb. 2011. <http://www.participations.org/Volume%204/Issue%201/ 4_01_attwood.htm>.

———. "Reading Porn: The Paradigm Shift in Pornography Research." *Sexualities* 5:1 (2002): 91-105. Sage. Web. 01 Oct. 2008.

Atwood, Margaret. "*The Handmaid's Tale* and *Oryx and Crake* 'In Context.'" *PMLA* 19: 3 (2004): 513-17. JSTOR. Web. 08 May 2010.

"Authors' Guidelines." *Silver Moon Books*. Shadowline Publishing Ltd, n.d. Web. 26 Jan. 2009. <http://www.adultbookshops.com/authors.html>.

Barthes, Roland. "The Death of the Author." *Image Music Text*. By Barthes. Trans. Stephen Heath. London: Fontana Press, 1977. 142-48. Print.

Bataille, Georges. "The Festival, or the Transgression of Prohibitions." *The Bataille Reader*. Ed. Fred Botting and Scott Wilson. Oxford: Blackwell, 1997. 248-53. Print.

———. "The Phaedra Complex." *The Bataille Reader*. Ed. Fred Botting and Scott Wilson. Oxford: Blackwell, 1997. 253-58. Print.

Baudrillard, Jean. "Dust Breeding." *CTheory.net*. Ed. Arthur Kroker and Marilouise Kroker. Trans. François Debrix. 10 Aug. 2001. Web. 07 Dec. 2010. <http://www.ctheory.net/printer.aspx?id=293>.

Beachy, Stephen. "Who is the Real JT LeRoy?: A Search for the True Identity of a Great Literary Hustler." *New York Magazine*. 10 Oct. 2005. Web. 07 Dec. 2010. <http://nymag.com/nymetro/news/people/features/14718/>.

Benedictus, Leo. "Embarrassing Bodies: medical porn or public health crusade?" *Guardian Unlimited*. 25 Jan. 2011. Web. 11 May 2011. <http://www.guardian.co.uk/lifeandstyle/2011/jan/25/embarrassing-bodies-medical-porn-or-crusade>.

Bergland, Betty. "Postmodernism and the Autobiographical Subject: Reconstructing the 'Other.'" *Autobiography and Postmodernism*. Ed. Kathleen Ashley, Leigh Gilmore, and Gerald Peters. Amherst: University of Massachusetts Press, 1994. 130–166. Print.

Berlant, Lauren. "The Female Woman: Fanny Fern and the Form of Sentiment." *The Culture of Sentiment: Race, Gander, and Sentimentality in Nineteenth-Century America*. Ed. Shirely Samuels. Oxford: Oxford University Press, 1992. 265–81. Print.

Bernardi, Daniel. "Interracial Joysticks: Pornography's Web of Racist Attractions." *Pornography: Film and Culture*. Ed. Peter Lehman. New Brunswick: Rutgers University Press, 2006. 220–43. Print.

———. "Racism and Pornography: Evidence, Paradigms, and Publishing." *Cinema Journal* 46: 4 (2007): 116–21. *Project Muse*. Web. 10 Oct. 2008.

Bersani, Leo. "Is the rectum a grave?" *October* 43 (1987): 197–222. *JSTOR*. Web. 02 Aug. 2008.

Birger, Jon. "Fortune 500: AT&T." *CNN Money*. 4 May 2009. Web. 27 June 2009. <http://money.cnn.com/magazines/fortune/fortune500/2009/snapshots/2756.html>.

Blum, Virginia L. "A response to Bruce Burgett." *American Literary History* 21:1 (2009): 87–95. *Project Muse*. Web. 25 May 2009.

Bone, James. "US paper admits rape images were net hoax." *Times Online*. 14 May 2004. Web. 02 Aug. 2010. <http://www.timesonline.co.uk/tol/news/world/iraq/article423443.ece>.

Bourke, Joanna. "Torture as Pornography." *Guardian Unlimited*. 07 May 2004. Web. 21 Oct. 2009. <http://www.guardian.co.uk/world/2004/may/07/gender.uk>.

Bouson, J. Brooks. "'It's Game Over Forever': Atwood's Satiric Vision of a Bioengineered Posthuman Future in *Oryx and Crake*." *The Journal of Commonwealth Literature* 39: 3 (2004): 139–56. *Sage*. Web. 08 May 2010.

Bozelka, Kevin John. Rev. of *Porn Studies*, ed. Linda Williams. *The Velvet Light Trap* 59 (2007): 69–71. *Project Muse*. Web. 28 Nov. 2009.

Breslin, Susannah. "To the Max." *The Reverse Cowgirl*. 06 Oct. 2008. Web. 09 Aug. 2011. <http://reversecowgirlblog.blogspot.com/2008/10/to-max.html>.

Bright, Susie. "Slash/Fraud: The Literary Origins of JT Leroy." *Susie Bright's Journal*. 12 Jan. 2006. Web. 04 June 2011. <http://susiebright.blogs.com/susie_brights_journal_/2006/01/slashfraud_the_.html>.

Brownmiller, Susan. "Women fight back." *Pornography: Private Right or Public Menace?* Ed. Robert M. Baird and Stuart E. Rosenbaum. Buffalo: Prometheus Books, 1991. 36–39. Print.

Bruner, Jerome. "The 'remembered' self." *The Remembering Self: Construction and Accuracy in the Self-narrative*. Ed. Ulric Neisser and Robyn Fivush. Cambridge: Cambridge University Press, 1994. 41–54. Print.

Burke, Jason. "Publishers battle to sign up Europe's sex sensation." *Guardian Unlimited*. 25 May 2008. Web. 20 April 2009. <http://www.guardian.co.uk/books/2008/may/25/news.germany>.

Butler, Heather. "What Do You Call a Lesbian with Long Fingers? The Development of Lesbian and Dyke Pornography." *Porn Studies*. Ed. Linda Williams. Durham, NC: Duke University Press, 2004. 167–97. Print.

Califia, Pat. "Introduction: Or it is Always Right to Rebel." *Public Sex: The Culture of Radical Sex*. By Califia. San Francisco: Cleis Press, 2000. xii–xxx. Print.

———. "The Obscene, Disgusting, and Vile Meese Commission Report." *Public Sex: The Culture of Radical Sex*. By Califia. San Francisco: Cleis Press, 2000. 42–53. Print.

Campbell, Peter. "The Lens of War." *New Left Review* 55 (2009): 65–72. Print.

Capino, José B. "Asian College Girls and Oriental Men with Bamboo Poles: Reading Asian Pornography." *Pornography: Film and Culture*. Ed. Peter Lehman. New Brunswick: Rutgers University Press, 2006. 206–19. Print.

Clover, Carol J. "Introduction." *Dirty Looks: Women, Pornography, Power*. Ed. Pamela Church Gibson and Roma Gibson. London: British Film Institute, 1993. 1–4. Print.

Cochrane, Kira. "A Literary Fraud Who is not a Fake." *New Statesman*. 28 June 2007. Web. 16 Dec. 2010. <http://www.newstatesman.com/north-america/2007/06/cochrane-leroy-albert-author>.

Codrescu, Andrei. "Adding to my Life." *Autobiography and Postmodernism*. Ed. Kathleen Ashley, Leigh Gilmore, and Gerald Peters. Amherst: University of Massachusetts Press, 1994. 21–30. Print.

Cohen, Derek. "Is Your Porn Collection Still Legal?" *Spanner Trust*. July 2008. Web. 06 Jan. 2009. <http://www.spannertrust.org/documents/possession_of_extreme_pornography_share.pdf>.

Collins, Ian. "Embarrassing Bodies: Collins On TV." *Ask Men UK*. IGN Entertainment, n.d. Web. 11 May 2011. < http://uk.askmen.com/entertainment/austin_500/596_embarrassing-bodies-collins-on-tv.html>.

Cooper, Dennis. "A JT Leroy riff." *Dennis Cooper's Blog*. 28 Oct. 2005. Web. 16 Dec. 2010. <http://denniscooper.blogspot.com/2005/10/jt-leroy-riff.html>.

Coward, Rosalind. "Sexual violence and sexuality." *Sexuality: A Reader*. Ed. Feminist Review. London: Virago, 1987. 307–25. Print.

Cowie, Elizabeth. "Pornography and Fantasy: Psychoanalytic Perspectives." *Sex Exposed: Sexuality and the Pornography Debate*. Ed. Lynne Segal and Mary McIntosh. New Brunswisk: Rutgers University Press, 1993. 132–52. Print.

Crisell, Luke. "The Lost Boy." *Guardian Unlimited*. 06 March 2005. Web. 07 Dec. 2010. <http://www.guardian.co.uk/books/2005/mar/06/fiction>.

Dean, Carolyn. "The Great War, Pornography, and the Transformation of Modern Male Subjectivity." *Modernism/Modernity* 3:2 (1996): 59–72. Project Muse. Web. 25 May 2009.

Dean, Tim. "The erotics of transgression." *The Cambridge Companion to Gay and Lesbian Writing*. Ed. Hugh Stevens. Cambridge: Cambridge University Press, 2011. 65–80. Print.

Deitch, Charlie. "Buchanan wins another online obscenity case." *Pittsburgh City Paper*. 11 March 2009. Web. 11 May 2011. <http://www.pittsburghcitypaper.ws/gyrobase/Content?oid=oid%3A60259 >.

DeJean, Joan. "The Politics of Pornography: *L'Ecole des Filles*." *The Invention of Pornography: Obscenity and the Origins of Modernity, 1500–1800*. Ed. Lynn Hunt. New York: Zone Books, 1996. 109–23. Print.

Deleuze, Gilles. "Coldness and Cruelty." Trans. Jean McNeil. *Masochism*. New York: Zone Books, 1989. 9–138. Print.

Dollimore, Jonathan. "Post/modern: On the Gay Sensibility, or the Pervert's Revenge on Authenticity." *Camp: Queer Aesthetics and the Performing Subject*. Ed. Fabio Cleto. Edinburgh: Edinburgh University Press, 1999. 221–36. Print.

Downing, Lisa. "What is 'Sex Critical' and why should we care about it?" *Sex Critical*. 27 July 2012. Web. 01 Dec. 2012. <http://sexcritical.blogspot.com/2012_07_01_archive.html>.

Downing, Lisa, and Robert Gillett. "Georges Bataille and Avant-Garde of Queer Theory?: Transgression, Perversion, and Death Drive." *Nottingham French Studies* 50: 3 (2011): 86–100. Print.

Dubs, Jamie. "2 Girls 1 Cup." *Know Your Meme*. Cheezburger Network, 2009. Web. 10 May 2011. <http://knowyourmeme.com/memes/2-girls-1-cup>.

Duggan, Lisa, Nan D. Hunter, and Carole S. Vance. "False promises: feminist anti-pornography legislation." *Sex Wars: Sexual Dissent and Political Culture*. By Duggan and Hunter. New York and London: Routledge, 1995. 43–63. Print.

Dunning, Stephen. "Margaret Atwood's *Oryx and Crake*: The Terror of the Therapeutic." *Canadian Literature* 186 (2005): 86–103. Literature Online. Web. 01 June 2010.

Dworkin, Andrea. "Against the Male Flood: Censorship, Pornography, and Equality." *Letters from a War Zone: Writings 1976–1987*. By Dworkin. London: Secker and Warburg, 1988. 253–75. Print.

———. "Pornography and Male Supremacy." *Letters from a War Zone: Writings 1976–1987*. By Dworkin. London: Secker and Warburg, 1988. 226–34. Print.

———. "A Woman Writer and Pornography." *Letters from a War Zone: Writings 1976–1987*. By Dworkin. London: Secker and Warburg, 1988. 31–36. Print.

———. "Women Lawyers and Pornography." *Letters from a War Zone: Writings 1976-1987.* By Dworkin. London: Secker and Warburg, 1988. 235-46. Print.
Dyer, Richard. "Idol Thoughts: Orgasm and Self-Reflexivity in Gay Pornography." *More Dirty Looks: Gender, Pornography and Power.* Ed. Pamela Church Gibson. London: British Film Institute, 2004. 102-09. Print.
Edelman, Lee. "Unbecoming: Pornography and the Queer Event." *Post/Porn/Politics: Queer Feminist Perspectives on the Politics of Porn Performance and Sex Work as Cultural Production.* Ed. Tim Stüttgen. Berlin: b_books, 2009. 194-209. Print.
Edelstein, David. "Now Playing at Your Local Multiplex: Torture Porn." *New York Magazine.* 28 Jan. 2006. Web. 16 June 2011. <http://nymag.com/movies/features/15622/>.
Egan, Susanna. "Auto/Biographical Impostures as Media Sensations." *Auto/Biography and Mediation.* Ed. Alfred Hornung. Memmingen: Universitätsverlag Winter Heidelberg, 2010. 131-37. Print.
Ellen, Barbara. "The debt all women owe to Jade and Wendy." *Guardian Online.* 12 Oct. 2008. Web. 16 June 2011. <http://www.guardian.co.uk/commentisfree/2008/oct/12/women-celebrity>.
Ellis, John. "On Pornography." *Pornography: Film and Culture.* Ed. Peter Lehman. New Brunswick: Rutgers University Press, 2006. 25-47. Print.
Ellmann, Lucy. "To bodily go . . ." *Guardian Unlimited.* 07 Feb. 2009. Web. 20 April 2009. <http://www.guardian.co.uk/books/2009/feb/07/ charlotte-wetlands-lucy-ellmann>.
Elsworth, Catherine. "US porn industry seeks multi-billion dollar bailout." *Telegraph.* 8 Jan. 2009. Web. 28 June 2009. <http://www.telegraph.co.uk/news/newstopics/howaboutthat/4165049/US-porn-industry-seeks-multi-billion-dollar-bailout.html>.
Falk, Pasi. "The Representation of Presence: Outlining the Anti-aesthetics of Pornography." *Theory, Culture & Society* 10:1 (1993): 1-42. *Sage.* Web. 20. Jan. 2011.
"FearFactorPorn.com hit with Cease and Desist." *AVN Business.* 15 Dec. 2004. Web. 20 May 2011. <http://business.avn.com/articles/video/FearFactor-Porn-com-Hit-with-Cease-and-Desist-41466.html>.
Findlen, Paula. "Humanism, Politics and Pornography in Renaissance Italy." *The Invention of Pornography: Obscenity and the Origins of Modernity, 1500-1800.* Ed. Lynn Hunt. New York: Zone Books, 1996. 49-108. Print.
Flood, Alison. "Is this the end of misery memoirs?" *Guardian Unlimited.* 20 Nov. 2008. Web. 27 Jan. 2011. <http://www.guardian.co.uk/books/booksblog/2008/nov/20/misery-memoirs-constance-briscoe>.
Foster, Hal. "Obscene, Abject, Traumatic." *October* 78 (1996): 106-24. *JSTOR.* Web. 02 Nov. 2009.

Foucault, Michel. "A Preface to Transgression." *Language, Counter-Memory, Practice: Selected Essays and Interviews*. By Foucault. Trans. Donald F. Bouchard and Sherry Simon. Ithaca: Cornell University Press, 1980. 29–52. Print.

Frappier-Mazur, Lucienne. "Truth and the Obscene Word in Eighteenth-Century French Pornography." *The Invention of Pornography: Obscenity and the Origins of Modernity, 1500–1800*. Ed. Lynn Hunt. New York: Zone Books, 1996. 203–21. Print.

Furedi, Frank. "An emotional striptease." *Spiked*. May 2007. Web. 27 Jan. 2011. <http://www.spiked-online.com/index.php?/site/reviewofbooks_article/3353>.

Geene, Stephan. "The Happiness of the Displaced Feeling: The Invisible Hand, Penis Surrogates, and Sex." *Post/Porn/Politics: Queer Feminist Perspectives on the Politics of Porn Performance and Sex Work as Cultural Production*. Ed. Tim Stüttgen. Berlin: b_books, 2009. 63–71. Print.

Gergen, Kenneth J. "Mind, text, and society: Self-memory in social context." *The Remembering Self: Construction and Accuracy in the Self-narrative*. Ed. Ulric Neisser and Robyn Fivush. Cambridge: Cambridge University Press, 1994. 78–104. Print.

Gilbert, Harriet. "So long as it's not sex and violence: Andrea Dworkin's *Mercy*." *Sex Exposed: Sexuality and the Pornography Debate*. Ed. Lynne Segal and Mary McIntosh. New Brunswick: Rutgers University Press, 1993. 216–29. Print.

Gilmore, Leigh. "American Neoconfessional: Memoir, Self-help, and Redemption on Oprah's Couch." *Biography* 33:4 (2010): 657–79. *Project Muse*. Web. 27 May 2011.

———. "Limit-Cases: Trauma, Self-Representation, and the Jurisdictions of Identity." *Biography* 24:1 (2001): 128–39. *Project Muse*. Web. 27 May 2011.

———. "The Mark of Autobiography: Postmodernism, Autobiography, and Genre." *Autobiography and Postmodernism*. Ed. Kathleen Ashley, Gilmore, and Gerald Peters. Amherst: University of Massachusetts Press, 1994. 3–18. Print.

———. "Policing Truth: Confession, Gender, and Autobiographical Authority." *Autobiography and Postmodernism*. Ed. Kathleen Ashley, Gilmore, and Gerald Peters. Amherst: University of Massachusetts Press, 1994. 54–78. Print.

Glaser, Mark. "Porn site offers soldiers free access in exchange for photos of dead Iraqis." *OJR: The Online Journalism Review*. 20 Sept. 2005. Web. 10 Nov. 2009. <http://www.ojr.org/ojr/stories/050920glaser/>.

Gordon, Bryony. "Why I've had enough literary sex." *Telegraph*. 27 Jan. 2009. Web. 20 April 2009. <http://www.telegraph.co.uk/comment/columnists/bryony-gordon/4361782/Why-Ive-had-enough-literary-sex.htm>.

Graham, Jane. "The Scheme: Gritty TV or Poverty Porn?" *Guardian Unlimited.* 28 May Web. 16 June 2011. <http://www.guardian.co.uk/tv-and-radio/tvandradioblog/2010/may/28/the-scheme-bbc>.

Griffo, Megan. "Ira Isaacs, Defecation Porn Shock Artist, Sentenced 4 Years In Prison." *Huffington Post.* 17 Jan. 2013. Web. 01 June 2013. <http://www.huffingtonpost.com/2013/01/17/ira-isaacs-defecation-por_n_2495505.html>.

Grinberg, Emanuella. "Georgia judge bars release of photos of hiker's nude, decapitated body." *CNN.* 11 March 2010. Web. 02 Aug. 2010. <http://edition.cnn.com/2010/CRIME/03/10/meredith.emerson.photos/index.html>.

Gronnvoll, Marita. "Gender (In)Visibility at Abu Ghraib." *Rhetoric and Public Affairs* 10: 3 (2007). 371–98. *Project Muse.* Web. 11 Nov. 2009.

Gubrium, Jaber F., and James A. Holstein. "The Everyday Work and Auspices of Authenticity." *Authenticity in Culture, Self, and Society.* Ed. Philip Vannini and J. Patrick Williams. Farnham: Ashgate, 2009. 121–38. Print.

Hansen, Christian, Catherine Needham, and Bill Nichols. "Pornography, Ethnography, and the Discourses of Power." *Representing Reality: Issues and Concepts in Documentary.* By Nichols. Bloomington: Indiana University Press, 1991. 201–28. Print.

Hardy, Simon. "The New Pornographies: Representation or Reality?" *Mainstreaming Sex: The Sexualization of Western Culture.* Ed. Feona Attwood. London: I. B. Tauris, 2009. 3–18. Print.

Harrison, Sophie. "And she seems like such a nice girl . . ." *Guardian Unlimited.* 01 Feb. 2009. Web. 20 April 2009. <http://www.guardian.co.uk/books/2009/feb/01/roche-wetlands-review>.

Hollibaugh, Amber. "Desire for the future: radical hope in passion and pleasure." *Pleasure and Danger: Exploring Female Sexuality.* Ed. Carole S. Vance. London: Pandora Press, 1992. 401–10. Print.

Howells, Coral Ann. "Margaret Atwood's Dystopian Visions: *The Handmaid's Tale* and *Oryx and Crake*." *The Cambridge Companion to Margaret Atwood.* Ed. Howells. Cambridge: Cambridge University Press, 2006. 161–75. Print.

Hunt, Lynn. "Introduction: Obscenity and the Origins of Modernity, 1500–1800." *The Invention of Pornography: Obscenity and the Origins of Modernity, 1500–1800.* Ed. Hunt. New York: Zone Books, 1996. 9–45. Print.

———. "Pornography and the French Revolution." *The Invention of Pornography: Obscenity and the Origins of Modernity, 1500–1800.* Ed. Hunt. New York: Zone Books, 1996. 301–39. Print.

Hunter, Nan D. and Sylvia A. Law. "Appendix A: the Fact Brief." *Sex Wars: Sexual Dissent and Political Culture.* By Lisa Duggan and Hunter. New York and London: Routledge, 1995. 207–47. Print.

Iyer, Aarti. "Misery loves cinematic company." *Columbia Spectator.* 04 March 2010. Web. 27 Jan. 2011. <http://www.columbiaspectator.com/2010/03/04/misery-loves-cinematic-company>.

Jenkins, Henry. "'He's in the Closet but He's Not Gay': Male-Male Desire in *Penthouse Letters*." *Pornography: Film and Culture*. Ed. Peter Lehman. New Brunswick: Rutgers University Press, 2006. 133–53. Print.

Jones, E. H. "Autofiction: A Brief History of a Neologism." *Life Writing: Essays on Autobiography, Biography and Literature*. Ed. Richard Bradford. Basingstoke: Palgrave Macmillan, 2010. 174–84. Print.

Jones, Steven. "Horrorporn/Pornhorror: The Problematic Communities and Contexts of Online Shock Imagery." *Porn.com*. Ed. Feona Attwood. New York: Peter Lang, 2010. 123–37. Print.

Juffer, Jane. "There's No Place Like Home: Further Developments on the Domestic Front." *More Dirty Looks: Gender, Pornography and Power*. Ed. Pamela Church Gibson. London: British Film Institute, 2004. 45–58. Print.

Kean, Danuta. "Are these taboo-breaking novels art or porn?" *The Independent*. 23 Jan. 2009. Web. 20 April 2009. <http://www.independent.co.uk/arts-entertainment/books/features/are-these-taboobreaking-novels-art-or-porn-1501292.html>.

Kernes, Mark. "Analysis: Karen Fletcher Pleads Guilty in 'Red Rose' Obscenity Case." *AVN Business*. 17 May 2008. Web. 09 July 2012. <http://business.avn.com/articles/legal/Analysis-Karen-Fletcher-Pleads-Guilty-in-Red-Rose-Obscenity-Case-52783.html>.

Kim, Victoria, and Aida Ahmad. "Fetish filmmaker convicted of obscenity charges." *Los Angeles Times*. 28 April 2012. Web. 09 July 2012. <http://articles.latimes.com/2012/apr/28/local/la-me-obscenity-trial-20120428>.

Kipnis, Laura. "How to Look at Pornography." *Pornography: Film and Culture*. Ed. Peter Lehman. New Brunswick: Rutgers University Press, 2006. 118–29. Print.

———. "(Male) Desire and (Female) Disgust: Reading *Hustler*." *Popular Culture: Production and Consumption*. Ed. C. Lee Harrington and Denise D. Bielby. Malden: Blackwell, 2001. 133–53. Print.

Klein, Marty. "Pornography: What Men See When They Watch." *Pornography: Film and Culture*. Ed. Peter Lehman. New Brunswick: Rutgers University Press, 2006. 244–57. Print.

Kleinhans, Chuck. "Virtual Child Porn: The Law and the Semiotics of the Image." *More Dirty Looks: Gender, Pornography and Power*. Ed. Pamela Church Gibson. London: British Film Institute, 2004. 71–84. Print.

Koch, Gertrude. "The Body's Shadow Realm." *Dirty Looks: Women, Pornography, Power*. Ed. Pamela Church Gibson and Roma Gibson. London: British Film Institute, 1993. 22–45. Print.

Krzywinska, Tanya. "Dissidence and Authenticity in Dyke Porn and Actuality TV." *Dissident Voices: The Politics of Television and Cultural Change*. Ed. Mike Wayne. London: Pluto Press, 1998. 159–75. Print.

———. "The Dynamics of Squirting: Female Ejaculation and Lactation in Hardcore Film." *Unruly Pleasures: The Cult Film and its Critics*. Ed. Xavier Mendik and Graeme Harper. Guildford: FAB Press, 2000. 31–45. Print.

Lane, Anthony. "Telling Tales." *The New Yorker* 82:4 (2006): 95. *The Shakespeare Collection*. Web. 15 Jan. 2011.
Lauritzen, Paul. "Arguing with Life Stories." *The Ethics of Life Writing*. Ed. Paul John Eakin. Ithaca: Cornell University Press, 2004. 19–39. Print.
Lehman, Peter. "Introduction: 'A Dirty Little Secret'–Why Teach and Study Pornography?" *Pornography: Film and Culture*. Ed. Lehman. New Brunswick: Rutgers University Press, 2006. 1–21. Print.
Leith, Sam. "Misery memoirs like Ugly by Constance Briscoe make pornography of personal pain." *Telegraph*. 19 Nov. 2008. Web. 17 Feb. 2011. <http://www.telegraph.co.uk/comment/columnists/samleith/3563600/Misery-memoirs-like-Ugly-by-Constance-Briscoe-make-pornography-of-personal-pain.html>.
Leonard, Sarah. "Pornography and Obscenity." *Palgrave Advances in the Modern History of Sexuality*. Ed. H. G. Cocks and Matt Houlbrook. Basingstoke: Palgrave Macmillan, 2006. 180–205. Print.
LeRoy, JT. Interview with Kevin Sampsell. "An Interview with JT Leroy." *Rain Taxi Online*. Winter 2001/2002. Web. 16 Dec. 2010. <http://www.raintaxi.com/online/2001winter/jtleroy.shtml>.
———. Interview with Litsa Dremousis. "An Interview with Fiction Writer JT Leroy." *Poets & Writers*. 15 Dec. 2004. Web. 16 Dec. 2010. <http://www.pw.org/content/interview_fiction_writer_jt_leroy?cmnt_all=1>.
———. Interview with Litsa Dremousis. "An Interview with J. T. Leroy." *Bookslut*. Dec. 2003. Web. 16 Dec. 2010. <http://www.bookslut.com/features/2003_12_001154.php>.
Lewin, Philip, and J. Patrick Williams. "The Ideology and Practice of Authenticity in Punk Subculture." *Authenticity in Culture, Self, and Society*. Ed. Philip Vannini and Williams. Farnham: Ashgate, 2009. 65–83. Print.
Longino, Helen E. "Pornography, Oppression, and Freedom: A Closer Look." *Pornography: Private Right or Public Menace?* Ed. Robert M. Baird and Stuart E. Rosenbaum. Buffalo: Prometheus Books, 1991. 84–95. Print.
Loontjens, Jannah. "Resisting the Author: JT Leroy's fictional authorship." *Image [&] Narrative: Online Magazine of the Visual Narrative* 22 (2008). Web. 05 Jan. 2011. <http://www.imageandnarrative.be/inarchive/autofiction2/loontjes.html>.
Lowe, Dave. "Travel Porn / trahvul-pohrn / (noun)." *The Lowe Road*, n.d. Web. 22 June 2011. <http://www.theloweroad.com/what-is-travel-porn/>.
Lowenstein, Adam. "Spectacle horror and *Hostel*: why 'torture porn' does not exist." *Critical Quarterly* 53:1 (2011): 42–60. *Wiley Online Library*. Web. 16 June 2011.
Lynch, Claire. "Trans-genre Confusion: What does Autobiography Think It Is?" *Life Writing: Essays on Autobiography, Biography and Literature*. Ed. Richard Bradford. Basingstoke: Palgrave Macmillan, 2010. 209–18. Print.
MacKinnon, Catharine A. "The roar on the other side of silence." *In Harm's Way: The Pornography Civil Rights Hearings*. Ed. MacKinnon and Andrea Dworkin. Cambridge, MA: Harvard University Press, 1997. 3–24. Print.

Maddison, Stephen. "'Choke on it Bitch!': Porn Studies, Extreme Gonzo and the Mainstreaming of Hardcore." *Mainstreaming Sex: The Sexualization of Western Culture*. Ed. Feona Attwood. London: I. B. Tauris, 2009. 37–53. Print.

Maher, Kevin. "Embarrassing Bodies; Waking the Dead: Last Night's TV." *Times Online*. 29 April 2008. Web. 11 May 2011. < http://entertainment.timesonline.co.uk/tol/arts_and_entertainment/tv_and_radio/article3834818.ece >.

Maldoro, Johnny. "Abu Gag!" *Village Voice*. 27 July 2004. Web. 10 Nov. 2009. <http://www.villagevoice.com/2004-07-27/people/abu-gag/>.

Man, Paul de. "Autobiography as De-facement." *MLN* 94: 5 (1979): 919–30. *JSTOR*. Web. 20 Jan. 2011.

Marcus, Laura. "Theories of Autobiography: Part One: The face of autobiography." *The Uses of Autobiography*. Ed. Julia Swindells. London: Taylor and Francis, 1995. 13–23. Print.

Masson, Jeffrey. "Incest Pornography and the Problem of Fantasy." *Men Confront Pornography*. Ed. Michael S. Kimmel. New York: Meridian, 1991. 142–52. Print.

Mazzola, Robert L. "Sade's Woman: Essential Pornography and Virtual Embodiment." *Gender Reconstructions: Pornography and Perversions in Literature and Culture*. Ed. Cindy L. Carlson, Mazzola, and Susan M. Bernardo. Aldershot: Ashgate, 2002. 108–24. Print.

McCaffrey, Shannon. "Hustler Magazine Asks for Crime Scene Photos of Slain Hiker Meredith Emerson." *The Huffington Post*. 08 March 2010. Web. 02 Aug. 2010. <http://www.huffingtonpost.com/2010/03/08/hustler-magazine-asks-for_n_490823.html>.

McClintock, Anne. "Gonad the Barbarian and the Venus Flytrap: Portraying the Female and Male Orgasm." *Sex Exposed: Sexuality and the Pornography Debate*. Ed. Lynne Segal and Mary McIntosh. New Brunswick: Rutgers University Press, 1993. 111–31. Print.

———. "Maid to Order: Commercial S/M and Gender Power." *More Dirty Looks: Gender, Pornography and Power*. Ed. Pamela Church Gibson. London: British Film Institute, 2004. 102–09. Print.

———. "Paranoid Empire: Specters from Guantánamo and Abu Ghraib." *Small Axe* 28 (2009): 50–74. *Project Muse*. Web. 19 May 2010.

McDowall, Iain. "The Scheme is misleading 'poverty porn.'" *Guardian Unlimited*. 13 June 2011. Web. 16 June 2011. <http://www.guardian.co.uk/commentisfree/2011/jun/13/scheme-bbc-onthank-scotland>.

Merck, Mandy. "The feminist ethics of lesbian S/M." *Perversions: Deviant Readings*. By Merck. London: Virago, 1993. 236–66. Print.

Mijnhardt, Wijnand W. "Politics and Pornography in the Seventeenth- and Eighteenth-Century Dutch Republic." *The Invention of Pornography: Obscenity and the Origins of Modernity, 1500–1800*. Ed. Lynn Hunt. New York: Zone Books, 1996. 283–300. Print.

Miller-Young, Mireille. "Let Me Tell Ya 'Bout Black Chicks: Interracial Desire and Black Women in 1980s Video Pornography." *Pornification: Sex and Sexual-*

ity in Media Culture. Ed. Susanna Paasonen, Kaarina Nikunen and Laura Saarenmaa. Oxford: Bera, 2007. 33–44. Print.

Mills, Claudia. "Friendship, Fiction, and Memoir: Trust and Betrayal in Writing from One's Own Life." *The Ethics of Life Writing*. Ed. Paul John Eakin. Ithaca: Cornell University Press, 2004. 101–20. Print.

"Minneapolis Ordinance, 1983." *In Harm's Way: The Pornography Civil Rights Hearings*. Ed. Catharine A. MacKinnon and Andrea Dworkin. Cambridge, MA: Harvard University Press, 1997. 426–33. Print.

Mooney, Gerry, and Lynn Hancock. "*Poverty Porn* and the *Broken Society*." *Variant* 39/40 (2010). Web. 16 June 2011. <http://www.variant.org.uk/39_40texts/povertp39_40.html>.

Murphy, Dina. "Embarrassing Bodies; Another Wonky Week." *Sabotage Times*. 12 March 2011. Web. 11 May 2011. <http://www.sabotagetimes.com/tv-film/embarrassing-bodies-another-wonky-week/>.

Nguyen, Tan Hoang. "The Resurrection of Brandon Lee: The Making of a Gay Asian American Porn Star." *Porn Studies*. Ed. Linda Williams. Durham, NC: Duke University Press, 2004. 223–70. Print.

Nichols, Bill. "Video shows beheading of American captive." *USA Today*. 11 May 2004. Web. 02 Aug. 2010. <http://www.usatoday.com/news/world/iraq/2004-05-11-iraq-beheading_x.htm>.

"Non Fiction PB: Week Ending: Sat, 28/05/2011." *The Bookseller*. 28 May 2011. Web. 03 June 2011. <http://www.thebookseller.com/node/44841>.

Noys, Benjamin. "'Monumental Construction': Badiou and the Politics of Aesthetics." *Third Text* 23:4 (2009): 383–92. *Informaworld*. Web. 05 Aug. 2009.

———. "Transgressing transgression: the limits of Bataille's fiction." *Les Lieux Interdits: Transgression and French Literature*. Ed. Larry Duffy and Adrian Tudor. Hull: Hull University Press, 1998. 307–23. Print.

"Official UK Top 50: Week Ending: Sat, 28/05/2011." *The Bookseller*. 28 May 2011. Web. 03 June 2011. <http://www.thebookseller.com/node/45028>.

Ogreenworld. "Shock Sites." *Know Your Meme*. Cheezburger Network, 2009. Web. 10 May 2011. < http://knowyourmeme.com/memes/shock-sites>.

O'Rourke, Meghan. "James Frey and JT LeRoy: Lying writers and the readers who love them." *Slate Magazine*. 12 Jan. 2006. Web. 16 Dec. 2010.<http://www.slate.com/id/2134214/>.

Paasonen, Susanna. "Epilogue: Porn Futures." *Pornification: Sex and Sexuality in Media Culture*. Ed. Paasonen, Kaarina Nikunen and Laura Saarenmaa. Oxford: Bera, 2007. 161–70. Print.

———. "Good Amateurs: Erotica Writing and Notions of Quality." *Porn.com*. Ed. Feona Attwood. New York: Peter Lang, 2010. 138–54. Print.

———. "Repetition and Hyperbole: The Gendered Choreographies of Heteroporn." *Everyday Pornography*. Ed. Karen Boyle. Abingdon: Routledge, 2010. 63–76. Print.

Paasonen, Susanna, Kaarina Nikunen, and Laura Saarenmaa. "Pornification and the Education of Desire." *Pornification: Sex and Sexuality in Media*

Culture. Ed. Paasonen, Nikunen, and Saarenmaa. Oxford: Bera, 2007. 1–20. Print.

Page, Benedicte, and Graeme Neill. "Gloom envelops the misery memoir market." *The Bookseller*. 23 May 2008. Web. 02 June 2011. <http://www.thebookseller.com/news/gloom-envelops-misery-memoir-market.html>.

Pasquinelli, Matteo. "Libidinal Parasites and the Machinic Excess: On the Dystopian Biosphere of Networks." *Post/Porn/Politics: Queer Feminist Perspectives on the Politics of Porn Performance and Sex Work as Cultural Production*. Ed. Tim Stüttgen. Berlin: b_books, 2009. 213–23. Print.

———. "WARPORN WARPUNK! Autonomous videopoiesis in wartime." *Generation Online*, n.d. Web. 18 May 2011. <http://www.generation-online.org/t/warporn.htm>.

Paterson, Tony. "Taboo-busting writer sets Germany abuzz." 17 Oct. 2008. *The Independent*. Web. 20 April 2009. <http://www.independent.co.uk/life-style/love-sex/culture-of-love/taboobusting-writer-sets-germany-abuzz-965189.html>.

Patterson, Zabet. "Going On-line: Consuming Pornography in the Digital Era." *Porn Studies*. Ed. Linda Williams. Durham, NC: Duke University Press, 2004. 104–23. Print.

Penley, Constance. "Crackers and Whackers: The White Trashing of Porn." *Porn Studies*. Ed. Linda Williams. Durham, NC: Duke University Press, 2004. 309–31. Print.

Petley, Julian. "Britain: Matters of Decency." *Index on Censorship*. 18 Jan. 2008. Web. 16 Feb. 2011. <http://www.indexoncensorship.org/2008/01/britain-matters-of-decency/>.

———. "Pornography, Panopticism and the Criminal Justice and Immigration Act 2008." *Sociology Compass* 3:3 (2009): 417–32. Print.

Pipe, Roger T. "Max Extreme 4." *Rog Reviews*. 08 March 1999. Web. 09 Aug. 2011. <http://www.rogreviews.com/10512/max-extreme-4/>.

Pollock, Griselda. "Art/Trauma/Representation." *Parallax* 15: 1 (2009): 40–54. *Informaworld*. Web. 01 Oct. 2010.

"Porn Jackass review PornJackass by Rabbit." *Rabbit's Reviews*. 22 Sept. 2004. Web. 22 March 2010. <http://www.rabbitsreviews.com/s507/Porn-Jackass.html>.

"Pornography." *The Oxford English Dictionary*. 3rd ed. 2006. Web. 24 Nov. 2009. <http://www.oed.com.ezproxy.sussex.ac.uk/viewdictionaryentry/Entry/148012>.

Preciado, Beatriz. "The Architecture of Porn: Museum Walls, Urban Detritus and Stag Rooms for Porn-Prosthetic Eyes." *Post/Porn/Politics: Queer Feminist Perspectives on the Politics of Porn Performance and Sex Work as Cultural Production*. Ed. Tim Stüttgen. Berlin: b_books, 2009. 23–33. Print.

Probyn, Elspeth. "Beyond Food/Sex: Eating and an Ethics of Existence." *Theory, Culture & Society* 16:2 (1999): 215–28. *Sage*. Web. 20. Jan. 2011.

Quandt, James. "Flesh and Blood: Sex and Violence in Recent French Cinema." *Artforum*. Feb. 2004. Web. 28 Nov. 2010. <http://artforum.com/inprint/id=6199&pagenum=0>.

Rich, B. Ruby. "Anti-Porn: Soft Issue, Hard World." *Sexuality: A Reader*. Ed. Feminist Review. London: Virago, 1987. 340–54. Print.
Roche, Charlotte. Interview with Decca Aitkenhead. " 'It should make you blush.' " *Guardian Unlimited*. 17 Jan. 2009. Web. 20 April 2009. <http://www.guardian.co.uk/books/2009/jan/17/interview-charlotte-roche-debut-novel-wetlands>.
———. Interview with Ed Caesar. "Charlotte Roche is an unlikely shock artist." *Times Online*. 01 Feb. 2009. Web. 20 April 2009. <http://entertainment.timesonline.co.uk/tol/arts_and_entertainment/books/article5612411.ece>.
———. Interview with Philip Oltermann. "Interview: Charlotte Roche." *Granta*. 10 May 2008. Web. 20 April 2009. <http://www.granta.com/Online-Only/Interview-Charlotte-Roche>.
———. Interview with Nina Power. "The Dirty Girl." *Salon*. 04 April 2009. Web. 20 April 2009. <http://www.salon.com/books/int/2009/04/04/charlotte_roche>.
Roush, Jason. "A gazillion little pieces." *The Gay & Lesbian Review* 14:3 (2007): 45. *The Shakespeare Collection*. Web. 20 Jan. 2011.
Rubin, Gayle. "The leather menace: comments on politics and S/M." *Coming to Power: Writings and Graphics on Lesbian S/M*. Ed. Samois. Boston: Alyson Publications, 1982. 192–227. Print.
Russo, Julie Levin. " 'The Real Thing': Reframing Queer Pornography for Virtual Spaces." *Julie Levin Russo*. Sept. 2005. Web. 09 Aug. 2011. <http://j-l-r.org/docs/jlr_netporn.pdf>.
Sánchez-Eppler, Karen. "Bodily Bonds: The Intersecting Rhetorics of Feminism and Abolition." *The Culture of Sentiment: Race, Gander, and Sentimentality in Nineteenth-Century America*. Ed. Shirely Samuels. Oxford: Oxford University Press, 1992. 92–114. Print.
Sanghera, Sathnam. "Misery Memoirs: The Final Chapter?" *Times Online*. 19 Nov. 2008. Web. 27 Jan. 2011. <http://women.timesonline.co.uk/tol/life_and_style/women/the_way_we_live/article5182916.ece>.
Sarler, Carol. "I'll tell you what's Ugly . . . this shameful appetite for misery porn." *Daily Mail*. 20 Nov. 2008. Web. 27 Jan. 2011. <http://www.dailymail.co.uk/femail/article-1087604/Ill-tell-whats-Ugly---shameful-appetite-misery-porn.html>.
———. "This new and peculiar pornography of grief." *Times Online*. 07 Sept. 2007. Web. 16 June 2011. <http://www.timesonline.co.uk/tol/comment/columnists/guest_contributors/article2402693.ece>.
Saunders, Kate. "Memoir: Fat Girl by Judith Moore." *Times Online*. 17 July 2005. Web. 02 June 2011. <http://entertainment.timesonline.co.uk/tol/arts_and_entertainment/books/article543384.ece>.
Savile, Anthony. "Sentimentality." *Arguing About Art: Contemporary Philosophical Debates*. Ed. Alex Neill and Aaron Ridley. London: Routledge, 2002. 315–19. Print.
Saxton, Libby. "Ethics, Spectatorship and the Spectacle of Suffering." *Film and Ethics: Foreclosed Encounters*. By Lisa Downing and Libby Saxton. Abingdon: Routledge, 2009. 62–75. Print.
Sears, P. Personal Interview. 27 Oct. 2009.

Sedgwick, Eve Kosofsky. "From 'Wilde, Nietzsche, and the Sentimental Relations of the Male Body.' " *Camp: Queer Aesthetics and the Performing Subject.* Ed. Fabio Cleto. Edinburgh: Edinburgh University Press, 1999. 207-20. Print.

Segal, Lynne. "Pornography and Violence: What the 'Experts' Really Say." *Feminist Review* 36 (1990): 29-41. JSTOR. Web. 05 Aug. 2010.

Shelton, Emily. "A Star is Porn: Corpulence, Comedy, and the Homosocial Cult of Adult Film Star Ron Jeremy." *Camera Obscura* 17:3 (2002): 115-46. *Project Muse.* Web. 09 Aug. 2011.

Smith, Clarissa. "Pleasing Intensities: Masochism and Affective Pleasures in Porn Short Fictions." *Mainstreaming Sex: The Sexualization of Western Culture.* Ed. Feona Attwood. London: I. B. Tauris, 2009. 3-18. Print.

———. "Pornographication: A Discourse for all Seasons." *International Journal of Media and Cultural Politics* 6:1 (2010): 103-08. Print.

Smith, Joan. "Book of the week: Wetlands by Charlotte Roche." *Times Online.* 29 Jan. 2009. Web. 16 June 2009. <http://entertainment.timesonline.co.uk/tol/arts_and_entertainment/books/fiction/article5614066.ece>.

Sontag, Susan. "Regarding the Torture of Others." *New York Times.* 23 May 2004. Web. 10 Nov. 2009. <http://www.nytimes.com/2004/05/23/magazine/23PRISONS.html>.

St. John, Warren. "The Unmasking of JT Leroy: In Public, He's a She." *New York Times.* 09 Jan. 2006. Web. 08 Feb. 2011. < http://www.nytimes.com/2006/01/09/books/08cnd-book.html?_r=1>.

Staruch, Peggy. "The 'reality' of a writers' strike." *Toronto Star.* 22 Nov. 2007. Web. 14 Feb. 2011. <http://www.thestar.com/entertainment/article/278772>.

Steinem, Gloria. "Erotica and Pornography: A Clear and Present Difference." *Pornography: Private Right or Public Menace?* Ed. Robert M. Baird and Stuart E. Rosenbaum. Buffalo: Prometheus Books, 1991. 51-55. Print.

Steintrager, James A. "Liberating Sade." *Yale Journal of Criticism* 18: 2 (2005): 351-79. *Project Muse.* Web. 02 Aug. 2008.

Stone, Laurie. "Introduction: Recalled to Life." *Close to the Bone: Memoirs of Hurt, Rage, and Desire.* Ed. Stone. New York: Grove Press, 1997. Print.

Stüttgen, Tim. "Before Orgasm: Fifteen Fragments on a cartography of Post/Pornographic Politics." *Post/Porn/Politics: Queer Feminist Perspectives on the Politics of Porn Performance and Sex Work as Cultural Production.* Ed. Stüttgen. Berlin: b_books, 2009. 10-21. Print.

———. "Disidentification in the Center of Power: The Porn Performer and Director Belladonna as a Contrasexual Producer: A Letter to Beatriz Preciado." *Post/Porn/Politics: Queer Feminist Perspectives on the Politics of Porn Performance and Sex Work as Cultural Production.* Ed. Stüttgen. Berlin: b_books, 2009. 41-55. Print.

Sullivan, Chris. "J T LeRoy: A brutally frank autobiography." *The Independent.* 9 July 2005. Web. 16 Dec. 2010. <http://www.independent.co.uk/arts-entertainment/books/features/j-t-leroy-a-brutally-frank-autobiography-498019.html>.

Swanson, David. "The Iraq War as a Trophy Photo." *TomDispatch*. 13 June 2006. Web. 10 Nov. 2010. <http://www.tomdispatch.com/post/91318/>.

Swash, Rosie. "Girls Aloud 'porn' blogger appears in court." *Guardian Unlimited*. 23 Oct. 2008. Web. 09 Jan. 2009. <http://www.guardian.co.uk/music/2008/oct/23/girls-aloud-porn-blog-trial>.

Tétreault, Mary Ann. "The Sexual Politics of Abu Ghraib: Hegemony, Spectacle, and the Global War on Terror." *NWSA* 18: 3 (2006): 33–50. Project Muse. Web. 11 Nov. 2009.

"Transgression." *The Oxford English Dictionary*. 2nd ed. 1989. Web. 18 June 2009. <http://dictionary.oed.com.ezproxy.sussex.ac.uk/cgi/entry/50256254?single=1&query_type=word&queryword=transgression&first=1&max_to_show=10>.

Trumbach, Randolph. "Erotic Fantasy and Male Libertinism in Enlightenment England." *The Invention of Pornography: Obscenity and the Origins of Modernity, 1500–1800*. Ed. Lynn Hunt. New York: Zone Books, 1996. 253–82. Print.

Vance, Carole S. "More danger, more pleasure: a decade after the Barnard Sexuality Conference." *Pleasure and Danger: Exploring Female Sexuality*. Ed. Vance. London: Pandora Press, 1992. xvi–xxxix. Print.

———. "Pleasure and danger: towards a politics of sexuality." *Pleasure and Danger: Exploring Female Sexuality*. Ed. Vance. London: Pandora Press, 1992. 1–27. Print.

Vernon, Polly. "This is the woman who played the man who became a transsexual and fooled the world for six years." *Guardian Unlimited*. 02 Nov. 2008. Web. 07 Dec. 2010. <http://www.guardian.co.uk/lifeandstyle/2008/nov/02/savannah-knoop-jeremiah-jt-leroy>.

Wachter, Phyllis E. "Annual Bibliography of Works about Life Writing, 2009–2010." *Bibliography* 33:4 (2010): 714–846. Project Muse. Web. 27 May 2011.

Ward, Paula Reed. "Porn producer, wife get 1-year jail terms." *Pittsburgh Post-Gazette*. 02 July 2009. Web. 11 May 2011. <http://www.post-gazette.com/pg/09183/981250-53.stm>.

Waugh, Thomas. "Homosociality in the Classical American Stag Film: Off-Screen, On-Screen." *Porn Studies*. Ed. Linda Williams. Durham, NC: Duke University Press, 2004. 127–41. Print.

Webster, Paula. "The forbidden: eroticism and taboo." *Pleasure and Danger: Exploring Female Sexuality*. Ed. Carole S. Vance. London: Pandora Press, 1992. 385–98. Print.

Weil, Rachel. "Sometimes a Scepter is Only a Scepter: Pornography and Politics in Restoration England." *The Invention of Pornography: Obscenity and the Origins of Modernity, 1500–1800*. Ed. Lynn Hunt. New York: Zone Books, 1996. 125–53. Print.

"Wetlands erotic novel goes on sale in Britain." *Telegraph*. 24 Jan. 2009. Web. 20 April 2009. <http://www.telegraph.co.uk/news/worldnews/europe/germany/4326359/Wetlands-erotic-novel-goes-on-sale-in-Britain.html>.

Wicke, Jennifer. "Through a Gaze Darkly: Pornography's Academic Market." *Dirty Looks: Women. Pornography, Power*. Ed. Pamela Church Gibson and Roma Gibson. London: British Film Institute, 1993. 62–80. Print.

Williams, Linda. "Pornographies On/Scene: or Diff'rent Strokes for Diff'rent Folks." *Sex Exposed: Sexuality and the Pornography Debate*. Ed. Lynne Segal and Mary McIntosh. New Brunswick: Rutgers University Press, 1993. 235–65. Print.

———. "Second Thoughts on *Hard Core*: American Obscenity Law and the Scapegoating of Deviance." *Dirty Looks: Women. Pornography, Power*. Ed. Pamela Church Gibson and Roma Gibson. London: British Film Institute, 1993. 46–61. Print.

———. "Skin Flicks on the Racial Border: Pornography, Exploitation, and Interracial Lust." *Porn Studies*. Ed. Williams. Durham, NC: Duke University Press, 2004. 271–308. Print.

Willhoit, Dana. "Wilson Will Avoid Jail In Plea Deal." *The Ledger*. 14 Jan. 2006. Web. 02 Aug. 2010. <http://www.theledger.com/apps/pbcs.dll/article?AID=/20060114/NEWS/601140413>.

Willis, Ellen. "Feminism, Moralism, and Pornography." *Desire: The Politics of Sexuality*. Ed. Ann Snitow, Christine Stansell, and Sharon Thompson. London: Virago, 1984. 82–88. Print.

Wilson, Elizabeth. "Feminist Fundamentalism: The Shifting Politics of Sex and Censorship." *Sex Exposed: Sexuality and the Pornography Debate*. Ed. Lynne Segal and Mary McIntosh. New Brunswick: Rutgers University Press, 1993. 15–28. Print.

Wimsatt, William K., and Monroe C. Beardsley. "The Intentional Fallacy." *The Norton Anthology of Theory and Criticism*. Ed. Vincent B. Leitch, et al. New York: W. W. Norton, 2001. 1374–387. Print.

Winograd, Eugene. "The authenticity and utility of memories." *The Remembering Self: Construction and Accuracy in the Self-narrative*. Ed. Ulric Neisser and Robyn Fivush. Cambridge: Cambridge University Press, 1994. 243–51. Print.

Wiseman, Eva. "Why Channel 4's Embarrassing Bodies is in rude health." *Guardian Unlimited*. 05 Sept. 2010. Web. 11 May 2011. < http://www.guardian.co.uk/tv-and-radio/2010/sep/05/embarrassing-bodies-channel-4-behind-the-scenes>.

Withers, James. "Streets of San Francisco." *The Gay & Lesbian Review* 12: 2 (2005): 45. *The Shakespeare Collection*. Web. 20 Jan. 2011.

Woolaston, Sam. "Last night's TV." *Guardian Unlimited*. 29 April 2008. Web. 11 May 2011. < http://www.guardian.co.uk/media/2008/apr/29/television?INTCMP=SRCH>.

Zornick, George. "The Porn of War." *The Nation*. 22 Sept. 2005. Web. 28 Nov. 2009. <http://www.thenation.com/doc/20051010/the_porn_of_war>.

Zucchino, David. "U.S. troops posed with body parts of Afghan bombers." *Los Angeles Times*. 18 April 2012. Web. 09 July 2012. <http://articles.latimes.com/2012/apr/18/nation/la-na-afghan-photos-20120418>.

Works Cited 227

Legal, Governmental, and Policy Documents

BBFC (British Board of Film Classification). "Annual Report 2003." *British Board of Film Classification*. 2003. Web. 05 Aug. 2009. <http://www.bbfc.co.uk/download/annual-reports/BBFC_AnnualReport_2003.pdf>.

Itzin, Catherine, Ann Taket and Liz Kelly. *The evidence of harm to adults relating to exposure to extreme pornographic material: a rapid evidence assessment (RAE)*. 28 Sept. 2007. Web. 05 Aug. 2010. <http://www.justice.gov.uk/publications/docs/280907.pdf >.

United Kingdom. HMSO. Criminal Justice and Immigration Act 2008. *Office of Public Sector Information*. May 2008. Web. 09 Jan. 2009. <http://www.uk-legislation.hmso.gov.uk/acts/acts2008/ukpga_20080004_en_9>.

United Kingdom. Ministry of Justice. "Further information on the new offence of Possession of Extreme Pornographic Images." *Ministry of Justice*. Nov. 2008. Web. 07 Jan. 2009. <http://www.justice.gov.uk/docs/extreme-pornographic-images.pdf>.

United States. Department of Justice. "Adult Entertainment Producer Sentenced to 46 Months in Prison on Obscenity Charges." *United States Department of Justice*. 03 Oct. 2008. Web. 09 Jan. 2009. <http://www.usdoj.gov/criminal/ceos/Press%20Releases/MDFL_MaxHardcore_10-03-08.pdf>.

———. "News Release." *United States Department of Justice*. 07 Aug. 2003. Web. 09 Jan. 2009. <http://www.usdoj.gov/criminal/ceos/Press%20Releases/WDPA%20Zicari%20indict%20PR_080703.pdf>.

Websites

Embarrassing Bodies. Channel 4, n.d. Web. 11 May 2011. <http://www.channel4embarrassingillnesses.com/>.

Simpsons: The XXX Parody. Full Spread Entertainment, 2010. Web. 27 Jan. 2011. <http://www.simpsonsporno.org/>.

Gag Factor. JM Productions, n.d. Web. 22 March 2010. <http://www.gagfactor.com/gagfactordotcom.html>.

Porn Jackass, n.d. Web. 22 March 2010. <http://tour.pornjackass.com/aa/index.php>.

Sicko Games. Redslip LLC, 2005. Web. 20 May 2011. <http://www.sickogames.com/fff.html>.

Skin Two Magazine. 2008. Web. 04 Nov. 2008. <http://www.skintwo.co.uk>.

Wilson, Chris. *Documenting Reality*, 2010. Web. 02 Aug. 2010. <http://www.documentingreality.com/forum/>.

Recordings

"American porn." *Frontline*. Writ. Michael Kirk and Peter J. Boyer. Dir. Michael Kirk. PBS. 7 Feb. 2002. Web. 27 June 2009. <http://www.pbs.org/wgbh/pages/frontline/shows/porn/view/>.

"Back to the Woods." *Family Guy: Season 6.* Fox. Writ. Seth MacFarlane and Tom Devanney. Dir. Brian Iles. Twentieth Century Fox, 2008. DVD.

centerback14, dir. "Two Girls one Cup reaction." *YouTube.* 08 Oct. 2007. Web. 11 May 2011. <http://www.youtube.com/watch?feature=player_embedded&v=N7aABa0N0Qc#at=31>.

"Embarrassing Bodies: Back to the Clinic." *Embarrassing Bodies: Series 4.* Channel 4. Prod. Emma Baron. 15 April 2011. Web. 11 May 2011. <http://www.channel4.com/programmes/embarrassing-bodies/4od#3178297>.

"Episode 1." *The Sex Education Show: Series 1.* Channel 4. Dir. Catherine Ellis and Aislinn McIvor. 21 May 2010. Web. 11 May 2011. <http://www.channel4.com/programmes/the-sex-education-show/4od#2924003>.

fartenewt, dir. "2 Girls 1 Cup # 1." *YouTube.* 21 Sept. 2007. Web. 11 May 2011. <http://www.youtube.com/watch?v=OtRzf_ZcM0U&feature=related>.

———. "2 Girls 1 Cup # 5." *YouTube.* 26 Sept. 2007. Web. 11 May 2011. <http://www.youtube.com/watch?v=HI4k0ORM-TI&feature=mfu_in_order&list=UL>.

———. "2 Girls 1 Cup # 9." *YouTube.* 02 Oct. 2007. Web. 11 May 2011. <http://www.youtube.com/watch?v=2w8c2Z4VN3w&feature=mfu_in_order&list=UL>.

Gag Factor 15. Dir. Jim Powers. JM Productions, 2004. Web. 08 Nov. 2009. <http://www.hotmovies.com/video/98641/Gag-Factor-15/?>.

giannidallatorre, dir. "Rocco Amica Chips (Non Censurato)." *YouTube.* 22 April 2007. Web. 27 Jan. 2011. <http://www.youtube.com/watch?v=ZXM3TPe7EvM&NR=1>.

Gilman-Opalsky, Richard. "This Event is Not Taking Place: Truth, Reality, and History in Baudrillard's Political Philosophy." *Engaged Citizenship Common Experience (ECCE) Speaker Series.* University of Illinois, Springfield. July 15 2009. MP3.

Jackass: The Lost Tapes. Perf. Dave England. MTV, 2009. DVD.

Jackass: The Movie. Dir. Jeff Tremaine. Perf. Ehren McGhehey. Paramount, 2007. DVD.

kevinsynder, dir. "MARINES 2 girls 1 cup reactions!!" *YouTube.* 02 April 2008. Web. 11 May 2011. <http://www.youtube.com/watch?feature=player_embedded&v=doZnJSojBtw#at=51>.

Lil Wayne feat. Drake. "Gonorrhea." *I am Not a Human Being.* Young Money, 2010. MP3.

lurknstock, dir. "Jenna Jameson Adidas Adicolor." *YouTube.* 26 Nov. 2010. Web. 27 Jan. 2011. <http://www.youtube.com/watch?v=6g4Zyh7fOXI>.

Rocco Ravishes LA. Dir. Rocco Siffredi. Evil Angel, 2009. Web. 06 March 2010. <http://www.hotmovies.com/video/159213/Rocco-Ravishes-L.A./>.

RTAmerica, dir. "US military 'War Porn' surfaces." *YouTube.* 18 April 2012. Web. 09 July 2012. <http://www.youtube.com/watch?v=zjGUjdcPbmg&fb_source=message>.

Sandy Insatiable. Dir. Rocco Siffredi. Evil Empire, 1995. Web. 08 March 2010. <http://www.hotmovies.com/video/133712/Sandy-Insatiable/>.

Simpsons: The XXX Parody. Dir. Lee Roy Myers. Hustler Video, 2011. DVD.
This Ain't Avatar: XXX. Dir. Axel Braun. Hustler Video, 2010. DVD.
"TOP SECRET What Solders [sic] Do With Iraqi Prisoners." *Need Bang*, n.d. Web. 02 Aug. 2010. <http://www.needbang.com/media/1507/TOP-SECRET-What-Solders-Do-With-Iraqi-Prisoners.html>.

Index

"2 Girls 1 Cup," 49–55, 60
abject, the, 38–41, 42, 47, 49, 52, 56–57, 130–131, 137–138
abolitionist materials, 109–112, 114–115
Abu Ghraib, 79, 80–81, 85, 106–109, 121–122, 182, 185
adult entertainment: authenticity in, 132–139, 175–176; and generic slippage, 67–68, 73–79, 90–91, 104–105; and parody; 151–152; versus pornography, 13–14, 57, 109–112, 120–121, 123, 142–143, 182, 185–186; versus sexually explicit memes, 52–56; written forms of, 11–13
affect: and disaffection; 92–93, 95, 100; and disgust, 42, 44, 46–47, 52–55, 137; generalized forms of, 90–91; in postmodern culture, 88–89; relationship with transgression, 78, 82–86, 143–144; *see also* intensity
Albert, Laura: *See* LeRoy, JT
anti-censorship feminism: *See* pro-sex feminism
anti-pornography feminism: common ground with pro-sex feminism, 25–27; influence of, 117–120; transgression within, 29–31, 33–34; use of sentiment, 112–114; viewpoints of, 21–23

Attwood, Feona, 2, 8–9, 10, 204n1
Atwood, Margaret, 89–91, 92–98, 99–102
authenticity: and anxiety, 149–150, 152–155, 176–177, 178–179; and confession, 148; as a definitional criteria for the pornographic, 59–60, 139, 149, 168–169; and marginality, 162–163; and postmodern culture, 92–94, 97, 129–131, 158–160; and prurience, 175–176; role in adult entertainment, 132–136, 151
authorship, 129, 148, 157–158, 161, 164–165
autobiography: generic instability of, 150–151, 160; and pornographic fiction, 139–140, 143; role of truth in, 139, 148, 159–160; and trauma, 154–155, 179

Badiou, Alain, 31, 45–46, 93–94, 131
Bataille, Georges, 18–19, 27–31, 33, 137–138; *see also* transgression
Baudrillard, Jean, 94–95, 129, 132, 170, 178–179, 180
BDSM, 7–8, 74–75
Bersani, Leo: on intensity, 64, 72, 122, 154 on the redemptive project of sex, 25–26; with Ulysse Dutoite, 85, 110

bodily fluids, 43, 137–138
body genres, the, 74–75, 137, 151
Butler, Judith, 108, 198n5

class, 3, 14, 17, 78, 162–163; *see also* distaste
confession, 139–140, 143, 148–149, 170
Criminal Justice and Immigration Act 2008, the, 6–7, 11, 52, 119–120
cynicism, 100, 129–130

disavowal, 34, 94, 145–147
displacement: of affect, 42, 60; of sex within 'the pornographic', 14, 56–57, 73–75, 77–78, 112; within sexuality, 179
disgust: cultural invisibility of, 42–44; in legal discourse, 6–7, 32; and 'the pornographic', 47, 55; and the powers of horror, 40–41, 58–59; reactions of, 50–52, 53, 71, 137–138; *see also* affect
distaste, 77, 82–83, 146, 187
Dworkin, Andrea, 22–23, 28–30, 32–33, 112–114, 117

Embarrassing Bodies, 56–61
Evil Angel, 134–135
execution videos, 81, 90, 93–94, 97–98, 99–100
Extreme Associates, 5–6, 67–68, 78

Foucault, Michel, 4, 42–44, 46, 58, 139, 148–149, 170
Flynt, Larry, 75–76, 78
frenzy of the visible, the, 2, 51–52, 74–75, 122, 138, 152–153
Freud, Sigmund, 71–73, 85

Gag Factor, 80–83, 106
genre, issues of, 13, 67–68, 148, 150–152, 153–154, 159–163
gonzo, 67, 108, 133, 136–137

Hardcore, Max, 5, 143–144
hoaxes, 149–150, 153–155, 157, 165, 176–179
horror: *See* body genres
Hustler: *See* Flynt, Larry

intensity: the body in a state of, 122–123, 131, 137–138, 166; and sexuality, 71–73, 85; theorists of, 63–65; and trauma, 85–86, 154, 179–180

Jacobs, Katrien, 4–5, 78, 88, 103–104
jouissance, 72, 77, 85–86, 137–138, 154, 179, 185
Juffer, Jane, 3, 24

Kendrick, Walter, 6, 11, 71, 118

LeRoy, JT, 126, 149, 157, 160–175, 178
lifestyle pornographies, 187–188

MacKinnon, Catherine A., 23, 33, 112, 119, 198n9
Marcus, Steven, 10
memes, 50, 52–54
misery porn, 139, 142–147, 152, 154, 162–163, 166–168, 175–176

Now That's Fucked Up, 103–105

obscenity: definitions of, 91, 122–123; and the Obscene Publications Act 1959, 12, 181–182; prosecutions for, 5–6, 12, 67–68, 104, 119
Oryx and Crake: *See* Atwood, Margaret
O'Toole, Laurence, 54, 68–69, 77, 181–182, 184

Paasonen, Susanna, 3–5, 11–12, 18, 52–53, 143, 146; with Kaarina Nikunen, and Laura Saarenmaa, 3

Index

paroxysms, 52, 55, 74, 137
Pasquinelli, Matteo, 9–10, 81, 85–86, 185
Porn Studies, 1–13, 16, 17–19, 184
pornographic, the: alternative definitional criteria for, 58–60, 75, 117–118, 121–124, 147, 150–151; expanded understandings of, 13–14, 47, 50–51, 105, 108–109, 111–112, 120, 139, 144–146, 177–178, 181–189
pornographication, 182–189
pornography: amateur, 12, 103, 133, 135–136; as a distinct cultural category, 69, 73; diverse history of, 68–71, 73; effects of, 22, 101, 119–120; photorealistic forms of, 11, 13, 133, 168; written forms of, 10–13, 139–140, 143–144
postmodernism, 88–89, 92–95, 97–99, 129–132, 158–160
poverty porn, 14
pro-sex feminism, 3, 5, 8, 23–29, 41, 186
prurience: anxieties about, 114, 144–147; definition of, 91; manipulation of, 115–117, 178; and the pornographic, 123, 149, 175, 188; wide-ranging character of, 91–92, 137
psychoanalysis: *See* therapeutic, the

queer theoretical approaches, 4–5, 201n6

race: in Porn Studies, 3, 5, 9, 19, 191n6; and transgression, 19, 78, 82, 84
Real, the, 92, 93, 98, 131, 133, 138, 154, 162–163, 166, 175, 179
repressive hypothesis, the, 43–44
Roche, Charlotte, 35–44, 47

Sade, Marquis de, 69–71, 143
sadomasochism: *See* BDSM

sentiment, 109, 111, 113–116
Sex Education Show, The, 49, 54–56
sex wars, the, 19, 21–34, 112, 118–120
sexual explicitness: displacement of, 63, 65, 104–106, 109, 120–121, 143, 145, 185; and diverse affects, 77, 83, 101
sexual minorities, 4, 5, 7–8, 45, 163
shock porn: *See* memes
Siffredi, Rocco, 133–136, 138
Sontag, Susan, 98–99, 106, 116
Smith, Adam, 116, 195n6, 198n7
Smith, Clarissa, 182–189, 192n8
spectacle, 89–92, 98, 103–104, 141, 197n1

therapeutic, the, 148, 161–162, 171
transgression: and approaches to pornography, 4, 8, 10, 14, 17–18, 37, 57, 123; and bad taste, 75, 77–78, 81–82; in feminism, 19, 24–34, 41; and the law or taboo, 18–19, 83, 86, 100; licensed forms of, 116–117, 145–146; as potentially a-political boundary crossing, 27, 33, 46; and sex, 36, 38, 42–43, 44–46, 70–71, 83–85, 119; *see also* Bataille
trauma: in misery porn, 154–155, 162–163, 175; and the real, 85–86; 130–131, 168–169, 179–180

violence: centrality to understandings of 'the pornographic,' 22–23, 30, 112, 117–120; displacement of sexuality onto, 74–75; as taboo, 18, 78, 82
viral videos: *See* memes
voyeurism, 58–59, 115, 145; *see also* prurience

warporn: in contemporary visual culture, 79–81, 83, 103–109; definitions of, 78; historical

warporn *(continued)*
  examples of, 87–88, 118
Wetlands: See Roche, Charlotte
Williams, Linda, 1, 2, 4, 7, 19, 51, 74–75, 91, 152

Wood, Marcus, 109–114, 116, 117, 145, 186

Žižek, Slavoj, 31, 44–45, 86, 92, 93, 98

www.ingramcontent.com/pod-product-compliance
Ingram Content Group UK Ltd.
Pitfield, Milton Keynes, MK11 3LW, UK
UKHW041942140426
5217IPUK00014B/623